Series Editors:
LUANNA H. MEYER, PH.D.
CHERYL A. UTLEY, PH.D.

Staying in School

SERIES EDITORS

Luanna H. Meyer, Ph.D.
School of Education
Syracuse University

Cheryl A. Utley, Ph.D.
Juniper Gardens Children's Project
Schiefelbusch Institute for
    Life Span Studies
University of Kansas

EDITORIAL ADVISORY BOARD

James A. Banks, Ph.D.
University of Washington

Eugene E. Garcia, Ph.D.
Office of Bilingual Education and
    Minority Language Affairs
Washington, D.C.

Margaret B. Spencer, Ph.D.
University of Pennsylvania

Ann Lieberman, Ed.D.
Teachers College
Columbia University

William L. Pollard, Ph.D.
Syracuse University

Barbara J. Shade, Ph.D.
University of Wisconsin–Parkside

Henry T. Trueba, Ph.D.
University of Houston

Alba A. Ortiz, Ph.D.
University of Texas–Austin

Children, Youth & Change
Sociocultural Perspectives

Staying in School

Partnerships for Educational Change

edited by

IAN M. EVANS
Binghamton University (SUNY)

TERRY CICCHELLI
Fordham University

MARVIN COHEN
Bank Street College of Education

NORMAN P. SHAPIRO
The City College of the City University of New York

LIBRARY

PUBLISHING C?

Baltimore • London • Toronto • Sydney

Paul H. Brookes Publishing Co.
Post Office Box 10624
Baltimore, MD 21285-0624

Copyright © 1995 by Paul H. Brookes Publishing Co., Inc.
All rights reserved.

Typeset by Brushwood Graphics, Inc., Baltimore, Maryland.
Manufactured in the United States of America by
The Maple Press Company, Binghamton, New York.

This book is printed on recycled paper. ♻

Library of Congress Cataloging-in-Publication Data
Staying in school : partnerships for educational change / edited by
  Ian M. Evans . . . [et al.].
       p.   cm. — (Children, youth & change)
  Includes bibliographical references and index.
  ISBN 1-55766-173-1
  1. College–school cooperation—New York (State)   2. Home and school—
New York (State)   3. Dropouts—New York (State)   4. Socially handicapped
children—Education—New York (State)   5. Educational change—New York
(State)   I. Evans, Ian M.   II. Series.
LB2331.53.S73   1995   94-37647
378.1'03—dc20   CIP

British Library Cataloguing-in-Publication data are available from the British
Library.

Sociocultural Perspectives

Also available in the
Children, Youth & Change Series:

Cooperative Learning and Strategies for Inclusion:
Celebrating Diversity in the Classroom
edited by JoAnne W. Putnam, Ph.D.

Contents

Contributors

THE EDITORS

Ian M. Evans, Ph.D., Professor of Psychology and Director of Clinical Training, Binghamton University (SUNY), Binghamton, New York 13902

Ian Evans served as Project Director for the Binghamton School Partnership Project, and is currently directing its successor, the Home and School Partnerships, funded by the U.S. Department of Education. His research program is in assessment and interventions for children with disabilities and significant social and emotional needs and he has co-authored or co-edited three books on these topics. He has general interests in the theoretical development of behavior therapy and of clinical psychology as a science. He is also a Fellow of the American Psychological Association.

Terry Cicchelli, Ph.D., Professor, Graduate School of Education, Fordham University, 113 West 60th Street, New York, New York 10023

Terry Cicchelli is a professor in the division of curriculum and teaching in the Graduate School of Education. Her major academic interests and writings include work in the areas of teaching and teacher development, along with urban youth and urban schooling issues.

Marvin Cohen, Ed.D., Senior Graduate School Faculty, Bank Street College of Education, 610 West 112th Street, New York, New York 10025

Marvin Cohen has been a member of the Graduate Faculty of the Bank Street College of Education in New York City since 1985. His interest in the reform of mathematics education and the change process in public schools led to his participation in the beginnings of the Center for Minority Achievement at Bank Street College. As Director of the Center, he was responsible for its replication in three new regions as well as for the Center's work in five New York City academies. Dr. Cohen is currently Director of the Baltimore City Early Adolescent Demonstration Project at Bank Street College.

Norman P. Shapiro, Ph.D., Professor of Education and Director of the Center for School Development, School of Education, The City College of the City University of New York, New York, New York 10031

Norman Shapiro served as Project Director for City College's Stay-in-School Partnership Program. As Director of the Center for School Development, he is currently directing a number of collaborative programs with secondary schools. Many of these programs were outcomes of the SSPP project including a new graduate program that synthesizes teacher education and school improvement; School–University Collaborative Houses in three high schools; the Consortium for School Development, a collaboration with four high schools who were part of the original SSPP program; and the Liberty Partnership Program. He also directs the Global Education Telecommunications Network, a program that links 60 New York City schools with schools around the world.

THE CHAPTER AUTHORS

Allison F. Alden, M.A.T., Co-Director, Home and School Partnerships Project and Doctoral Candidate, School of Education and Human Development, Binghamton University (SUNY), Binghamton, New York 13902

Allison Alden has coordinated the Binghamton School Partnership Project since its creation, acted as Assistant Director of the Center for Educational and Social Research, and now coordinates a federally funded research project. Her work focuses on the positive initiatives that help mitigate factors at home and school that place children at risk for school failure and dropout.

Immaculate M. Amuge, Ed.D., Associate at the New York State Education Department, Bureau of Professional Career Opportunity Programs, CEC 5664, Albany, New York 12230

Mary Amuge coordinated the activities of the Stay-in-School Partnership Program funded by the New York State Legislature and administered by the Office of Equity and Access. Originally from Uganda, she has a major interest in increasing the number of historically underrepresented and underserved students to be retained in school and to be supported in the pursuit of studies that lead to careers in scientific, technology, and health-related fields.

Richard E. Baecher, Ph.D., Professor, Division of Curriculum and Teaching, Fordham University, 113 West 60th Street, New York, New York 10023

Richard Baecher is Director of the Bilingual Teacher Education program at Fordham. His research interests include children at risk, students with limited English proficiency, and two-way bilingual programs.

Michael N. Bazigos, M.A., Assistant Dean for Educational Outreach, School of Education, Pace University, 1 Pace Plaza, New York, New York 10038

As Dean for Educational Outreach Programs, Michael Bazigos is involved in developing and directing programs addressing critical issues in urban education. He is currently President of the Associated Youth Partnership Programs, a 23-college consortium of directors of programs serving at-risk students in public schools, and serves as development associate for the International Center on Cooperation and Conflict Resolution at Teachers College. Dean Bazigos trains educators in grant writing, program evaluation strategies, and organizational development in both faculty and consultant capacities.

Jeffrey Beaudry, Ph.D., Senior Associate in Programming, Northwest Regional Educational Lab, Portland, Oregon 97207

Jeffrey Beaudry served as program evaluator for St. John's University SSPP program. His scholarly interests focus on multicultural education and program evaluation.

Amy Coffey, M.S.Ed., Assistant Dean, St. John's College of Liberal Arts and Sciences, St. John's University, 8000 Utopia Parkway, Jamaica, New York 11439

Amy Coffey teaches at-risk children and youth and is involved in minority teacher training. Working with drop-out prevention and retention programs are among her chief professional interests.

Warren Crichlow, Ed.D., Assistant Professor, Warner Graduate School of Education and Human Development, University of Rochester, 302 Latimer Hall, River Campus, Rochester, New York 14627

Warren Crichlow was an administrator with the Rochester City School District during the SSPP years, specializing in program evaluation. He contributed to the Nazareth College SSPP in such areas as outcome measurement and monitoring student progress. Currently, he is Assistant Professor of teaching and curriculum at the Warner Graduate School of Education and Human Development, University of Rochester. He is co-editor of *Race, Identity, and Representation in Education* (Rutledge, 1993), and of "Toni Morrison and the Curriculum," a special issue of the journal, *Cultural Studies* (1995).

John Devine, Ph.D., Adjunct Professor, School of Education, New York University, 32 Washington Place, New York, New York 10003

John Devine is director of the Liberty Partnership Program at New York University's Metropolitan Center for Urban Education. He also directs the School, College, and University Partnership Program and Project Achieve. During the 1994–1995 academic year he is conducting research on school violence under a grant from the Harry Frank Guggenheim Foundation.

Mary Gibbons, M.S., School Principal (Retired)

Mary Gibbons was a classroom teacher for many years before becoming a building principal in Jamaica, Queens. Ms. Gibbons served as Program Coordinator for St. John's University SSPP.

Aaron W. Godfrey, Ph.D., Professor, SUNY Stony Brook, Stony Brook, New York 11794-5318

Bill Godfrey has been a lecturer in the classics and comparative literature at SUNY Stony Brook since 1965. With strong involvement in the education of young people, he was Director of Upward Bound for 20 years. He has also been Director of other programs, including Stay-in-School Partnership Program, Liberty Partnerships Program, and the Teacher Opportunity Corps.

Charles F. Graber, M.S., Assistant Commissioner for Higher Education, Director, Bureau of Grants Administration, Cultural Education Center, Room 5B68, State Education Department, Albany, New York 12230

Charles Graber began his career in education as a classroom teacher. He is currently administrator of a number of programs to support educational innovations statewide and has a specific interest in children with special needs.

Joseph C. Grannis, Ph.D., Professor, Institute for Urban & Minority Education, Teachers College, Columbia University, New York, New York 10027

Joseph Grannis was a social worker and teacher before receiving his Ph.D. in Education. He is an active researcher in the nature of schools and educational processes. Most of his fieldwork has been in urban schools, especially evaluations of dropout prevention programs and alternative schools, but his work also includes a 3-year action-research project on student stress in school, and the Teachers College SSPP project.

Berj Harootunian, Ph.D., Professor of Teaching and Leadership, Syracuse University, Syracuse, New York 13244-2280

Berj Harootunian's studies investigate how teachers solve problems and create successful environments for students and themselves. His published works include numerous articles, chapters, and books that reflect these interests, including a new monograph he co-authored on school violence and aggression in youth.

Luanna H. Meyer, Ph.D., Professor, School of Education, Syracuse University, Syracuse, New York 13244-2340

Luanna Meyer is Coordinator of the Inclusive Elementary and Special Education Teacher Preparation Program and Director of the Consortium for Collaborative Research on Social Relationships of Children and Youth. She also coordinates the doctoral program in special education at Syracuse University. Her research and publications have focused on children's social relationships, positive approaches to challenging behaviors, middle-school curricular strategies, and theoretical and practical issues surrounding the implementation of innovative practices in education.

Akiko Okifuji, Ph.D., Clinical Psychology Program, Binghamton University (SUNY), Binghamton, New York 13902

Akiko Okifuji was a research assistant in the Binghamton School Partnership Project. She had responsibilities for program evaluation and was a psychological consultant on family issues. She is at present a research associate with the Western Psychiatric Institute in Pittsburgh, where she participates in clinical studies in health psychology and pain management.

Rhoda Pearl Peltzer, M.B.A., High School Teacher, New York City Schools, c/o Center for School Development, City College (CUNY), Convent Avenue and 138th Street, New York, New York 10031

Rhoda Peltzer has been released full time for the past 9 years by the New York City Board of Education to work at City College's Center for School Development. She served as the College's SSPP Project Co-Director and is currently Division Director for the Consortium for School Development.

Alean Rush, M.A.Ed., Professor, Nazareth College of Rochester, Smyth Hall, 4245 East Avenue, Rochester, New York 14610

Alean Rush is Director of Special Projects and Programs at Nazareth College. She is an educator, a community activist, and an international ecumenist. Her interests include specialty teacher preparation and direct services to children deemed to be at risk.

William Sanders, Ph.D., Associate Professor of Education, St. John's University, School of Education, Grand Central and Utopia Parkways, Jamaica, New York 11439

William Sanders was Director of St. John's University SSPP program. He is currently Coordinator of Secondary Programs and is involved in the Teacher Opportunity Core. His professional concerns focus on both gifted students and at-risk students.

Alan Steinberg, M.S., Supervising Director of Secondary and Middle School Education, Syracuse City School District, Syracuse, New York 13210

Alan Steinberg was Co-Director of Syracuse University's SSPP project. His interest is in seeing all children succeed to their full potential. He has been a classroom teacher as well as a district administrator, and has taught education courses as an adjunct faculty member at Syracuse University.

Alison D. Thomas, M.A., Doctoral Candidate, Clinical Psychology, Binghamton University (SUNY), Binghamton, New York 13902

Alison Thomas's work has centered on the influence of social support on academic achievement in African American children. She is also investigating other issues related to children's social relationships such as friendship stability and peer rejection.

Dilafruz R. Williams, Ph.D., Associate Professor of Educational Policy, Foundations, and Administrative Studies, Portland State University, P.O. Box 751, Portland, Oregon 97207-0751

Dilafruz Williams is interested in the moral issues related to inclusion. She has studied the nature and formation of communities in urban schools, primarily at the middle school level, as well as multicultural approaches to teaching and curriculum. She is the president of Holistic Education, a special interest group of the American Education Research Association.

Preface

Criticizing America's public schools has become something of a national pastime. And just about everyone has a solution: let business run the schools; introduce choice and vouchers; only total restructuring of education will solve the problems; the future is in computers and technology; let's get back to basics. This book offers a constructive alternative to criticism and panacea. We have chronicled the experiences of a variety of different projects that were all part of a practical initiative by New York State to develop working partnerships between universities and school districts, designed to address the needs of students considered at risk of school failure and dropout. This effort was called the Stay-in-School Partnership Project, affectionately known as "SSPP" and sometimes "S²P²."

By discussing numerous, pragmatic aspects of these partnerships, we have attempted to make this volume relevant for many different readers, certainly not just for educators in New York State. After all, New York is highly variegated and the SSPP programs included several types of school districts and communities, from large, inner-city schools to smaller rural and suburban settings. Thus, the lessons of our experiences, we hope, will have wide general applicability. The projects also involved very close collaboration between university faculty, teachers, school administrators, and policy makers, and so we believe that the understanding that emerged will have relevance for all of these constituents.

We are most fortunate that this work was selected by Luanna Meyer and Cheryl Utley to be the second volume in their book series, *Children, Youth & Change: Sociocultural Perspectives*. This multidisciplinary series will incorporate a wide range of perspectives and innovations that foster understanding of how best to meet the needs of children and youth in today's changing world. The first volume in the series, *Cooperative Learning and Strategies for Inclusion: Celebrating Diversity in the Classroom*, edited by JoAnne W. Putnam, set the stage—and the standard—for the present work. JoAnne Putnam provides a rich and practical guide to instructional strategies designed to accommodate the fascinating range of differences in culture, family background, and academic strengths found in contemporary public schools. Whereas many social commentators bemoan the difficulties created by heterogeneity, JoAnne Putnam, as her subtitle emphasizes, sees diversity as an advantage.

The *Children, Youth & Change* series, guided by its distinguished advisory board, will address current social challenges in a positive way—the same spirit with which the chapter authors of this volume set out to support schools and address the needs of those children and youth for whom the educational system has failed to provide equitable opportunities. Because the SSPP programs themselves were funded through universities and colleges, these chapters tend to tell the story from that perspective. Thus, there are observations about difficulties in forming partnerships with schools that are not balanced with comments by school personnel on the problems of working with universities. However, every SSPP program had strong links with school administrators and teachers, without whose constant support and dedication none of the work would have been possible. Thus, we trust that educators of every kind will find the information in this volume valuable and the messages presented here important in enhancing learning opportunities for all school children.

Not every SSPP program is represented in this book, which is regrettable. When the original idea emerged that our experiences were so unique that their documentation would be important, we wrote to participants from each of the programs and asked them to submit a chapter based on their insights. Only some were able to do so, and of these some had to be edited or modified in the interests of the length and balance of the final volume. We have tried hard to maintain the original flavor and emphasis of the chapters submitted, yet greatly appreciate the willingness of the many authors to succumb to our sometimes heavy-handed editing. Editorial responsibility shifted over time as we worked on each other's contributions, and so the order of editorship, after myself, is simply alphabetical. My editorial assistant, Susan Marx, did an excellent job of coordinating the final stages of the project, and deserves many thanks. We are especially indebted to Luanna Meyer of Syracuse University for her considerable involvement and support in editing—many of the contributions benefited enormously from her suggested revisions and comments.

Finally, we are forever grateful to Mary Amuge and Charles Graber, who were primarily responsible for the administration of the various programs by New York State's Education Department. Their management skills, tolerance for academic noncompliance, and enthusiastic ability to get all of the eventual 17 programs to work positively together were largely responsible for the success of the program over the years. It was their encouragement that allowed the vision of many state legislators to be translated into effective action. Although the Stay-in-School Partnership Project is officially over, its impact continues, as this book demonstrates. We believe the taxpayers were well served, both by their representatives in the legislature and officials in the State Education Department. We hope you will agree.

Ian M. Evans

*This book is dedicated to the children
of New York, including ours*

Staying in School

Prologue

The Evolution of a
School–University
Partnership

JOHN DEVINE

O ne snowy weekend in February, 1985, I attended a group retreat on Long Island with 10 New York City high school principals and some officials from the central Board of Education. The principals had been selected by Dr. Victor Herbert, the Dropout Prevention Coordinator for New York City, to attend a kind of think-tank weekend because their schools had the highest dropout rates in the city. It was a relaxed setting, and the principals were far from being on the defensive. One principal's remark captured the mood: "with dropout rates this high, we must be doing something wrong."

I was attending the retreat as a representative of a group of New York University (NYU) faculty members who had expressed a desire to become more deeply involved in the crucial issue of school dropout. After my presentation, I was chatting with Mr. Louis Santiago, principal of Bushwick High School, at the evening reception. "How do you think we might be helpful to Bushwick?" I asked. "Believe me, we could use all the help the university could give us," was his reply.

On one level, this exchange had all the earmarks of the all-powerful university parachuting in to rescue the poor beleaguered high school—such clichés are never easily shed. But in the ensuing years (in 1995, the university is in its 10th year of collaboration with Bushwick High School) I have often had occasion to reflect on how almost every resource at the university's disposal could, in fact, be profitably deployed in assisting this

1

large, overcrowded, and highly troubled school. Still, no one would argue that such massive assistance alone could create an *effective* school, the central concept underlying the school-reform literature.

AN IDEA IS BORN

A few weeks after the retreat, Mr. Santiago convened a meeting of myself and his key advisors: his assistant principals for social studies, for guidance, and for English as a Second Language (ESL)/foreign language, as well as his school's Dropout Prevention Coordinator. We decided to begin our joint effort in the most uncomplicated way possible. We would design a simple strategy based on three significant statistics: 1) the student population at Bushwick was 75% Latino, 2) Bushwick had the second worst dropout rate of the city's 120 high schools, and 3) most of the students who dropped out did so during 9th grade. Since a very large proportion of these students were recent immigrants, our initial approach involved identifying NYU graduate students with three distinct characteristics: all of them had been trained in ESL techniques; had been exposed to the principles of bilingual/bicultural education; and were training as bilingual counselors, and could therefore be of particular help to students who were immigrants.

Our next task, that of locating an appropriate tutoring room or "coaching corner" in the school, was facilitated by the Brooklyn Superintendent, who, on a tour of the school, discovered a fairly large and currently unused recreation room in the basement. This room was put at our disposal, and soon the Assistant Principal for ESL and Foreign Languages, Mrs. Emilia Cardona, was referring 9th graders to us. Our nine graduate-student tutors (two of whom were paid, thanks to a small grant from the Board of Education, and seven of whom were volunteers) began visiting the school 3 days a week. Such was the beginning of our pilot project at Bushwick High School in the spring of 1985.

That same spring, some significant political events were taking place in the New York State capitol. The President of New York University, John Brademas, had gone to Albany to plead with the legislature not to cut tuition assistance to NYU and other universities. Meeting with the Speaker of the Assembly, President Brademas learned that several legislators felt that the colleges and universities were not doing enough to tackle the dropout issue. Back at the university, Brademas brought together Dean Robert Burnham and other faculty to begin work on a draft of legislation that, over the course of the summer, developed into the plan for the Stay-in-School Partnership Project (SSPP). In its first year, SSPP provided $1.5 million to 10 colleges and universities throughout the state to allow them to ally themselves with public school districts in their dropout prevention efforts. Our small pilot program at Bushwick High School thus served as one of the precursory models for the design of the legislation. Thanks to the funds provided through SSPP, we continued our efforts at Bushwick in September of 1985 and extended the program to three additional inner-city high schools that same year.

QUESTIONS FOR THE NEW PARTNERSHIP

Somewhat worrisome to the university personnel involved in SSPP was the fact that New York City educators had a reputation, whether deserved or not, for rejecting outside intervention. If one did not come up "through the system" it was assumed that he or she wouldn't understand the problems of the public schools. I myself had had no experience working in a public school setting, having been steeped, both as student and teacher, in the traditions of Jesuit educational institutions, whose world-wide reputation as elite, orderly, and well-disciplined places was, at least in my experience (in the 1940s through the 1960s) not far off the mark. I didn't need teachers to remind me, as they sometimes did, that when you are working in inner-city public schools, prior experience in private schools doesn't count. I was constantly wondering myself, as I ventured into Bushwick, what relevance my "elitist Jesuitical" background would have in a turbulent New York City high school.

In retrospect it is easy to recognize our initial mistakes, our naiveté, and our meager understanding of the complexities of today's large urban schools. We were aware of the warnings about the dangers of "band-aid" approaches to educational reform, about inadequately evaluated dropout-prevention efforts, and about the need for school officials to get on with the serious internal business of restructuring schools rather than bringing in outside programs. But we were not trying to take on the whole world. We were just starting tutoring programs for 50–75 students in several schools with populations ranging from 2,200 to 3,800. We harbored no illusions that our tutoring program was synonymous with school reform. But if any of us assumed that a tutoring program would be narrowly focused on cognitive skills, he or she was soon disabused of that notion.

I did not need to convince the graduate students, all of whom were receiving assistantships in 1986, of their need for training—everyone involved in the project felt it necessary to get together each week to talk about what we were doing and where our efforts were leading. We decided to meet in seminar style for two hours—a course that the university soon endorsed with six graduate credits. But what would be the content of such a course? When we began, we felt that the graduate students, who were the front-line staff of the program and in daily contact with the high school students, would need support and training in some very specific areas: most importantly, ESL, counseling techniques, math education, and literacy acquisition. But it became increasingly clear that the curriculum, the graduate training, and our whole approach would have to be broadened considerably if university students were to be adequately prepared for the challenge of communicating directly, one-to-one, with students in some of the riskiest schools in the city. For one thing, we would have to address a much wider range of issues. But, more basically, we had to determine how we were to forge an identity for ourselves. How were we to present ourselves to high school students? We had created this new kind of educator who was neither classroom teacher nor guidance counselor nor disciplinarian nor special educator. And most of the titles that were suggested—"role model," "big sister/brother," "tutor," "advisor," "mentor," and even "educational advocate"—didn't quite fit. We had to ask ourselves not only who we were, but also how we could prepare ourselves for the demanding task of working productively with adolescents on an individual basis without infringing on the roles of counselors, psychologists, or classroom teachers. Although we felt a close kinship with those who worked with street youths, in the final analysis we were still teachers, but teachers who provided individualized instruction.

New Demands as the Program Evolves

Perhaps the best way to explain how our self-concept evolved is to describe the gradual change in our seminar curriculum, which initially focused on tutoring techniques and methods for imparting study skills. "Begin where the student is!" is good advice, but it is also oversimplistic in most cases. In the everyday interactions between the university tutors and the young adults they were working with, countless issues arose that provided windows into the lives of these inner-city students, and not all of these situations could be dealt with simply by "listening to the voice of the students," as some educational ethnographers imply. For one thing, adolescents (and adults as well, in fact) may react differently to a given situation depending on the circumstances and on who else is present at the time; for example, if a student is asked the same question in different contexts by a tutor, a peer, and the school principal, he or she is likely to respond very differently to each. But matters become even more complex when one considers that we were not simply running a program for adolescents by ourselves, but rather were conducting a collaborative program, and that there are many ways in which the goals of a university program and a large public high school, even if generally smoothly integrated, can conflict.

How does one react, for example, to a student whose teacher gives him or her high grades in English for copying articles wholesale from the encyclopedia? Students may have the impression from teachers or counselors that they are progressing well, when, compared to a general student population, they are not as advanced or doing nearly as well as they believe. How do you let students know that their competition is not just their own classmates, but also their peers throughout the country, many of whom are attending more-demanding schools?

The challenge of simultaneously helping a high school student while still holding him or her to high standards academically and, especially, behaviorally, is often a new one for a university graduate student. Not everyone is comfortable confronting students on academic issues, much less on ethical ones. In the informality of the tutoring room students may reveal perceptions, attitudes, or behaviors that reveal racial prejudice, homophobia, or self-destructive reactions to everyday situations. A student may divulge quite spontaneously that she or he is sexually active without using birth control or protection against sexually transmitted diseases. Tutors in our program needed to do more than just develop a degree of comfort in handling such sensitive matters, they had to present themselves in such a way that students would feel that they could speak openly. They needed to sharpen their listening skills. But they also needed the emotional support of other graduate students and faculty to assist them in learning how to skillfully confront students, when necessary, without alienating them. In recruiting tutors/mentors, we have learned how important it is to select young people who have a sense of who they are, of how to function on a team, and of how to work with adolescents in a highly stressful situation, all while maintaining their sense of humor.

Learning Is a Two-Way Street

How does one prepare graduate students for one-to-one or small-group encounters with adolescents from such diverse backgrounds? Certainly the main idea is to foster strong, meaningful relationships, but it is not enough to simply preach mutual respect and the golden rule. Training graduate students for work in inner-city schools must begin with reflection on our own attitudes and an examination of our own implicit sociocultural assumptions. Since the late 1960s, sociolinguists and anthropologists, among others, have been documenting the fact that adolescents and children who appear to be unable to respond properly in school or who seem to lack verbal ability are often found to be very good communicators when interacting with their own peer group or family outside of school. Prior to that time, some theorists were prone to deprecate the communication skills of these students, regarding them as the result of "cultural deficits" or failures of the home. Unfortunately, one still hears teachers blaming students' failures in school on their "deficient" home situation, but more recent ethnographic studies have shown that in the heterogeneous mix of today's urban schools there are a wide variety of linguistic and cultural configurations at work. Standard English and American culture are but two among many valid systems of speech and culture. Fundamental to the development of the contemporary educator is learning to appreciate the fact that students bring from the home patterns of speech, verbal etiquette, habits such as taking turns (or not taking turns), and ways of communicating that may be different from those of the teacher. It is not necessary for a teacher to have a detailed knowledge of the cultural traits of each student, but he or she must realize that her or his own ways of speaking and cultural/class/gender norms are not universal. And yet these considerations should not obscure the fact that street/drug culture, with its styles, demeanor, and attendant ethos of violence and fear, has crept into many homes, as well as into schools and other institutions of society, and that a basic understanding of this culture can be very important to the inner-city educator.

Consider how one might fashion a university curriculum to respond to some of the following situations. These excerpts from my field notes and from graduate student logs were selected without deliberately avoiding conflictual situations, but also without singling them out.

> Violence continues to be a feature of their everyday lives. A lot of these kids are actively engaged in creating and sustaining the violent environment. I believe that J (another tutor) has written in his log about a group of boys who have been attending sessions in the tutoring room. They are all 9th graders fresh from the local Junior High School. When we first met, I asked them what they wanted out of school. "Man, we want to rule this place like we did JHS----." I inquired how they were going to accomplish this, to which they responded, "We're gonna beat some heads, we'll show them who rules." All of this was said in an energetic boastful way which made it seem that they were talking about a football game, not a life or death reality where guns and knives are the ball. To be sure, they were showing off a bit, engaging our interest so that we would not perceive them as naive freshmen. But the implications of what they said were very serious and very real. They talked of getting "props," or respect, and the only way to achieve this was by "busting heads," or at the very least, never backing away from a fight.

> Last week I started working with a new student. Her name is N. N represents to me what many of the students are in this school: very sweet, very smart, and willing to learn. However, N has to show herself as tough, street wise, and acts like she knows it all. N's mother died last year. This has been a great loss for her. She feels like a lot is missing in her life. She now has to live with her brother, a 21-year-old man whom she hardly knows. Her brother left the house when he was 12 and has lived apart since then. He

now has to take care of his younger sister. N complains that she is having a lot of trouble with her brother. "He treats me like I am somebody from the street," she complained.

We mailed a questionnaire to an educational magazine, and in the process of doing so I discovered Jose (9th grader) could not address an envelope. Apparently no one ever showed him how.

A quote from one of the high school students: "Well, in our home country, it is the men who decide whether a couple should use birth control."

M is a very rough case first referred to me by his English teacher. All teachers agree that M is a handful and a nuisance in the classroom. One teacher commented that he doesn't ever participate in classroom conversation and just sits at the back of the room making animal noises. After working with M for a few weeks, I realized that most of this was true and wanted to know why. I found out that M was not understanding most of the material in his classes and is basically too shy to ask questions for fear of being made fun of by other students. Because of this he falls further behind with every class. M is a student who needs constant individual attention in order to work. He is great at manipulating teachers and other students to do what he wants, so one must be careful when getting involved with him. Basically what he thrives on is attention.

At this point I have my work cut out for me just to keep the hats and Walkmen off and their eyes on their work. D will not keep his Walkman off. I told him I would rather not take it away from him since he was old enough to be treated with more respect, but after many reminders I finally decided to hold onto his headphones for the duration of the session. He seemed almost relieved by this. My sense is that these kids are dying for some kind of aesthetic experience. They have so much inside of them which often has no outlet that if we can tap into it we'll find a gold mine of resources.

While we worked, several other students came by to bother D. One of these students, W, came by, started fooling around, and D asked him to leave. "That's OK, man," said W, "I can't read for shit either." "We're trying to study here, so I'd appreciate it if you'd leave," said D. W complied and after he left, D gave me a goofy grin and said, "Man, I don't know what's happening to me. I just said that without any kind of attitude at all."

Incidents like these rebut the contention that, by the time they reach high school, it is too late to work with these kids. And this last episode is not just a self-congratulatory success story. It demonstrates what we see over and over again every day in our tutoring rooms—that even the toughest adolescent, when exposed to someone who shows genuine interest, to someone who cares, will, even without conscious reflection, "code-switch" behavior away from the tough stance and begin to emulate the tutor.

Implications for Teaching

The point of presenting such a wide array of episodes, performances, and reflections on everyday events is to illustrate the need for a curriculum that not only addresses study skills, test preparation, literacy, and math (essential though these are), but for one that is also responsive to differences in emotional awareness and styles of speaking and that recognizes the unique problems of recently immigrated adolescents, some of whom may initially appear to be illiterate in their native language as well as in English. A graduate seminar that concentrates only on literacy, mathematics instruction, and high school curricular issues ignores an eclectic series of critical topics: violence, AIDS, adolescent culture, Creole languages, gender issues, and aesthetics, to name just a few. More fundamentally, graduate students, as reflective educators, need to be sensitive to their own prejudices and cultural assumptions. This requires an examination of societal and political issues, as well as a critique of the whole enterprise of Western thought and civilization. A pedagogy that blindly accepts the modernist rationality that underlies much of traditional educational discourse does a disservice to the student in allowing his or her education to proceed as if critical or postmodern scholarship had never existed.

The teaching and learning that goes on between tutor and student is truly "constructive" in the sense that it is meaningful learning that arises out of the real context of the students' lives. I am often asked, sometimes somewhat cynically, how one measures the success of the Stay-in-School Partnership Program. And I have often thought that a count of the looks of concentration and of the smiles on the faces of students actively engaged in the learning process in our tutoring room might satisfy even the most recalcitrant positivist educational researcher.

It is important to bear in mind that New York University's version of SSPP was only one possible variation on this theme. The design of the SSPP legislation and the supportive way in which the program was administered allowed institutions of higher education to construct their own models of public school–university collaboration. Some colleges worked with preschoolers, others organized parent groups, others concentrated on teacher and staff development. One of the basic assumptions underlying our own program was that we did not set out to "reform" or "restructure" the schools with which we allied ourselves. The schools themselves were abuzz with such plans. Our intentions were more modest: we hoped, in each building, to have some effect on the lives of about 100–150 students (in schools with total enrollments of more than 3,000). To do this, we created teams of NYU graduate students that were truly multiethnic, multilinguistic, and multidisciplinary. Our teams had to be assembled this way not just because it was politically correct, but because this diversity was an absolute educational necessity. The "zoned" schools in inner-city areas had one feature in common: none had any white students. High school students sitting in the tutoring room and observing black, white, Latino and Asian tutors interacting with one another would often ask: "Are you guys friends? Do you guys hang out and party together on weekends?" A typical team consisted of both women and men from several of many different homelands— Trinidad, Ghana, Puerto Rico, Canada, and China—and Americans from a wide spectrum of the states. We learned that, even more than individual role models, these adolescents needed exposure to a "corporate role model," to the reality of young industrious adults of different racial and ethnic backgrounds working together, playing together, having fun together, studying together, arguing with one another at times, but also resolving conflicts in a mature way. In short, they needed to be exposed to and become part of a community.

CONCLUDING COMMENTS

This, then, was what the original SSPP tutoring program at New York University evolved into: a community of learners—of adolescents and young adults who could share with the youth an appreciation of jazz, admiration for Malcolm X, or a critique of rap lyrics, as well as help with an algebra problem or counseling on dealing with violence or a pregnancy.

The various research projects that grew out of these encounters all had a common perspective. To paraphrase Clifford Geertz, they sought to comprehend the students' own understanding of what they and their peers were up to as they moved through the toughest of inner-city schools and neighborhoods. How much more convincing and compelling was this research, which arose from intimate involvement in the everyday life of the schools, than the usual run of dissertations emanating from graduate schools of education, with their surveys, questionnaires, content validity schemes, post-tests, and chi-square statistics? If we assume that the central goal of educational research is to ameliorate the current system, rather than supplant it (as the voucher system clearly proposes to do), we must also realize that this can only come about through the work of people who understand how the current system functions. And there is no better way to understand the system than by observing first-hand how students and teachers interpret it, how it forces students through its factory-like buildings and security apparatus. Our work in the schools, then, does have important implications for school restructuring at the grass-roots level, even if this was not directly intended in the original design.

Reflecting on high school students' resistance (or lack thereof) to the values and ideology of the dominant culture as it is translated to them through the mediation of the schools necessarily requires researchers to reflect on their own collusion, complicity, or critiques of these same value systems. We are thus led to acknowledge that there is no "final stage" in the evolution of a tutoring program. The tutor's self-concept, having blossomed into that of tutor/mentor/ethnographer, undergoes a daily reconceptualization in the maelstrom of life in today's urban high schools.

Although SSPP funding is, regretably, no longer available, our project at Bushwick High School and at six other large New York City high schools has continued through 1995, thanks to various state, federal, and private sector funding sources. All of these schools now consider the program to be an integral part of their institutions—and the need is as great, if not greater, in 1995 as it was in 1985.

1

New York State's Stay-in-School Partnership Program
Overview and Evaluation

CHARLES GRABER, IMMACULATE M. AMUGE,
ALEAN RUSH, AND WARREN CRICHLOW

The term "partnership" has been somewhat overused in educational contexts, but when the Stay-in-School Partnership Program (SSPP) first began, the word was not, as it is today, on everyone's lips. In fact, the term had something of a double meaning for us, since SSPP referred to both a partnership between a state education department and a diverse collection of universities or colleges in New York, and to alliances between the universities and the public schools. Later, many of the projects engendered other meaningful relationships—between home and school, high school teachers and college faculty, students and mentors—and these too are documented in this volume. In this introductory chapter, we will concentrate on explaining SSPP, how it came about, the needs it was designed to address, and a little about the various activities that emerged from it. We believe that many of the lessons learned through this project could serve as valuable guides to what might be accomplished by other agencies.

This chapter represents a blend of two narratives prepared for us by the four authors listed; order of authorship is arbitrary. We have also added some material that was provided by other chapter authors but that had to be deleted from their commentaries in the interests of avoiding redundancy. We are grateful to the contributors for allowing this flexibility; any errors are our responsibility. *The Editors*

The concept of the school–university partnership is a major theme addressed by Sirotnik and Goodlad (1988). A partnership known as the Metropolitan School Study Council has continued to function in New York City since 1941. Recently, Goodlad has been a notable participant in the Southern California Partnership and the Puget Sound Educational Consortium, alliances that have been actively attempting to define and negotiate educational agendas and sustain the pursuit of mutual goals through the collaborative efforts of superintendents, principals, deans, and faculty members. However, their concerns have been primarily directed toward solving the organizational problems of administrators at the district and building level and addressing the inservice needs of teachers. Less emphasis has been placed on the educational needs of students. In his prologue, John Devine provides a personal synopsis of the creation, development, and purpose of our type of partnership. His particular program at New York University was one that involved placing university graduate students as tutors in a complex and challenging urban school environment. He uses his description of that program to interweave a variety of important themes that echo throughout the following pages: the relationship between the public school and the university, the insights and revelations of university faculty, the recognition that new skills will be needed by tomorrow's teachers, the complexity of students' needs, the difficulties of formally evaluating a multi-faceted program, and the interplay between the demands of a direct, hands-on program and the ultimate requirement of educational change.

IDENTIFYING THE ISSUES

For the past 10 years or so, one of the most talked about and important policy issues in American education has been the so-called "dropout problem." While the calculation of precise statistics is difficult, best estimates are that approximately 25% of 1994's 9th graders will not finish high school within 4 years; the percentage is even higher (up to 50% or more) in the metropolitan districts of America's larger cities (Hammack, 1986). One reason for the concern is the issue of equity—an unequal distribution of children drop out among various groups in American society. Black, Latino, and less-affluent Americans of all ethnic groups and nationalities drop out at far higher rates than members of other groups, especially in the inner cities. Students who have a history of poor school performance and attendance are also more likely to eventually drop out. Being over-age in 8th grade is another powerful predictor, as is high school pregnancy, marriage, and employment accompanied by poor academic performance (Ekstrom, Goertz, Pollack, & Rock, 1987; Wehlage & Rutter, 1987). The implications of a future generation that includes both large numbers of underachievers and as many as one in four adults who have not completed high school are sobering in a society that values literacy, technology, and democratic participation by its citizenry and that must confront serious social, economic, and environmental challenges.

Considerable research has been conducted on who drops out and why, including substantive longitudinal studies such as Project TALENT, Youth in Transition, the National Longitudinal Survey of Youth Labor Market Experience, and the High School and Beyond reports. The variables that have been correlated with dropping out of school and underachievement include various demographic characteristics for which schools cannot be held directly accountable (see above). However, there is a wealth of information to suggest that many variables predictive of school failure and alienation are indeed within the school's sphere of influence. Some respondents say they dropped out because they were failing anyway, because they could not get along with their teachers, or because they simply did not like school. In addition to negative attitudes toward school, other student social–psychological characteristics that seem to be associated with dropping out are low educational and occupational motivation, weak sociability, low self-esteem, external locus of control, and discipline problems (though a caveat is in order, as attempts to determine the exact relationship of these variables to dropout status have yielded inconsistent findings). Unlike the background characteristics listed earlier, these variables would seem to be modifiable by schools on a year-by-year basis, and even by teachers from day to day. Knowing that poverty is associated with school failure should encourage government agencies concerned with children's welfare to mandate policies and practices that could have an impact on the demographic characteristics related to dropout.

A second important policy issue that emerged somewhat earlier than concern over the dropout rate was the growing awareness among policy makers, educators, and the business community that Americans— even those who managed to graduate from high school—were not learning very much in school. Many high school graduates were found to be deficient in basic skills and many seemed to have only minimal knowledge of academic subjects. Some graduates were deemed functionally illiterate, unable to utilize their capabilities in the tasks demanded of them by society. Compared to students in other industrialized nations, Americans often performed poorly, regardless of the subject matter.

EFFORTS IN NEW YORK STATE

By the 1980s, New York Governor Mario Cuomo, the state legislature, and the Board of Regents had all become gravely concerned about the high dropout rates in the state's public schools, especially in the cities of

New York, Buffalo, Rochester, and Syracuse. The *New York Times* (1990) reported that about one-third of New York City public high school students graduate with conventional diplomas in 4 years and, after 3 more years, another 23% receive either a diploma or an "equivalent certificate." Thus, 7 years after starting high school, approximately 44% of the students in New York City have neither a diploma nor an equivalent secondary-level certificate.

Comprehensive and integrated approaches are therefore needed to ensure that students learn and benefit from the educational system by earning a high school diploma and becoming productive members of the work force. In concert with the state's goal of providing equal opportunity for post-secondary education among all citizens, it was seen as imperative that efforts be made to increase graduation rates, especially among those students most at risk for dropping out of school. The New York State Education Department (1987b) issued a working paper entitled *Increasing High School Completion Rates: A Framework for State and Local Action*. This document presented several effective strategies for restructuring and managing schools to accommodate the needs of students at risk of dropping out. Among the Board's recommendations are using more appropriate instructional strategies, improving learning environments, and increasing parent and community involvement.

A number of important points can be made regarding such pronouncements. One is that there is already a great deal of information indicating how schools can and should change in order to improve educational outcomes for all students. However, such change is difficult and unlikely to emerge simply as the result of a state educational agency issuing eloquent documents. More practical, direct mechanisms are required—in addition to funding—to assist school districts in fulfilling the mandates laid down by educational policy makers. This book documents several such practical mechanisms and explains how they came about.

The Stay-in-School Partnership Project

The practical programs described in this volume emerged because of a special funding opportunity. Many people deserve credit for SSPP, but it is important to mention that the program was an initiative of the New York State Legislature and was supported by a number of influential legislators. The regulations were passed in 1986 in accordance with the provisions of Chapter 53 of the Laws of New York State to mandate the provision of services related to dropout-prevention programs conducted on a cooperative basis by institutions of higher education offering graduate degrees in education, social work, and the social sciences (psychology, sociology).

It made excellent sense to channel the funding through universities. First, universities and colleges have a fundamental stake in increasing high school graduation rates and thus ensuring that students are properly prepared to enter and succeed in post-secondary education. Second, personnel from the variety of departments, and especially Schools of Education, at universities and colleges could be expected to have the high levels of expertise in various special topics that seem to be necessary to help school districts ensure educational improvement. However—and this is a third proof of the ingenuity of the SSPP plan—these same colleges and universities had traditionally had very little contact with public schools that involved actually assisting in educational reform. In his prologue, John Devine honestly describes how personally ill prepared he was to work in the chaotic environment of an inner-city school, and most SSPP project directors later related similar stories. In fact, it can be said that the relationship between public schools and universities has traditionally been very one-sided. Universities have used school districts as convenient sites for teacher training or for conducting research, and the relationship has been rather unidirectional. With SSPP, it became imperative for schools and universities to work together. Chapters 4 (Grannis) and 10 (Godfrey) describe with candor how difficult it was to establish the kind of trust and commitment that enable a working and equitable partnership to emerge—this was one of the most salutary lessons learned in all of the SSPP programs.

Another valuable decision made when creating SSPP was to fund the individual programs through competitive grants. The initial appropriation of $1.5 million for the first year of the project was divided into 10 awards (less administrative costs for the NY State Education Department). The guidelines for proposals were quite general, but they described the kinds of activities that SSPP was designed to support. Funds were provided as service grants, rather than for basic research, but the inclusion of an evaluation component was encouraged. The universities had to establish a collaboration with a school district that contained buildings that were eligible for aid from the Attendance Improvement/ Dropout Prevention (AIDP) Program. This ensured that those buildings with the greatest need for dropout prevention would be approached by the university/college project designers. Some educational programs are designed to attract high school dropouts back into diploma granting programs; SSPP projects were all designed to prevent students from dropping out in the first place.

The relatively wide latitude in the Request for Proposals yielded some very interesting results. The focus of the effort was clearly on dropout prevention and the presumption was that proposed programs would be aimed at middle school and high school students with very poor records of attendance, persistent tardiness, academic performance that was below that predicted by tested ability, numerous suspensions, negative attitudes toward school, and limited English proficiency. However, some applicants recognized that such difficulties often begin to develop very early in a student's educational career, such that true prevention really needed to begin in elementary school (one such multi-faceted support program is described and evaluated by Terry Cicchelli and Richard Baecher in Chapter 3). For example, the proposal submitted by the State University of New York at Binghamton (see Chapter 2) was designed to address the needs of high-risk students in the earliest elementary grades kindergarten through 3rd grade. Later, staff of the SSPP project in the State Education Department confided to the Binghamton group that this proposal had been quite startling, since it had been assumed that the projects would focus on high school students who had or were about to drop out, or perhaps middle school students who were most vulnerable (see Chapter 5). However, after reading the Binghamton proposal it was felt the case had been made that prevention could and should start in the earliest grades, and the Binghamton proposal was funded, along with nine others.

The diversity in programs that these flexible regulations allowed proved to be very important to the long-term health and success of the project. For there were, in fact, some disadvantages in the early stages of the project. For one thing, the original announcement of the funding came out in the summer, with little lead time for universities to develop proposals. The fact that the funding was granted for only 1 year at a time created enormous administrative difficulties for the directors of the various projects, as most of them were faculty members in the universities, in some cases deans and other senior administrators, who relied on project coordinators to carry out the nitty-gritty details of programs. Anxiety caused by the uncertainty of continued funding tended to interfere with the smooth development of the projects. In Chapter 9, Michael Bazigos offers a formal conceptualization for examining a working partnership in which a variety of conflicts might arise; organizational management theory helps us to understand why educational problems can rarely be solved by throwing money at them—even if the money is essential.

These various points are emphasized because similar programs are now being initiated by other states and at the federal level. For instance, in New York State, a closely related program, the Liberty Partnership Project, emerged after SSPP. The relationship between SSPP and Liberty became very complicated, exacerbated by the fact that SSPP was a legislative initiative and Liberty was created through the Governor's initiative. For a while both programs existed concurrently, and many directors of SSPP projects applied for and received Liberty funding. However, the stipulations in the Liberty guidelines were much more restrictive and narrowly focused than those for SSPP, so that, for example, the Binghamton emphasis on kindergarten through 3rd grade was not allowable under Liberty funding guidelines, forcing Binghamton to develop an entirely new project for middle and high school students in order to receive Liberty funds. At various points in this volume, authors comment on the pros and cons of funding of this nature, and by documenting these facts here we hope to help educational policy makers to learn from our experiences.

In the section below, we describe a good example of the type of project that was originally funded and use this project to discuss some of the issues that arose in the evaluation of SSPP.

The Nazareth College/Rochester City School District Project

Nazareth College collaborated originally with two, and later with four, secondary schools in Rochester that met the criteria for buildings with significant dropout problems. The Rochester City School District serves approximately 33,000 students, 70% of whom are classified as members of minorities (African American, Latino, Asian, and Native American). This student population is served by a teaching staff of about 2,500, 19% of whom are themselves members of minority groups. The demographics of the students are similar to those in many larger cities: 41% of the students live in single parent households; the annual dropout rate is 9%; almost 33% of the 9th grade class will drop out by the time their class graduates; junior high school failure in core academic subjects approaches 55%; suspensions number in the thousands per year; of those students who do graduate, only 34% are self-reported to be college bound (Center for Educational Development, 1986).

Each school in the Rochester district collaborated with the college staff to design its own curriculum and activities, but all programs had the same general features, which were quite similar to those of many of the other SSPP partnerships. These were:

Individual, in-school tutoring in math, reading, and writing provided by graduate students enrolled in a master's degree program in education

Student support, including mentoring by graduate students, employment opportunities, and cultural enrichment activities provided for high school students and their families

Family communication and support through parent training.

Staff and curriculum development for teachers, guidance counselors, and paraprofessionals that emphasized multicultural awareness and strategies for teaching at-risk students

The long-range goal of the ongoing intervention efforts was to significantly increase the number of students who successfully graduate from high school.

Identification Criteria   The State Education Department's Office of Education Planning and Support Services developed a screening instrument designed to aid in the identification of students at risk for dropping out. It should be remembered that students with identifiable disabilities are likely to already be receiving special education or remedial services. The population of students served by SSPP were those who tended to fall through the cracks between educational services: often students known to be failing in school but not presenting sufficient emotional, behavioral, or academic problems to justify special programming. It was the experience of most SSPP personnel that although these students might be known to individual teachers or counselors, there were few systematic efforts to track and identify them (see Grannis's discussion of providing attendance data to teachers, Chap. 4, this volume). The Nazareth/Rochester project therefore developed specific criteria for identifying students in 8th grade, going into 9th grade, who were at risk of dropping out:

1.   Standardized Achievement Test scores from the preceding spring in the 36th percentile in Reading or the 37th percentile in Math
2.   Failures in two or more core subjects in 8th grade
3.   One or more retentions at any time in school career
4.   Average daily attendance for preceding year below 81%
5.   Two or more days lost to suspension during the preceding school year

We found, however, that the profile cutoffs required some adjustment and that not all potentially at-risk students will be identified through these criteria alone. We therefore encouraged teacher, counselor, or self-referral, since some students' frustrations with school or with personal or domestic problems may not be immediately apparent through just the criteria in the profile. We are also cautious to avoid labeling students, a significant risk inherent in this approach. All SSPP personnel expressed concern, at one time or another, about singling out students and informing them, however subtly, that they were considered to be at risk.

Evaluation Design   The basic evaluation design requested by the State Education Department called for measures of student achievement, attendance, and behavior (e.g., suspensions) at the end of the program year and comparisons to the students' figures for the previous year. The Nazareth project also conducted an attitude/orientation survey of students themselves (*Wisconsin Youth Survey*, National Center on Effective Secondary Schools, no date) and recorded site observations to evaluate qualitative changes among identified students. The reasons for this last type of information was that it was felt that there was some need to better understand the process of becoming "at risk" in Rochester schools. We assume that this does not happen overnight, but is a long developmental process involving interaction between school organization and student-background factors. Later chapters discuss these interactions in some detail.

We have assumed that the process of becoming at risk affects students' attitudes toward school, adult institutions, and society as a whole. If school programs are to be at all meaningful, then they must certainly have an impact on students in areas that are not necessarily related to achievement. We must also look at the underlying attitudes that make students bond to school in purposeful ways, or at the external factors that interfere with bonding, increasing student disaffection. Examining student attitudes and orientation may also be helpful in developing curricula, teaching strategies, and staff development in future projects (Crichlow, 1988).

GENERAL ISSUES IN EVALUATION

The SSPP programs were not designed as basic research studies; pre–post comparisons provide useful information, but it is not as definitive as that derived from the random assignment of participants to intervention and control groups. Even measure of change within the identified group proved to be difficult. Grades vary as a function of teachers' different grading policies; achievement tests are not administered every year; suspension rates are often influenced by specific building and district policies that vary from year to year. Students in this population often lead unstable lives: students in SSPP move in and out of districts quite frequently, may be assigned to foster families, and sometimes withdraw from participation in a program.

Because each SSPP program was required to report various statistics to the state agency administering the grants, it was possible, on a yearly basis, to compile descriptive statistics about the program as a whole. After 4 years, these statistics were summarized and yielded the following findings:

1. The vast majority, averaging 96% annually, of the students who initially participated in one of the programs were still in school. All programs at the high school level were reporting that some participants were indeed graduating, and individual success stories indicated that SSPP students were, in some cases, going on to post-secondary education.

2. Project reports generated from a variety of different data sources indicated that program activities helped motivate students to study, resulted in improved self-esteem, fostered family involvement, and improved home–school communication.

3. SSPP preservice activities included training a cadre of 393 college students to work effectively with students at risk.
4. SSPP inservice training activities provided more than 1,000 teachers and school staff with effective instruction in strategies for working with students considered to be at risk for school failure.
5. SSPP encouraged post-secondary institutions to review and revise college curricula and enabled them to develop effective strategies for responding to the needs of students at risk.

Each of these outcomes will be discussed in different contexts in the ensuing chapters. Obviously, an overall evaluation of effectiveness is difficult to conduct. All programs provided, as the Nazareth College– Rochester City Schools partnership illustrates, a complex array of services at a variety of different levels. Some programs have described efforts at systemic reform of teaching practices, building policies, and teacher preparation—Chapters 5 (Meyer et al.) and 6 (Cohen) provide details on such reforms at the middle school level. Other projects focused on the specific services provided to students on an individual basis; at the high school level these included such interesting activities as carefully designed visits to a university (see Chapter 7) and the creation of smaller, enriched organizations, called "houses," within schools (see Chapter 8). No matter where on the spectrum a project fell (and it was often on more than one dimension), the funded activities were still completely intertwined—confounded, if one prefers the scientific language—with a variety of superordinate considerations. The most important of these was the sense of caring and concern that was communicated to participating students by those conducting the projects. Whether expressed through tutors, mentoring, enrichment activities, curriculum reform, or family support, the importance of a commitment to finding some strategy to assist in the education of the most disadvantaged group of children in public education cannot be dismissed, but neither can it be easily evaluated.

One important form of evaluation is self-evaluation. Chapter 11 by Norman Shapiro and Chapter 12 by Allison Alden both explore the impact of SSPP on the university programs themselves. With hindsight, most of the SSPP project personnel recognize how the need to examine teacher-preparation programs and policies has become paramount. These issues are addressed in a number of chapters and are emphasized in the Epilogue, in which the editors make a series of recommendations of relevance to anyone concerned with the effective education of all students.

I

THE EARLY YEARS

2

Home–School Partnerships
Involving Families
in the Educational Process

IAN M. EVANS,
AKIKO OKIFUJI,
AND ALISON D. THOMAS

After many years of relative prosperity as a manufacturing community, the town of Binghamton has lately been faced with numerous social concerns—a declining tax base, job loss and high unemployment, immigration from Southeast Asia and central Europe, growing drug traffic on the supply lines between major cities, increasing juvenile crime, high rates of infant mortality, and rapidly increasing numbers of children born to single parents. In the surrounding rural areas, the decline of the farming economy has resulted in increasing poverty and decreasing opportunities for students once they graduate from school. The scenarios below illustrate the effects of these changes on some of the families in Binghamton, and especially on the academic life of the town's children:

> Cindy was hurt, angry, and confused. As a single parent of four children, she had always felt she was doing pretty well for her family. When the notes started coming home from school about her oldest daughter, Sarah, she resented the way they were written and the negative terms used by the teacher to describe Sarah's noncompliant and aggressive behavior. She did not see why there was so much concern about keeping her home from

We would like to thank Allison Alden, Brenda Brown, and Mary Chanecka for their invaluable input, as well as Dr. James Lee, Superintendent, Binghamton City Schools, for his enthusiastic support and cooperation.

kindergarten sometimes to help around the house and babysit the younger ones. Cindy felt school didn't really teach many useful things, especially not in kindergarten. She particularly disliked the note that implied that perhaps Sarah could not learn as well as the other students. Cindy remembered that those were the kinds of things that were said about her when she was in school. Instead of responding to the notes or complying with what was requested, Cindy decided that she would keep Sarah home *more* often and would refuse to attend the parent—teacher conference coming up soon.

Mr. Rossi was known in the faculty lounge as a difficult parent. Only that week he had called the elementary building principal and yelled obscenities into the phone. In the fall, he had stormed out of the parent—teacher conference, complaining that his son's 2nd grade teacher was incompetent; Mrs. Rossi, looking embarrassed and anxious, had quickly followed him. They claimed that the teacher was publicly humiliating their son Tony by constantly criticizing his reading errors in front of the class. Tony started to say he hated school and was showing reluctance to get up in time to catch the school bus. Previous attempts by the Rossis to talk to the principal had not gone well: he had pointed out that this teacher was one of the best in the school, with high standards—her classes always showed impressive gains in reading scores on achievement tests.

Scenarios like these are repeated every day across all the small-city and rural school districts in which educators and educational researchers and interventionists are working. Cindy lives in considerable poverty and isolation with her boyfriend in a trailer on a secluded dirt road; she has no car or telephone. Mr. Rossi has been unemployed for almost a year; Mrs. Rossi's state job as a direct care worker for people with developmental disabilities has helped maintain their neat home in a blue-collar neighborhood, but her husband's drinking and bouts of depression are becoming a serious strain. What can be done to assist families like Cindy's to help diminish the risk of their children experiencing academic failures and dropping out of school? A few key steps are to increase proactive parental involvement, improve communication between home and school, and establish collaborative partnerships between parents and teachers.

The Binghamton School Partnership Project (BSPP) was developed as a preventive model based on such a strategy. During the project, two university departments (Education and Psychology) collaborated with a small-city school district and later a number of rural districts in the surrounding region. The state university is a well-known undergraduate liberal arts institution with growing strength in graduate-level research. The majority of its students come from downstate, and the university has traditionally remained uninvolved with the local community. In fact, the usual town—gown conflict has been endemic, and even the School of Education has generally interacted with the community only in the context of practicum training sites, predominantly in the suburban, upper-income districts. Collaboration was thus a new departure for everyone involved, creating an unusual alliance between the university and the local community.

With the American public school system being so decentralized and community based—in New York State alone there are over 700 school districts—and controlled by democratically elected school boards, the possibility that there might *not* be close cooperation between parents and the school system seems quite anomalous. And yet the degree of active parental involvement in the educational process is really quite limited (Moles, 1987). On one level, this could be seen as a desirable result of the professionalization of education. In cases in which parents have intruded into decisions such as those regarding what books should or should not be read, what curricula should be emphasized or de-emphasized, or which teachers might or might not be acceptable, the motivation has often reflected narrow sectarian interests, and the outcome has generally been regressive. Thus, there is often a reluctance on the part of educators to be influenced by the wishes and needs of parents and families. If the issue is seen as a struggle for control between opposing parties (Lightfoot, 1978), then parental involvement is indeed something to be shunned. However, if the concept of a partnership is fostered, new opportunities arise that can benefit both schools and families (New York State Education Department, 1987a). The literature on parental involvement strongly supports the contention that such partnerships can lead to improvements in student achievement, self-concept, and behavior (Henderson, 1986; Sattes, 1985).

Currently, the predominant arenas for parent contact and participation are those traditions, common in America's school system, of Parent–Teacher Associations, open houses, parent nights, parent–teacher conferences, and notes sent home with students. All too often, these activities seem to have two major characteristics. One is that they represent an expansion of the control concept and usually reflect the greater power of the school, as most of these activities are one-sided and involve the transmission of information *to* parents, rather than true exchange or dialogue (see Darling, 1983; Roos, 1979). The other is that they appeal to, and are most often utilized by, a limited segment of the parents in any given district, namely those who are members of the middle class or those families with the most economic resources. In working with a district serving a wide range of socioeconomic groups, we in the BSPP have been particularly struck by the extent to which these traditional activities fail to attract, benefit, or recognize the more disadvantaged segments of the populace (Salisbury, 1987). Meetings held at night may be difficult to attend because child care and transportation are unavailable, while meetings scheduled during the teacher's work day may be difficult to attend because these parents are least likely to be able to take time off from work. Additionally, teacher or principal contact with these parents usually implies a problem rather than an accomplishment on the part of the student, so they may be understandably reluctant to interact with educators and administrators.

To develop a true educational partnership, what is needed is a new set of assumptions, goals, and models of how the school system can interact with parents for the benefit of students. In this chapter we discuss and attempt to clarify these assumptions and present an argument for the value of effective collaboration between teachers and parents. We describe different ways in which parents can become involved in their children's education and the potential benefits of this involvement. We also discuss the efforts made by BSPP to promote and foster home–school interaction and describe in more detail some of the strategies that seem to have been particularly successful, as well as some of the common barriers to effective interaction. Finally, we relate the discussion to the specific benefits that family–school collaboration has in the prevention of dropout and in increasing the effectiveness of the educational process.

CONCEPTS OF FAMILY INVOLVEMENT

It is tempting, when discussing the importance of home–school partnerships, to focus on the need to help families with their problems. That is to say, the school tends to be seen as a social agency capable of providing services to those families judged to be at risk in some way. But the psychological conditions that seem to benefit children can be identified independently of the superficial structure or economic circumstances of the family. Loving, nurturing caregivers who protect children from physical abuse, pain, and other hardships are not found only within traditional family structures. Democratic childrearing styles that encourage responsibility and the development of moral principles are healthier for children than either neglect or excessive control. The effectiveness and quality of family systems, therefore, seem to be very much matters of degree. Attempts to categorize individual families as good or bad, or high risk or low risk, tend to be problematic. Within social work fields, the most encouraging trends are those that focus on family "preservation" (Whittaker, Kinney, Tracy, & Booth, 1990)—that respect the dignity and well-meaningness of all families. There are various concepts of family involvement that respect these assumptions.

Extending School into the Home

One of the most widely adopted approaches to family involvement is the practice in early education of directly involving parents as the "first teachers" of their children. Much is now known about the aspects of home life that are important for enhancing cognitive development. Ways that parents should talk to their children, engage them in intellectual activities, spend time reading with them, and play with them in order to stimulate intellectual growth are quite well understood (e.g., Meyerhoff & White, 1986).

Head Start programs, for instance, have developed this kind of parent education into a very elaborate network (see Weiss, 1989). When extended into the elementary school years, the focus is especially strong on reading, helping with and encouraging the completion of homework, and finding cognitively enriching activities for the summer (Rich, 1985). In the BSPP project, we focused considerable attention on all three of these areas, although the schools already had an active program in place called PARP—Parents As Reading Partners—to encourage parents to read to their children. We implemented a backpack-lending program whereby children could take home a set of entertaining educational materials, some of which they got to keep and some of which were returned with the backpack the next school day. We also initiated a "Get Set for Summer" program that we encouraged the teachers themselves to take over. Free pizza, create-your-own lapel buttons, helium filled balloons, and information about public summer activities were all interspersed with direct demonstrations by teachers to show parents how they could locate enriching activities for their children.

While there is much support for this strategy, and some good evaluation of its efficacy at a variety of ages (e.g., Burkett, 1982), it is important to ensure that the influence of such activities is not one-sided (Swap, 1990). Educators need to be careful not to take responsibility for knowing how parents should be behaving, judging whether they are functioning in these sanctioned ways or not, or undertaking to teach them if they consider the parents to be at risk in terms of providing their children with appropriate cognitive stimulation. It may well be that there are elements of the families' culture that promote intellectual development in ways that are not readily perceived or valued by the school culture. For instance, there may be a strong focus at school on reading, whereas some families convey information through an oral tradition based on story telling or singing songs. Simply requesting that families make changes may mistakenly convey the message that parents are the cause of a student's problems. Such communication is detrimental to both the family and the school, as it increases antagonistic feelings between the two.

Another major concern about this model is that it fails to assess the *reasons* why the parents are not providing an intellectually stimulating environment. Often, it is not because they do not understand the value of cognitive interactions with a young child, but because their own lives are so stressful or problematic that they have little time, energy, or enthusi-asm to devote to the task. Mothers who are depressed, who are being physically abused, or who have difficulty in dealing with their young child's behavior and engaging his or her attention are unlikely to sud-denly be able to provide a new range of stimulating activities after they have attended some school-based group or workshop on how to support academic work at home. And the parents who are perhaps least able to make the necessary changes in their family routines are also those least likely to attend sessions or to act on recommendations (e.g., Wahler, 1980).

Families' Attitudes Toward School

Based on our intensive interactions with many families, we have become convinced that an important feature of family involvement is not so much direct participation in school activities, but the kinds of attitudes that parents convey to children about school. What is it that parents say about school and learning that communicates to their youngsters the value of school and the activities that take place there? Little is known about such variables. But drawing from our experiences with parents judged by teachers to be at risk, we have the strong impression that many of these parents were themselves unsuccessful in school. As a result, they have rather negative impressions of school and memories of highly aver-sive things happening to them there. Thus, they are not easily able to communicate to their own children the value of education, particularly, perhaps, in districts in which there is considerable stability—many of our parents went to the same schools at which their children are now experiencing early signs of failure.

A somewhat related topic has been explored by Epstein (1986) through her survey of parents' attitudes about helping their children and of the way they perceive teachers' efforts to involve them in the academic development of students. Epstein found that parents value specific sug-gestions made by teachers concerning home-based activities, but some-times doubt their own ability to help their children, especially in the higher grades. Epstein (1987) has generated recommendations for school administrators regarding the types of teacher activities that promote pa-rental involvement through the higher grades.

Parental Decision Making: The Special Education Example

There is an interesting lesson that can be drawn from special education regarding parental involvement. In this arena, parents have had a long history of having to fight for appropriate educational services for their children. Prior to PL 94-142, the Education for All Handicapped Children Act of 1975, parents of such children often considered themselves lucky if they could simply secure a school placement for their child. (PL 94-142 was updated by PL 101-476, the Individuals with Disabilities Education Act of 1990 [IDEA].) In many cases parents had to form their own schools, as happened in the early Association for Retarded Citizens programs and among parents of children with autism. This situation has dramatically affected the attitudes of parents of children with disabilities toward the appropriateness of educational placements and procedures. This fighting spirit was most noticeable in the statutory language of PL 94-142, which gave parents a wide variety of rights and responsibilities regarding educational programs. The best example of this principle can be found in the legal requirement of the development of an individualized education program (IEP) for each student.

If the IEP is seen as an individual curriculum for a student with a disability, then the requirement that parents participate in the development of the plan is a quite radical approach, and one that general education has not yet begun to approximate. Of course, there are data suggesting that the actual degree of participation by parents in such planning varies; there are accounts of professional teams presenting parents with a written plan and expecting them to simply accept and sign it without further discussion (Turnbull & Leonard, 1981). Related service personnel, such as school psychologists, can be instrumental in encouraging and improving parental input by obtaining insights from parents regarding a child's needs, by avoiding jargon or explaining the meaning of terms and tests, and by recognizing the value of different perspectives on the student (Fine, 1984).

We have conducted a variety of studies on parental involvement in general and special education. Salisbury and Evans (1988) showed that parents of children in special education are much more involved and feel more positive about their involvement than do parents of children in general education. By high school, parents of typical students feel that they have little participation in their children's education. Comer (1984) has emphasized the importance of representative governance procedures and an involvement of parents in decision making that gives them, as well as teachers and students, a clear sense of direction and purpose. We believe that the example of special education clearly demonstrates the value of such a policy.

Parent Empowerment

The statutory mandate for parental involvement in special education suggests that parents should play a much more significant role in improving schools. Sometimes this involvement takes the form of active parental participation in securing funds, assembling equipment, physical plant maintenance, or any of a whole host of other activities, including participation in the classroom as aides, tutors, and role models (e.g., Henning-Stout & Goode, 1986). While, in general, we see value in the spirit behind this effort, there is always a danger that such active participation will result in the domination of the school's educational policies by a small, active, select group of parents. Furthermore, it has the danger of following a charity model, with parents directly providing those services that the school should be responsible for. Often, the need for these parental supports does not arise out of a desire for collaboration, but out of the regrettable fact that there are insufficient funds available to otherwise provide playground equipment, classroom amenities, or additional tutors.

Another important facet of parental empowerment is professionals' ability to provide help to families in ways that encourage self-sufficiency and equity. As we mentioned earlier, assistance can foster feelings of helplessness in the recipient, as well as causing dependency, lowered self-esteem, and resentment (Dunst & Trivette, 1987). Dunst has used family systems theory to develop intervention strategies that *enable* families by focusing on activities that foster parents' self-efficacy beliefs, "conveying a sense of cooperation and joint responsibility [partnership] for meeting needs and solving problems" (Dunst & Trivette, 1987, p. 452).

Cochran (1987) argues that empowerment is a *process* involving several steps, rather than an outcome. Interestingly, he suggests that this process begins on an individual level, with parents changing the extent of their self-regard. When they become more comfortable with themselves, parents begin to expand their networks, first to personal friends and relatives (close others), and then toward more impersonal organizations, such as schools, government agencies, and so on. It was on the basis of this conceptualization that we designed certain rules for our efforts to encourage families. The home-visitor model developed by BSPP always had as a primary consideration that the strengths and assets of the home would be respected and fostered. Unlike the typical communication from the schools, during our home-visits, BSPP personnel studiously avoided any suggestion of blame or criticism of the families, instead trying to suggest simple ways that parents could begin to test their abilities to make changes.

Promoting True Collaboration

If community members can become involved in a school for any reason, it seems a wonderful accomplishment. If community members get together to contribute to the school—not because the school is too financially strapped to provide its own amenities, but because they wish to express their commitment to and support of the local school—then the enterprise can be of immense value. Such efforts also convey to youngsters that adults care about their education and about the buildings in which they spend so much of their young lives. Similarly, it communicates that teachers and professionals appreciate the support and assistance that they receive from families, particularly from those considered difficult or "problem" families.

A true collaboration model assumes mutual respect and recognition. Some teachers blame families for children's difficulties, and if parents are asked to comment on the cause of their child's problems they are likely to identify the teacher as disliking the youngster or being unwilling to bend in order to assist him or her. In general, conflict is more likely to occur when two parties have experienced different styles of socialization. For example, a particular family may be accustomed to aggressive, authoritarian styles of communication and may not appreciate more democratic decision making. Because the child has a long history of learning within the family prior to school attendance, the child's behavioral style may be perceived by teachers as maladaptive. Teachers may readily label a child as, for example, "spoiled," or the parents as "inadequate," failing to recognize that there is a conflict between the styles of socialization at home and school (Okun, 1984). Thus, in some cases there is active conflict between home and school. A collaborative model assumes that such conflicts are themselves failures, regardless of where the blame might objectively lie, and conflict resolution strategies require acceptance of responsibility by both parties.

Interestingly, parents are increasingly encouraged to work constructively with school personnel. Indeed, why would educators not encourage collaboration? Surely, no matter what the problem, it is essential for parent and teacher to work together. We were impressed by such popular items as a magazine article entitled "Educating Parents" (Baldwin, 1990), the author of which recommended the following strategies for allowing parents to work *together* with schools: 1) mutual respect, 2) observing the child's behavior together, 3) openness to the issues involved, and 4) responsible problem solving by avoiding such strategies as denial of the seriousness of issues, just trying to wait the problem out, blaming the teacher, being unwilling to try, encouraging counter-aggression in the child, getting angry, or believing that some other school can do much better.

Similar advice could be given to school personnel. They, after all, are the professionals and should possess an understanding of children's behavior and why it is occurring. Blaming parents and families for their problems does nothing to help solve them, and yet we have observed teachers with very limited knowledge of family dynamics or of the origins and maintenance of children's emotional difficulties doing just that. In the following sections we discuss specific strategies and methods that can be adopted to ensure that true home–school partnerships are fostered and that meaningful communication takes place between teachers and parents for the benefit of students.

GENERAL ISSUES IN HOME–SCHOOL COLLABORATION

How Teachers View Parents

It is obviously impossible to generalize about teachers' attitudes toward families, but, as we have already suggested, teachers' lack of knowledge about the problems and issues faced by today's families would seem to be something that can be readily addressed through preservice courses (see Chap. 12, this volume, by Allison Alden) or workshops. One of the workshops that BSPP provided for teachers was based on research conducted by college faculty and teachers who collaborated to gather information on the changing demographics of the American family. Training of this kind sensitizes teachers to such issues as how to handle having students make greeting cards for mothers' or fathers' day when some of them may have single parents or step parents. Such workshops can be a valuable first step in ensuring that teachers, especially in the elementary grades, are familiar with the home situations from which their students will likely be coming.

There are also other specific strategies that can be used. Drop-in centers and telephone "hotlines" allow easy contact before problems are blown out of proportion, whereas in one of our elementary schools parents were required to give 48 hours notice if they intended to visit the school! Attempt to include in planning committees, career exploration activities, and other school-related events those parents least likely to volunteer for such activities. Community-based organizations, such as cooperative extensions, emphasize collaboration between home and school in community projects. We provided communication-skills workshops for teachers on such subjects as perspective taking, listening skills, and providing positive feedback. Teachers' evaluations of this training were not particularly positive; they generally felt that they understood these principles already, although our own observations suggested they were certainly not practicing them. Some authorities (e.g., Schnorr, Ford, Davern, Park-Lee, & Meyer, 1989; Walker, 1989) have suggested that it would be preferable to encourage parents and teachers to work according to the same principles of cooperative learning that we encourage in classroom instruction (Johnson & Johnson, 1982).

How Parents View Teachers

Obviously, the focus of this volume is on changing schools and school policies. We may not, as educators, have much power to change families or eliminate social problems, nor is it necessarily our responsibility to do so. But one strategy that school systems *can* employ begins with finding out what parental perceptions are of the district and its policies. BSPP has been conducting such a survey for some years, and we believe that it can serve as a useful model for other districts. It would not be difficult for schools to obtain such systematic evaluation from an independent organization. We hear a great deal in the press about schools across the nation getting "report cards," but what does this really mean? Usually it refers to the opinions of some committee or findings from standardized test scores. Most teachers are well aware of the serious limitations of such data and quite justifiably resent such information being used to judge their efforts. But parental perceptions of the schools and their atmosphere provide a community-based report card that is meaningful and should be taken seriously.

Our parental questionnaire revealed that while most parents were generally satisfied with the school program, there was a small but angry minority who had very specific complaints that they expressed in detail. Very often these complaints were related to the attitudes of the principal or the school administrative staff, rather than to teachers.

SPECIFIC MODELS OF HOME–SCHOOL PARTNERSHIPS

The findings from our anonymous questionnaire revealed clearly that there are families who have highly negative perceptions of schools. It is unlikely that these families could be brought into a partnership through the efforts of the school itself. Thus, the home-visitor model developed by BSPP seems to have real promise for fostering home–school cooperation. Below, we first describe the general model and then provide some details on a specific project designed to help students whom the teachers and parents considered to be having special difficulties at school.

The School-Partner Concept

Our home-visitor model evolved over time in response to our perceptions of need. The general principles underlying the project were that we had to avoid labeling children, that we should try to ensure that students are not identified as being at risk, and that we needed to be cautious not to blame the victim by scapegoating the student or the family. Our home visitors were therefore labelled as *School Partners* and their tasks were to serve as mediators and go-betweens, to be advocates for both the parents and the teachers, and to interpret each group's needs (Alden, Brown, & Chanecka, 1988).

This required the selection of people who knew the community well, who could work with families, and who the teachers and school administrators would view as being credible. In the original model, the School Partners made contact with the families of children who had been referred by teachers as having difficulties and with families chosen at random from those who returned a consent postcard indicating they were willing to participate in a project designed to foster cooperation between families and the school.

The Design of Formal Interventions

It was important that we would not attempt to provide traditional, intensive mental health services, of which the main target is usually the child and family. The procedures that we developed can potentially be incorporated into the general school system at minimal cost, utilizing, as much as possible, resources already available to most public school systems. In our model, the children are not identified and labelled as "patients," and the interventions take place in the natural contexts of home and school rather than in a clinic. The primary emphasis of the intervention is on strategies that promote home–school communication and collaborative problem solving.

After referral by either teachers or parents, the home visitors met with teachers and parents independently to obtain clarification on the areas of concern. They brought this information back to the BSPP project staff and obtained consultation from one of two clinical child psychologists or from one of two doctoral students in clinical psychology. With assistance from the graduate student, a "diagnostic profile" was developed in which all identified areas of concern were placed into a hypothesized causal model of influence (see Evans, 1985). Using this causal model, potential areas for change were identified and a series of treatment goals developed for the subsequent intervention plan. Interventions were designed around four elements considered essential components of behavioral interventions with children (see Evans, 1989): 1) ecological change (to modify eliciting and setting events—those social and physical stimuli that trigger emotional responses); 2) manipulation of consequences; 3) teaching more adaptive alternatives; and 4) teaching longer-term, preventive (usually cognitive) strategies. In all cases these interventions involved changes in teacher and parent behaviors, since the home visitors did not work directly with the children themselves.

Intervention plans were explained to teachers and parents during classroom or home visits. Home visits were scheduled at the parents' convenience and sometimes occurred in neighbor's homes, local diners, or other settings in which the parents were most comfortable or most willing to meet. A standard goal of each intervention plan was to ensure direct contact between families and school personnel. This might involve a visit by the parent to the school, written notes, telephone contact, or the teacher going to the parents' home. Often, there had been a history of conflict between family members and school personnel, and standard mediational techniques were used to resolve these.

Specific behavior problems were addressed with direct suggestions for how behaviors could be handled by teachers and parents. The principal of each school building was kept apprised of the student's involvement, since the school retained responsibility for the student's welfare, for providing a complete educational service, and for dealing with crises (e.g., aggressive outbursts requiring suspension, unlawful behavior in the community resulting in police involvement). Toward the end of the maximum number of home visits designated in the protocol, the home visitors would begin to propose more-general problem solving strategies that the parents could use. For the classroom teacher, more-general strategies might include educative interventions (Evans & Meyer, 1985) including curricular and attitudinal change, positive acceptance of the student, and understanding the student's problems in the light of the home situation. Only a minimal amount of information about the home was transmitted to the teacher by the home visitor, in part to preserve the parents' right to privacy, but also in order to encourage direct communication between parents and teachers themselves.

The home visitors were responsible for obtaining informed consent from parents willing to participate in the project, gathering all data from the families, and keeping the consultants informed of new or unusual problems. Involvement in the project did not prevent the school or families from seeking other help or educational services to which the student might be entitled. A formal evaluation was conducted in which the results of the home-visitor effort were compared to figures for a control school in which only the first and last (data-gathering) visits took place, and it showed that the home-visitor intervention significantly reduced the number of students referred for and placed in special education services. Teachers reported improvement in the classroom behavior of students involved in the project, but this was not significantly greater than that reported for the control students. Parents in the participating group, however, reported a very significant decrease in the problems that had been identified as the targets of the intervention. Both parents and teachers who participated agreed that communication between home and school had been much improved. Where there was agreement that communication was better, there was also a significant improvement in the teachers' reports of the academic progress of the students (Evans & Okifuji, 1992; Evans, Okifuji, Engler, Bromley, & Tishelman, 1993).

PSYCHOLOGICAL ISSUES

When teachers find that a child has a particular difficulty at school, more-detailed information may be needed in order to develop intervention strategies. Dimensions of problem behaviors, such as duration, intensity, and frequency, are difficult to estimate from the limited observations that teachers can make within the school setting. Problems may be chronic and generalized, such that a student might almost always be non-compliant, but, conversely, they may be selective; for example we have had one or two students referred who would not converse at school but were talkative and friendly at home. In this latter situation, teachers might simply assume a lack of academic and cognitive abilities in such children, without knowing much about their masked potential for academic achievement. Such assumptions could in turn be detrimental to the child's attitude towards school and have a negative effect on later academic life.

It is also helpful for teachers to know what parents expect their children to learn at school. There may be significant differences in what contemporary school children are expected to master at a given age and what their parents were expected to learn at the same age when they were in school. Some parents may simply not be aware that children should be completing certain assignments, and as a result they may fail to insist that their children complete homework.

At times, however, problems go beyond mere misunderstandings regarding expectations; more serious concerns may accompany teachers' perceptions that the parent's own communication style is inadequate. In such cases, rather than becoming emotionally involved and feeling sure that the source of the child's difficulty has now been identified, teachers should proceed accordingly to the working hypothesis that the child may be facing considerable stress due to different communication styles required at school and at home. It is helpful to conceptualize this by recognizing that both the family and school are systems, and that both set standards for certain behaviors. When these standards differ between home and school, or are incompatible, the child faces considerable conflict, resulting in confusion, anxiety, and frustration. This same concept is important for those conducting direct intervention, who need to be certain that the same rules and standards that are being encouraged by the school are implemented in other settings in order to ensure the maintenance and generalization of behavior (Blechman, Kotanchik, & Taylor, 1981).

RECOMMENDATIONS

Based on our 5 years of developing a better understanding between home and school, we have developed a number of specific recommendations. Some of these are easier and less expensive to follow than others, but all are practical and within the current capabilities and resources of most school districts. Some of the recommendations simply seem logical, and some have a certain amount of empirical support. However, they cannot be considered rules, but are rather proposed as guidelines that districts might find useful as they try to enhance their involvement with parents and families. Our recommendations are as follows:

Provide inservice training or workshops for teachers on demographics and trends in the contemporary American family in order to increase sensitivity to the varieties of family structures that are possible and that can be effective. Supply teachers and principals with materials that emphasize working *with* parents (e.g., Henderson, Marburger, & Ooms, 1986).

Create a variety of possible ways that parents and teachers can meet each other. Do not attribute parental nonparticipation in events to apathy or lack of interest; view it instead as evidence that the school has not yet found a meaningful and motivating structure to encourage parents to attend activities.

Encourage small groups of teachers and parents to work together to set up committees to review school policies that might be aversive or intimidating to families. Use cooperative teaming principles in conducting these groups.

Identify those families who seem to be least likely to participate in traditional activities and provide them with some structured activity conducted in cooperation with teachers; a good possibility would be organizing a parent–teacher group to review material sent home by the school to see that it is positive in tone and not lecturing or critical.

Utilize small grants (e.g., from a teacher center, or union funds) specifically to encourage teachers to devise new projects that will foster home–school cooperation. Examples of such projects are: 1) starting a newsletter written by the classroom teacher that is positive and that identifies *all* students in some desirable way, rather than singling out only the brightest children for attention; or 2) enhancing communication at, and structuring of, parent–teacher conferences (Mcloughlin, 1987).

For the earlier grades, develop a system of supplying fun educational materials that can go home for parents and families to use. The lack of such materials in low-income homes might really surprise many school personnel. A back-pack lending program is one example of such an approach.

Establish some system or arbitrator for mediating parent–teacher conflict, such as a telephone hotline, community service coordinator, home-visitor, or neutral third party.

Utilize auxiliary personnel such as school counselors, school psychologists, school social workers, or assistant principals, as problem solvers *before* serious crises are allowed to develop. These personnel can utilize procedures such as the BSPP protocol, but there are also various other strategies that are valid as long as the intent is to solve problems through home–school cooperation, rather than by blaming the parent.

Conduct regular, independent evaluations of how the school's atmosphere and communications are being interpreted by families in the district. Make sure that such surveys reach those families who might be most alienated or least likely to participate in home–school projects. Take pride in positive evaluations, but recognize that each negative comment, no matter how unjustified it may appear to be, represents a family who is not supporting education in collaboration with their child's school, and that this situation cannot be beneficial for the student.

Create a policy that establishes the school as an integral part of the community and that supports the diversity and uniqueness of its members, rather than working with or valuing only the contribution of the more-privileged minority. Base the underlying philosophy of your effort on the recognition that there is no such thing as a parent who does not value educational opportunity for his or her own child.

CONCLUDING COMMENTS

It is clear that a model of education that fails to encourage the active involvement of families as partners is no longer functional in our society. Just as professional medicine has relinquished its ideology of "knowing best" in favor of encouraging self-knowledge and enlightenment in consumers of medical services, so education has to accommodate the needs, aspirations, and goals of families. In this way, children's educational development becomes the responsibility of parents and teachers working together. The model of collaboration that we have developed is one of true partnership, not one of patronage in which the school provides services for families in order to remedy their "deficiencies."

Although it is easy to subscribe to the logic and philosophy that underly such partnerships, it may be more difficult to formulate strategies to achieve effective collaboration. This is because over the years schools have adopted practices that have served to distance parents and limit their involvement, while at the same time recognizing that ultimately the public school system does serve at the behest of the families as taxpayers. This duality creates an uncomfortable situation, since parents, demanding more say in the management of the institutions that they finance, may be attempting to exert control over schools regardless of whether or not they are qualified to do so. Empowering parents is an odd concept, since it is already the parents who finance, and hence run, schools, though they may not have a proper working relationship with school personnel, a relationship based on understanding and respect.

We have described various practical strategies that can be adopted in order to foster such understanding. We do not necessarily advocate greater intrusion by parents into the educational process. We value and welcome the specific and technical knowledge of educators and fully recognize that parents do not always have the independence of judgment and wisdom to be able to regulate many of the facets of education. But parents do know their children and they do know what they wish to see as the result of education, and thus they are perfectly capable of entering into an effective partnership with schools. Such a partnership will create an entirely new context for education in the years ahead. Parents are likely to want to and be able to participate in the process to varying degrees providing schools with one of the most exciting opportunities for harnessing people's potential currently available. The concepts we have outlined here might contribute to a change in the design of a system that already has established implicit standards for parental involvement, but has not begun to realize the potential of such involvement. Once the construct of an equitable partnership is accepted and implemented, new opportunities will be created to the extraordinary benefit of both parents and teachers. This was what happened with our two original examples:

> After trying to connect with the parent for 2 months, the School Partner finally succeeded in meeting with Cindy in her home. A good relationship was established and they began to meet regularly. Their meetings centered on three main items, though crises took priority as they arose. First they discussed Cindy's feelings about the teacher and why she felt this way. The School Partner helped Cindy recognize that keeping Sarah home was only going to convey to her that school was unimportant, and that as a result, she might perform poorly and experience failure. Cindy did not want Sarah to have the same kind of school experience that she had as a child; Sarah began to attend school regularly.
>
> Next, Cindy and the School Partner talked about how to improve the relationship between Cindy and the teacher. The School Partner helped Cindy write a positive note about the things that she felt her daughter was enjoying in school. A positive reply from the teacher (after a great deal of support and coaching from the School Partner) then came home from school. This problem-solving instructional process continued slowly until Cindy had become a regular parent volunteer and was helping to sew costumes for a school play.
>
> Finally, the School Partner helped Cindy to examine some of the parenting techniques she was using at home and make changes in favor of more sensitive and effective methods. Cindy also recognized that a number of

other major issues affected her own life and her ability to provide a healthy environment for her children. She decided, with the School Partner's support, to seek counselling for herself.

The School Partner met with the Rossis and listened carefully to their concerns. By the second visit they were confiding to her that this was the first time anyone connected with the district had seemed interested in them for any reason other than simply to blame them for Tony's poor academic progress. The School Partner asked Tony's teacher to send home a couple of positive notes; at first she resisted, saying that Tony should be evaluated for a learning disability, but when she had heard a little more about the pressures on the family (no specific details were given her), she relented and sent home a reinforcing note drawn from some samples provided by BSPP.

The principal, surprised when Mr. Rossi called and apologized for his outburst, agreed to support a series of short workshops on new approaches to teaching reading. The workshop leader was a School of Education faculty member who provided a series of suggestions regarding reading instruction through the use of children's books and stories. Once the teacher was more comfortable with this approach based on literature, she agreed to meet with the Rossis and make suggestions about books Tony could read at home. The meeting, arranged by the School Partner, took place at the school library after school. The Rossis admitted that they had been trying to help their son by drilling him with flash cards they had bought at the supermarket. Together, the teacher and parents set up an alternative arrangement by which the Rossis would take out books from the public library. Later, Tony received a certificate from the school principal for the number of books he read over a vacation. The certificate is framed and hanging in the Rossis' kitchen. Mr. Rossi is still unemployed and there continue to be some stresses at home, but Tony is no longer experiencing academic problems.

3

Early Intervention
Linking Education and Social Services with Care

TERRY CICCHELLI
AND RICHARD E. BAECHER

The Fordham project began with the clear realization that dropping out of school is not an isolated event, but rather is just one step in an interactive process involving a wide range of school- and home-related factors. First, we saw the role of the family as a crucial component in any early intervention model. It may seem obvious, but as Rumberger, Ghatak, Poulos, Dornbusch, and Ritter (1988) point out, families exercise a powerful influence on the educational well-being of students and so must be involved in any effort designed to produce either immediate or long-range student achievement gains (see also Goodson & Hess, 1975; Houston & Joseph, 1994). For example, increased parental involvement has been related to significant improvements in the academic performance and attendance of students with a history of doing poorly in school (Sattes, 1985; Seeley, 1984; Walberg, 1984; see also Cohen, Chap. 6, this volume). Furthermore, we recognized that even during the elementary school years, intervention designed to improve children's academic self-concepts would be complex and difficult. As early as the primary level, students can already perceive low teacher expectations (Brookover, Brody, & Warfield, 1981) and may be-

---

An earlier version of this chapter was published as T. Cicchelli & R.E. Baecher (1993, Fall/Winter). School restructuring: A school–university partnership. *The School Community Journal*, 3(2), 27–44.

gin to react by gradually withdrawing from learning in the classroom (Rist, 1970).

Seemingly, the problematic nature of providing an early intervention dropout program for both parents and students demands different ways of delivering services to each. Moreover, these service delivery models involve the kinds of interactions that occur between parents, students, and the "system," along with the kind of structure used to support these interactions. What and how teachers would teach were important considerations, but equally critical would be whether the school could communicate to children and their families an "ethic of personal caring" (Smey-Richman, 1991).

Using this construct of personal caring as the framework for our efforts required that parents and students not be anonymous or invisible to the school. Instead, the problems, both academic and social, of children and their families would be acknowledged and respected, and both educators and social workers might be involved in this process. We decided to accept the responsibility of helping learners at risk and their parents not only with education-related problems, but also, through consultation and encouragement, with meeting their social needs. Ours would be a school-based model linking educators, social workers, students, and families through a shared sense of purpose and a commitment to follow through with educational and social work resources. The primary goal of Fordham University's Stay-in-School Partnerships Program was to enact dropout-prevention strategies with both parents and young learners in grades K–3 (with follow-up to the 5th grade). Our practices would be grounded in the literature showing that specific techniques are not as important to the academic and social progress of low achievers as is the way that these practices are combined to engender a sense of community—an ethic of caring—in order to foster positive student and family development (Hersh, 1982; Rutter, Maughon, Mortimer, Ouston, & Smith, 1979). Such a perspective extends the usual academic focus to include a more holistic concern for the well-being of students and parents. Moreover, we also believed that positive personal interactions that occurred while linking academic and social resources would promote the kind of psychological and educational development in parents and students that fosters a connection or bond with the school, leading to improvements in academic achievement (Comer, 1986).

THE PROJECT: DESCRIPTION AND LESSONS LEARNED

This university–school partnership project began in 1986. Fordham University's graduate schools of Education and Social Services teamed up initially with three, and later with a total of five, New York City public schools that each served a diverse student population. The goal of our program was to prevent youngsters from dropping out of school. We believed that this could best be realized by working to increase school attendance, improve achievement in math and reading, enhance self-esteem, and increase the quality of child care and levels of social living. In general, we wanted to ascertain the impact that our activities had on the attendance rate and academic and social learning of children in the primary grades who were regarded as being at risk. In doing so, we focused specifically on testing an "ethic of caring" approach in providing related educational and social services to students and their parents.

Partnership Structures Become Partnership Practices

Forging ahead, we initially encountered some of the typical issues associated with launching a university-initiated project in urban public schools. We had no prior working relationship with the personnel at these schools, and so had to establish one. At the onset, we conceptualized an integrated program of education and social services that would be delivered by school-based, building-level teams, each comprising one education service liaison from the School of Education, three social workers from the School of Social Work, and three Spanish-speaking tutors from the College at Lincoln Center; thus, we would be placing a seven-member team from the university at each school. These school-based teams were obviously critical, as they were charged with engendering a school community capable of providing direct services to students and their families, but their day-to-day activities also had to fit within the context of the greater system—actually the two greater systems: the bureaucracies of the university and of the public school system. We had to create a collaborative-governance model that included personnel from three units of the university and the school staff at each building. For the most part, governance issues were addressed in formal meetings, but these did not preclude typical "power and turf" conflicts that arose between and within units. Such situations included:

A principal who informed us that he just couldn't find the "space" for the project, but would continue to look—and proceeded to do so for 2 months, while in the meantime the building-level team at the school discovered an abandoned bathroom and creatively designed private tutoring and play-therapy spaces out of the stalls. Naturally, the principal eventually wanted that space back! And, also naturally, the project staff who had made the space attractive and useful were angry!

Social workers, educational liaisons, and tutors all thinking themselves most important to the project, were at times competing with one another rather than putting their energies into collaborative efforts on behalf of students and parents.

But situations that cause cognitive conflict or complexity can also serve as catalysts to generate questions and encourage inquiry (Dillon, 1982). Members "learned" to collaborate using conflict-resolution strategies. One such strategy involved using the three Ps (purpose, process, and payoff) as a framework for conducting our meetings. Briefly, the purpose phase included establishing the direction and focus for the meeting. During the process phase, general procedures for conducting the meeting were established based on whether the agenda items required problem solving, decision making, or information sharing. During the payoff phase, we focused on outcomes and results that would benefit all of the participants. We first tested these strategies on problems not directly related to members—for example, the removal of a principal charged with child abuse in his school or the decision regarding whether to include siblings in the project. As we became more comfortable with the three-Ps strategy, we targeted problems more directly related to members, such as determining who was responsible for different aspects of the program. While a painful process in the short haul, a long-term commitment required working through problems to develop community collaboration and interdependence among participants. But one important lesson we learned is that, as advocates of collaborative service models point out, those who would serve school subsystems must fundamentally change the way that they operate and relate to one another (Levy & Copple, 1989).

Operational Notions and Program Implementation

Our day-to-day activities provided a focus for the organizational partnership. Decisions had to be made regarding the identification of students and the descriptions of parent characteristics and problems, as these factors would be reflected in the service-coordination approach taken by the social workers.

Student Identification and Participation   School–university staff and the building teams jointly identified the appropriate target children for the program using the following criteria: 1) more than 15 absences in any academic year, 2) achievement in reading below average for grade level, and 3) a likelihood of being retained or referred for special education services. These criteria resulted in the identification of 20 students per school site. This selection process proved to be easy, particularly since parental permission was granted during home visits and personal contacts on Back-to-School nights. During these personal contacts, conducted in both English and Spanish, the educational liaisons, social workers, and tutors consciously engaged in nonthreatening, facilitative interactions with parents, which were designed to foster an ethic of caring—especially important at this initial operational stage of the program. While we saved time during this phase, we quickly lost it when we were forced to gather our own baseline academic data because records at each school were either incomplete or nonexistent.

Fortunately, we had chosen the Kaufman K-TEA Brief Form (Reading and Math subtests with a reported reliability of .76–.84) to be used in the program as a measure of achievement. Thus, we were able to use this instrument to provide our own baseline academic data for each student. The test was and continues to be individually administered to each student admitted.

Over a period of 5 years we served 220 children in five schools in Districts 4 in Manhattan and 10 in the Bronx; 30% of these children were African American and 70% Latino. Many of the Latino children and their families spoke Spanish as their first language. Our original design was longitudinal, with 20 children to be selected per site. However, we also accepted new students as, each year, students in the program moved on to junior high school or moved out of the school district. Consequently, there was an average 30% student turnover in the program each year. After the students had been identified, we moved on to working with their parents.

Parent Characteristics and Needs   Social workers made home visits to gather baseline data on parents' social problems. In all of their activities, social workers were committed to a case management approach in working with students at risk and their parents to provide psychological services in order to prevent or reduce emotional problems. This was done by initiating "collaborative" relationships within the school and community whenever problems were of such magnitude that they affected the quality of a child's learning and school functioning. Our services thus included providing assistance to families with educational, medical, legal, or financial problems—in other words, the full range of problems that contribute to school dropout. For many students, some or all of these difficulties were a major source of interference with their attendance and learning at school.

While the public schools typically purport to employ this model, one social worker in the existing system must serve many more families than the ratio of 1:7 we were able to support in our program. The combination of a sound social work approach, coupled with a reasonable caseload, allowed project social workers to interact quickly and consistently with parents.

We found that our parents reported the following:

Seventy-five percent are single heads of household.
Ninety-five percent never finished high school.
Most mothers reported not having enough money.

Most felt that they had few friends or family members.
Most felt that they had no one to count on for help.

Since these families moved from crisis to crisis, the education of their children sometimes seemed a low priority in the greater scheme of things, according to one social worker's report. Essentially, parents were consumed with survival issues, suggesting the urgent need to provide, as quickly as possible, a set of parental intervention strategies that met their needs.

Related Education and Social Work Activities in Operation

We next set into motion a series of coordinated education and social work activities for students and their families. Targeting parents' needs, we first implemented a series of workshops, offering an average of 10 each year. Workshop fliers in English and Spanish were distributed via the mail and home visits by building-team members, school principals, bilingual coordinators, and even the students themselves. Fliers indicated the education-related topics of each workshop, such as "How you can help your child at home," "Parental strategies in teaching reading and math," and "How to motivate students," and, most importantly, parents received a stipend of $15 per session to cover babysitting and other expenses. As a result of the mass distribution of fliers, the timely topics, and the stipend incentive, an average of 12 out of 20 parents attended these formal workshops at each school. Further, workshops followed an interactive design whereby the presenter and parents engaged in a lively interchange using both English and Spanish.

In addition to the formal workshops, each site had a "parent drop-in" center where parents could come on their own or by invitation to receive counseling on issues related to health services, welfare assistance, child abuse problems, and so on. Early on, parents became aware that the purpose of the parenting interventions was not to punish or blame, but to help them work through problems. Clearly, the nature of the positive interactions between parents and school-based staff helped to foster the atmosphere of caring that we were trying to achieve and that we felt was a necessary condition for the healthy psychological development of parents. Moreover, social workers spent 60 minutes each week in play therapy with each child. At the beginning of the project, these sessions were conducted one-on-one, but by the 4th year of operation, play-therapy activities were engaged in by small groups of children of mixed ages and grades. Our supervision of these activities was nondirective; children were encouraged to take part in board games, arts and crafts, and even academic games focused on reading and math.

While families participated in these ongoing social work activities, the educational liaisons and tutors also spent 40 minutes each week with each student. Initially, we followed a diagnostic-prescriptive, direct-instruction model for reading and math skills development. Unfortunately, achievement measures failed to show a significant improvement in these areas after these first 2 years of the program. Consequently, we altered our curriculum content and teaching strategies and adopted an across-the-curriculum orientation integrating reading, writing, speaking, and mathematics. Our new approach used high motivation "Big Books" and other materials based on whole-language concepts. In addition, we tested small groups of children of different ages in our tutoring sessions. By the 4th year, our effect-size data showed consistent improvement in reading and math achievement by the participating students. We had clearly learned the value of the careful use of evaluation data in modifying our approach, and with good results!

In fact, after each year's evaluation report, the building team and university staff developed alternative related services where needed. As a result, both education staff and social workers moved away from the one-to-one model toward small group and cooperative-learning type models for delivering direct academic support services and play therapy, respectively. In our judgment, this cooperative-group approach was not only functionally related to improvements in student performance, it was also a far more efficient use of instructional time for tutors, social workers, and students. Furthermore, we observed—and reinforced—prosocial behaviors that were now occurring in our multi-age grouping, a phenomenon that Goodlad and Anderson (1987) have also described. Through our annual review and responsiveness to the evaluation data, we were able to experiment with a variety of direct-service models, always remaining mindful of the way we delivered our services. Essentially, the evaluation process drove whatever changes were made in our programmatic efforts.

EVALUATION: A DISCUSSION OF
FORMAL AND INFORMAL OBSERVATIONS

To evaluate related education and social work activities for students and parents, we systematically collected data using the evaluation tools listed in Table 1. Data yielded by these tools were analyzed by means of a pre–post test design using difference-score effect size (ES) as the metric for most of the data (Feltz, Landers, & Becker, 1988). Effect sizes (as opposed to statistical effects) were used to ascertain the magnitude and direction of the educationally practical effects of SSPP in the areas of absenteeism, achievement in reading and math, adequacy of child care, and self-esteem. ES scores were calculated by subtracting the pretest scores of target children from their corresponding post-test scores and dividing by pooled, pretest standard deviations, yielding an effect size in score units.

Table 1. Project objectives and corresponding evaluation tools for The Fordham Project

Objective areas	Evaluation tools
Attendance of target population	Attendance lists (September–June)
Educational achievement	Kaufman K-TEA, brief form (Reading and Math subtests; reported reliability of .70–.84)
Adequacy of child care	Childhood Level of Living Scale (reported reliability of .64–.88)
Self-esteem	Coopersmith Self-Esteem Inventory (reported reliability of .87–.92)
Social service activities	Logs and levels of social work services
Tutoring	Tutoring logs and educational service plans
Special education referrals	List of referrals submitted
Parental training	Workshop attendance and evaluation

Formal and Information Observations and Discussion

The major formal observations yielded by the evaluation tools at the end of the 5-year project are summarized in Table 2.

Reduction in Absences   Over a 5-year period, absenteeism decreased significantly from an average of 41 days in 1985–1986 to an average of 21 days in 1990–1991—an impressive decrease of 48%. While results at individual sites in the Bronx and Manhattan varied from year to year, SSPP accomplished one of its major goals in reversing the negative effects of not attending school. Evaluation of monthly attendance records revealed February and April as "out of control" months for some project children. The pattern of absenteeism suggested that some students tended not to return to school after holiday breaks in the school calendar, so that the usual weeks off in February and in the spring (generally at the beginning of April) were followed by truancy. This suggested that breaks in contact between the home and the school were self-perpetuating, such that our frequent-contact model might indeed be expected to act as a powerful influence on this negative pattern. We had a hunch that both the kinds and frequency of contacts that the social workers maintained with parents, school officials, and community agencies would make a difference. Our contact was substantial, such that in any given year approximately:

1,000 contacts were made with parents about individual problems.
500 contacts were made in reference to family problems.
800 contacts were made with school officials.
200 contacts were made with agencies.
1,150 telephone conversations took place.

Table 2. Formal data on Fordham Project activities

Objective	Evaluation tool	District[a]	1986–1987	1987–1988	1988–1989	1989–1990	1990–1991
Reduction in absences (days absent)	Monthly lists	4	42	38	25	21	21
		10	N/A	52	48	20	29
Improvement in Reading (effect size data)	Kaufman K-TEA (brief form)	4	+.005	–.08	+.28	+.46	–.08
		10	N/A	N/A	+.21	+.37	–.25
Improvement in Math (effect size data)	Kaufman K-TEA (brief form)	4	–.09	+.25	+.32	+.19	–.02
		10	N/A	N/A	+.95	–.48	–.37
Home care condition (effect size data)	Childhood Level of Living Scale	4	+.39	+.69	+.60	+.60	+.02
		10	N/A	N/A	N/A	+.73	–.11
Self-esteem (median raw scores)	Coopersmith Self-Esteem Inventory	4	N/A	52	60	56	62
		10	N/A	N/A	52	52	68
Special Education referrals	End-of-year referrals	4 & 10	2	1	2	2	3

Spring-to-spring data sources.
[a]The two sets of numbers refer to two different districts, 4 and 10.

49

These figures illustrate the nature and extent of interactions between project personnel and children and their families. Furthermore, this information should also be viewed in light of the context in which we worked—one of overcrowded urban schools lacking in such basics as telephone availability or tutoring space, as evidenced by the earlier example of the school in which an abandoned bathroom was converted into our "office" and the stalls became our "tutoring cubes."

Reading Achievement   Although significant improvements in reading achievement did not occur at all five schools, effect-size data demonstrated a positive, upward trend in reading achievement as measured by the Kaufman K-TEA (Kaufman & Kaufman, 1985). ES ranged from −.08 to a moderate impact of +.46 across all sites (Baecher & Cicchelli, 1992; see also Table 2). One interpretation is that the variation in ES is a function of differences in the amount of tutoring time each child received at each site; the manner in which Fordham staff implemented SSPP at each site; and the range of reading approaches employed, which progressed from a diagnostic-prescriptive approach in years 1 and 2 to a more whole-language approach in the last 3 years. Another explanation is the possibility that increased attendance actually accounted for much of the improvement—children who attend school regularly are in a far better position to learn what is being taught while they are there.

Math Achievement   Inconsistent fluctuations in math achievement occurred over the course of the project at all sites. In 1988–1989, the 4th project year, one school district recorded a small positive gain in math achievement. Effect sizes showed wide variability, ranging from −.48 to a high of +.95 in one district. It should be pointed out that, originally, our SSPP program did not include improved math achievement as one of its objectives—reading had been our original focus—but math tutoring was included for selected children because of school staff requests on their behalf.

Child Home-Care Conditions   We used the Childhood Level of Living Scale (Polansky, Chalmers, Buttenwieser, & Williams, 1978) as a measure of the child care conditions in the homes of each of our target children. We found that most of our students' homes continued to score in the "neglectful" category as perceived by social service interns scoring this measure. A separate research study of 20 families at one of our schools was conducted in 1990 by social-service staff, who used the McMaster Family Assessment Device (McMaster, 1982) to measure family functioning and found a moderate increase in general positive child care and a significant increase in abilities to solve problems that threatened the integrity of the family.

Self-Esteem   Self-esteem data yielded by the Coopersmith Self-Esteen Inventory (Coopersmith, 1986) were found to be strongly correlated with improved academics (.29 with reading in particular) and increased attendance; students who made gains in reading apparently also felt better about themselves. In addition, the majority of target children moved into the medium self-esteem interquartile range (52–68) as the program progressed, another indicator of SSPP's overall impact.

Special Education Referrals   During the 5 years of our project, 10 referrals for special education services were made out of a total of 220 children in five schools—a referral rate of 3%.

Parental Involvement   In our judgment, parental involvement was critical to bringing about positive changes in absenteeism and the rate of special education referrals. Specifically, 75% of the parents made use of SSPP services related to housing, social security, public assistance, day care, legal issues, after-school care, substance abuse, and medical and psychological services. We also noted some informal observations that are worth sharing. First, with regard to families, we observed that in times of crisis, parents would often come to school with a brochure in hand that identified a community service and ask us for help. Concrete assistance, such as help with making appointments for agency services, following up, or accompanying a parent or child for a medical checkup served two purposes: we obviously helped the family to obtain the specific service they needed at the time, but we also provided them with models of how to negotiate community-agency systems. While there may indeed be many community agencies and services available to assist families in crisis, unless the families feel comfortable approaching these agencies and are knowledgeable about how to do so, those services may never be accessed. We also worked with families who initially did not appear to want to access needed services. With these families, we found that the parents were amenable to help if the social worker persevered and was deliberate in guiding the parent to the needed assistance.

The program also had an effect on parental involvement. After 5 years, about half of the parents had become involved in some aspect of school life—for example, assisting in bake sales, chaperoning class trips, and so on. At least 10% of those mothers who did not work outside the home became involved in the PTA as a direct result of the program. And finally, as a result of tutoring and play therapy, the level of trust that emerged in the children was extended to the parents. Some parents would say, "My child talks about you all the time, and I just came in to meet you."

As for the students, many of them became active participants in their education, taking responsibility for their own learning. For instance, one child entered tutoring sessions stating that a classmate had told her that she couldn't read. Feeling self-righteous, she asked her tutor for a book and proceeded to prove that she could in fact read. In another case, a child with serious truancy problems (85 absences) during her first year became class valedictorian after 4 years of active involvement in project activities. Additionally, several students who were themselves already participating recommended their peers and siblings as candidates for the project should it be expanded.

Relationships were perhaps our most valued outcome. In sharing space, time, and activities, the students, tutors, social workers, and education liaisons—"the team"—formed stable and cohesive friendships over time. For the students in particular, this encouraged the development of peer relationships and a greater sense of comfort with perceived authority figures—valuable outcomes for these young people. Essentially, a community had been established.

The Practice Profile

We adopted a Practice Profile in order to summarize program components and requirements in a standardized, systematic, and cost-effective way (Loucks & Crandall, 1982). For our project, the profile consisted of seven components or behaviorally anchored categories that were identified by social service and educational staff: assessment, record keeping, play therapy, tutoring, coordination, family problem solving, and parent-awareness workshops. Our purpose in describing this conceptual tool is to facilitate communication among users, evaluators, and potential adopters of innovative practices. Since many funded (and unfunded) programs claim to be innovative in responding to the needs of students at risk and include a wide range of descriptions of philosophies, goals, and strategies, we decided to put ours to the test and apply the practice profile concept to the Fordham program. In addition to on-site observations, this entailed a critical analysis of documents (proposals, manuals, forms, etc.) and interviews with project personnel who were responsible for implementing the educational and social service goals of SSPP. Examination of these data, derived from observations of actual practices, context analysis of documents, and responses to open-ended questionnaires, resulted in the practice profile summarized in Table 3.

To develop our practice profile, we followed these guidelines:

1. A manageable number of service components are identified.
2. Each component is described behaviorally.
3. Variations describe differences, from the developer's perspective, between the ideal use of each component, acceptable use, and unacceptable use.
4. The components focus on actual practice.

When we used the profile to evaluate our own project performance, we found that our performance on components related to assessment,

Table 3. Practice profile for Fordham Project, 1986–1991

Ideal	Acceptable	Unacceptable
Component 1: Assessment		
Students are assessed through a combination of tests, teacher judgment, and other probes.	Students are assessed using teacher judgment alone.	Students are not assessed individually.
Component 2: Record keeping		
Individual records are kept current for purposes of counseling and tutoring.	Individual records are occasionally updated.	No individual records are kept.
Component 3: Play therapy		
Students participate in 45 minutes of play therapy per week.	Students participate in 45 minutes of play therapy each week. Time varies for each student.	Students do not participate in at least 45 minutes of play therapy per week.
Component 4: Tutoring		
Students receive 20 minutes of personal tutoring per day. Activities are dictated by a performance contract that is cooperatively developed by the classroom teacher and the educational liaison.	Students receive 40 minutes of personal tutoring per week, but activities are not dictated by a performance contract.	Students do not receive at least 40 minutes of personal tutoring per week.
Component 5: Coordination		
Communication and consultation are maintained among the SSPP team and the site staff.		Communication is not maintained
Component 6: Family problem solving		
Families of children at risk for school failure and dropout acquire strategies and skills to solve problems through counseling and other supportive means.		Families are not taught essential problem-solving strategies.

record keeping, and tutoring were in the acceptable range, while we came closer to the ideal category on components related to play therapy, coordination, family problem solving, and parental workshops. None of our program components fell into the unacceptable category.

RECOMMENDATIONS

Our data on family and child outcomes were good, as was the evidence regarding the fidelity of our implementation of the model. Thus, we can be reasonably confident in asserting that the strategies that we employed in schools over a 5-year period are effective: they do indeed provide services to children and their families and are evidence that a model of an ethic of care can affect school attendance and achievement. But aside from these data—and perhaps more practically—we learned some lessons from the range of experiences that we ourselves had during the Fordham Program. We offer our colleagues in universities, schools, and funding agencies, as well as those in the business and social service communities, a summary of our observations:

Linking and delivering education and social services simultaneously is a powerful strategy in working with parents and children during the early school years. In particular, prevention and intervention strategies should not be employed in a piecemeal or fragmented fashion, but rather as parts of a holistic approach to solving home–school problems.

Time is a critical factor to be taken seriously when engaging in collaborative efforts among members of different institutions. Specifically, issues related to governance and power can lead to conflict, so sufficient time must be set aside to deal with problems through an ongoing, open process that includes both formal and informal conflict resolution approaches. Members of different institutions who have never really worked together before are themselves going to have to adjust to an essentially new way of doing things—through collaboration.

It is possible to demonstrate short-term benefits to children and their parents in the early stages of the onset of at-risk behaviors that seem destined, if unchanged, to lead to school dropout. However, careful and deliberate documentation and yearly evaluation of program activities is critical in developing a broad database that will be helpful in guiding the planning of necessary programmatic changes. In fact, these data provide project managers with support to try, test, and experiment with different instructional strategies and social work delivery systems. Innovations should be based on performance and carefully selected outcome measures, rather than the opinions of project staff and school personnel.

Emphasizing an ethic of caring was at the core of our intervention. We believe that having a firm value base such as this is as important as the particular nature of any intervention strategy. Our direct service personnel—the educational liaisons, tutors, and social workers—demonstrated a great sensitivity and commitment to children and parents alike. Knowing our "clients" by name, personalizing relationships and getting involved, and conveying high expectations for appropriate and positive behaviors were daily goals, which undoubtedly had an impact on the quality of services provided by everyone involved.

CONCLUDING COMMENTS

Finally, based on our own experiences and support from the literature, we offer the following recommendations to colleagues interested in implementing similar early intervention programs:

While early intervention programs can produce benefits for parents and students, *a commitment must be made to provide continued support and follow-up throughout elementary school and the transition to secondary school.* Very early efforts at working with children at high risk and their parents can be powerful; when successful, they serve as workable and effective strategies for prevention that focus on alleviating the antecedents of problems, rather than on the problems themselves (Dryfoos, 1991). But the needs of children at risk are obviously great, and they do not end when a 5-year project does. The bottom line may well be that any intervention worth implementing is probably an intervention that should take on a life of its own, becoming, in actuality, an integral part of the school experience itself.

The school is the obvious place to center interventions. In particular, no other institution can address such a broad range of needs and problems, or is as well-equipped to serve children and their parents. Furthermore, schools should be the locus of academic and nonacademic interventions concerned with health, welfare, and social support, simply because that's where the children *are* for most of the day, especially in the early grades (Dryfoos, 1991).

Restructuring must follow a school-based model, bringing together parents, students, social workers, and educational system personnel. Positive interactions among these individuals are absolutely necessary to promote the kinds of psychological and cultural development in students that encourages school bonding and ultimately leads to improvements in academic achievement (Comer, 1986).

Successful strategies such as those employed in the Fordham early intervention model need further testing in other contexts. By using a specific process such as the Practice Profile and carrying out systematic evaluation of all project components, including implementation, we can build a meaningful knowledge base on what works, and under what circumstances, for youngsters at risk and their parents.

II

THE MIDDLE YEARS

4

Starting a University–School Partnership in a High-Risk School

JOSEPH C. GRANNIS

In January 1990, staff at the Institute for Urban and Minority Education (IUME) at Teachers College, Columbia University, completed a 3-year evaluation of the New York City Dropout Prevention Initiative (DPI). A surprising amount of the information conveyed in the Institute's eight-volume report was digested by the Board of Education and reflected in the guidelines that they published in May 1990 for Project Achieve, a new dropout prevention program (Grannis, 1991).

DPI had combined six components of service provided to students identified as being at risk of dropping out: attendance outreach, guidance and counseling, health examinations and referrals, linkage between middle school and high school, alternative educational programs, and facilitation of the program by a teacher/administrator. Alternative placements in the middle schools emphasized career education and remedial instruction, but in most schools did not extend to the students' general curriculum. Overall, the initiative did not interrupt the steady decline in targeted students' attendance and only temporarily suspended their failure rate.

This chapter benefited greatly from the work of the Institute for Urban and Minority Education (IUME) staff of the Teachers College–Amerigo Vespucci project: Nancy Adams, Jeannette Betancourt, Rebecca Dyasi, Daniel Fishbein, Kavitha Mediratta, Erwin Reyes-Meyer, and Steven Simons. The author is equally indebted to the staff and students of the host school; though they cannot be individually named, their contribution was essential. Still, the author is solely responsible for the opinions expressed and for errors that might remain in the chapter.

A principal conclusion of the evaluation was that interventions needed to bring about change at the very core of students' educational experience, rather than just adding services to a school's outer shell. The very concept of "services" was seen as implying that student absences and academic failure were symptoms of a pathology of the students and their families, rather than indications that the schools needed to be reformed. Taking a different approach would involve adapting the curriculum and methods of teaching, as well as developing programming geared more toward changing students' learning modes and the exigencies of their lives in and outside of school, rather than following a rigid and routine curriculum. The evaluators took the position that more services, or, less disparagingly, *supports* for students—for example, positive communications between home and schools—should be provided by the core staff of a school, especially teachers, though not necessarily at the cost of losing the supplementary staff that programs like the Dropout Prevention Initiative provided for. Basically, the emphasis in dropout-prevention programs needed to be shifted from students to schools themselves as risk-producing or risk-reducing places.

INITIAL DEVELOPMENT OF THE TEACHERS COLLEGE PROGRAM

Just as the evaluation was coming to an end, we saw in the Stay-in-School Partnership Project an opportunity to try out some of the Dropout Prevention Initiative recommendations in a hands-on program. We approached the superintendent of one of the city's community school districts and were referred by him to an intermediate school that, as it happened, had been one of the 29 middle schools included in the earlier dropout-prevention evaluation, which had identified it as a school where the attendance gains of students enrolled in the initiative had not been matched by gains in achievement.

Through our initial discussions with staff at what in this chapter will be called the Amerigo Vespucci School, we learned that they had just voted to become one of the first wave of schools to adopt Chancellor Joseph Fernandez's School Based Management/Shared Decision Making (SBM/SDM) initiative, known as the Chapter 1 Schoolwide Project. Partly to simplify the narrative, but also to validly reflect the priority of the contexts in which SSPP operated, this chapter will first concentrate on the partnership itself, and only later will turn to how the partnership has interacted with the SBM/SDM effort in the school. The chapter draws extensively on ethnographic journals kept by Teachers College personnel, as well as school documents and other more quantitative data.

The School

For several years, Amerigo had enrolled a student population of about 1,850 6th-, 7th-, and 8th-graders; 68% were Latino, 29% Black, and 3% Asian American. The proportion of students with limited English proficiency (LEP) had increased from 16% in 1986–1987 to 22% in 1989–1990. The School Profile shows that in 1989–1990, Amerigo had a high student mobility rate (36%), low attendance, a high number of students who were eligible for free or reduced-price lunches (87%), many students who were eligible for Chapter 1 services (62%), and poor average math and reading scores. Starting in 1988–1989, a new principal and the Community School Improvement Plan committee at Amerigo reorganized it into three subschools that, between them, included eight clusters of four to nine homerooms each. Teachers College was initially asked to work with two Amerigo clusters that included students who were officially identified as being at risk: Mi Casa, a cluster for Spanish speaking students with LEP, and JET (Job Employment Training, i.e., career education).

In the very first SSPP meeting at Amerigo, the principal and an assistant principal emphasized the contribution that Teachers College could make in helping the school to understand itself, its student body, and how staff could respond to students. Great emphasis was placed on how deeply the neighborhood was affected by unemployment, poor housing, drugs, limited knowledge of English (or, indeed, of Spanish), and limited schooling, among both children and parents, who sometimes came from another country in which they had received only a few years of primary school.

The Original Plan

To qualify for SSPP funding, the Teachers College proposal had to include most of the very same service components that the DPI evaluation had found insufficient to stem the tide of students disengaging themselves from school. However, another thrust of SSPP, coordination of the various state and federally funded programs that themselves provide these services in a school, invited a proposal to work more centrally in a school. The novelty of the Teachers College–Amerigo plan was that in choosing service components, it would involve the students themselves in the information-gathering and interpretation process that the school leadership wanted Teachers College to undertake. Students would participate in focus groups and later a survey process to research the environment of the school and would conduct interviews with people in the school and community—parents, high school students, teachers, and so forth—to learn about different educational and health resources, life histories, and careers. Students, in short, would become part of the solution instead of just being considered the problem. Also, Teachers College would profile students' attendance and grades as these developed during the year, further contributing to our information-seeking and goal-oriented approach to promoting students' staying in school.

A Teachers College team was assembled with the author, a professor in urban education, as Program Director, a psychologist specializing in counseling and organizational development as Program Coordinator, and a staff member experienced in bilingual education and staff development as Program Associate.

At the beginning of September 1990, Amerigo staff returned to school, and we learned of two developments that would seriously affect the plan. First, the assistant principal who had helped negotiate the proposal had had to leave the school due to a health emergency. And second, the principal decided that the distribution of outside funds would be more equitable if SSPP dropped JET, which already received funding from another source, and instead served another cluster, "Farm," so named because some of its teachers had involved the students in cultivating a nearby plot of land during their weekly enrichment period. The Mi Casa cluster included nine homeroom teachers and a teacher-coordinator, who between them were responsible for one 6th-, four 7th-, and four 8th-grade classes. The Farm cluster consisted of eight class teachers and a teacher-coordinator, responsible for five 7th- and three 8th-grade classes.

The proposed focus groups, surveys, and interviews were meant to serve as vehicles for transforming the curriculum and for increasing the general education teachers' involvement in activities to foster students' careers and health education, their planning for their future education with increased support from their families, and the development of their self- and mutual-esteem. In a traditional, departmentalized intermediate school, these goals are usually thought to be more the responsibility of counselors and special teachers or auxiliary staff than the mission of the teachers in general, especially if homeroom periods allow only enough time to take attendance and distribute information. The intention to work systemically also led to our deciding to establish a task force within each of the two clusters.

THE PLAN VERSUS THE REALITY
OF THE FIRST WEEKS OF SCHOOL

Thus far, this is the story from the point of view of Teachers College. For the teachers in Farm and Mi Casa, the greatest concern during the first

3 weeks of school was the uncertainty of their classroom rosters. Many students whose names appeared on lists created in the spring did not come to the school in the fall, and new registrants trickled in to take their places. This was complicated by the fact that the newly installed, city-wide, Automate-The-School computerized attendance system could not keep up with the registration changes during the initial weeks of the school year, such that the daily printouts of the official rosters did not reflect changes as they occurred.

It soon became apparent that the teachers at Amerigo already had enough to deal with during the first weeks of school without Teachers College coming in with an entirely new agenda. Farm had not even been consulted during the proposal planning—only the coordinator of Mi Casa had been involved. The Mi Casa and Farm teams did begin the process of selecting several teachers for each of the task forces, but the reaction of both teams to the proposal that focus groups be formed to examine the school environment was the same: "What do you need to gather information for, when everyone already knows what the problem is? We want you to tell us what can be done!" A better use for the project money, some teachers thought, would be to provide incentives for students to attend school and complete their work, rather than, as they saw it, rewarding students for their absences from school.

For Teachers College, the overriding goals of the project were for students to become more engaged in their education and for school staff to foster and support that engagement. The dilemma that faced Teachers College staff at this time was that the goal of increasing student engagement pressed them to move swiftly, whereas the goal of involving school staff in the process meant building gradually on staff members' perceptions of what problems needed to be solved. We anticipated that students' attendance would be highest in September and would decline steadily throughout the course of the school year. Teachers' remarks in the very first meetings quickly confirmed another of our suspicions: that many teachers were likely to blame home situations for falling attendance, regardless of whether attendance was high at the beginning of the school year.

Short- and Long-Term Responses to Need

Our short-term response to this dilemma was to work with the Farm and Mi Casa teachers on a matter that began to preoccupy school staff early in the fall, the necessity of 8th-grade students' completing their high school applications. Teachers College and Amerigo staff planned luncheons for the parents of 8th-grade students in the two project clusters—preparing information in both English and Spanish, planning the meal, and developing a presentation to explain the application process. Parents of over 60 children—one fourth of the 8th-grade class—attended. This was considered a good turnout, although it still fell far short of the number who might have needed to be reached, and despite the fact that only a handful of the parents came back to a follow-up focus group.

Our long-term response took two forms. The first was talking to various staff members individually, gradually gathering different perceptions of the school and of what was needed. Site-based management had not yet been implemented at the school, and so was not yet a possible conduit for this exploration. The second response was a strategy that had already been used in the SSPP programs at the Bank Street College of Education and at SUNY-Binghamton: converting staff-development funds into mini-grants to allow members of the Farm and Mi Casa task forces themselves to propose and carry out projects designed to increase students' engagement in school. This restructured budget allowed each teacher to request up to $200 in educational materials.

Creation of the Social Service Network

A principal result of interviewing staff members individually was the development of a Social Service Network (SSN), a schematic of which is provided in Figure 1. Many Amerigo staff members reported that although there were numerous psychological and social personnel at the school, including members of the guidance department, family workers, representatives of the Victims Service Agency, substance-abuse counselors, and the School-Based Support Team, there had been little effort by these individuals to act as a cohesive unit. Too often, it was felt, members of each particular service had acted independently and in a self-protective and/or competitive fashion, resulting in a lack of mutual support and limited exchange of information and ideas. Discussion with these personnel and with other school staff did reveal their desire for greater coordination of services, but also a perceived lack of ability to effect such a change. Some of the barriers preventing coordination were time constraints, inflexible scheduling, and most of all fear that other staff members would not approve particular ideas.

A series of half-day and all-day planning and training sessions, several of them at Teachers College, in the winter and spring, were attended by not only the psychological and social support staff, but also the assistant principals and the teacher coordinators of the Mi Casa and Farm mini-schools. The resulting SSN group designed and began to implement a referral process whereby cluster teachers would discuss and write up a student case and then take it to an SSN meeting for further discussion and coordinated action. SSN staff themselves conducted workshops with the Farm and Mi Casa teams to train the teachers in observation techniques to help them make informed referrals. The most immediate gain

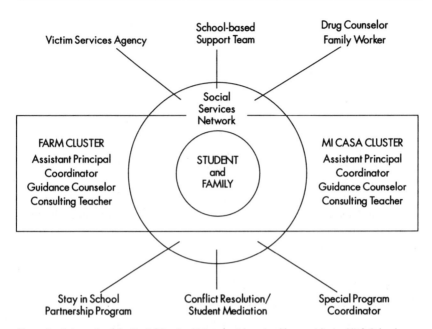

Figure 1. Schematic of the Social Service Network at Amerigo Vespucci Junior High School.

was to the staff members themselves, as they became more comfortable seeking assistance from each other and began to feel more professional in their interactions with one another. Very few students, however, became focuses of the formal referral process. The SSN staff's perception was that the teachers needed further training in how to assess behavior, as opposed to simply making summary judgments about students. Teachers, however, felt that they did not have time to write up observations, and that the brief comments that they wrote on attendance- and conduct-rating sheets were sufficient. Teachers College staff, who participated in both cluster and SSN meetings, concluded toward the end of the year that there was simply not enough time to review student cases during the one cluster staff meeting scheduled each week. There was an increase in spontaneous discussions about students among staff, but not in more deliberate discussions and actions. Teachers College made two recommendations at the end of the year: first, that each cluster staff schedule two meetings per week in 1991–1992, one to focus on student cases and the other on curriculum and general school business; and second, that SSN staff take notes on the teachers' discussion of students and facilitate the write-up of each case.

The SSN also revived a dormant interest at the school in student–peer mediation and conflict-resolution processes. Just as SSN staff completed a workshop and started training students, however, the school staff person who was in charge of such programs had to take an extended sick leave, so this project was rescheduled for the following year. SSN staff also started to discuss the possibility of an advisory system in the school, beginning with the two subschools that included Mi Casa and Farm. SSN staff were to begin their research by visiting several secondary schools in the city that had already implemented advisory systems. But these plans were overwhelmed by school governance issues toward the end of the year and were not likely to be continued in 1991–1992 without encouragement and support from outside the school. The type of system being considered would have involved adults in the school, each being responsible for advising a small group of students (Carnegie Council on Adolescent Development, 1989; Lipsitz, 1984). An exploration of the advisory concept in Amerigo a couple of years before had foundered due to the difficulty of getting a sufficient number of staff interested.

THE MINI-GRANT PROCESS AND CLUSTER CURRICULUM DEVELOPMENT

The mini-grant process turned out to be similar in certain respects to the SSN process. First of all, there was a period, lasting through most of October, during which the Teachers College staff felt that we were not plugged into the teams, that school staff had various agendas that we were not a part of. The mini-grant strategy was in fact a response to this more general malaise as much as to the specific failure to implement the original SSPP ideas for activities with students. But even this strategy might not have engaged the teachers if project staff had not also gone into classrooms and assisted with enrichment activities, thus winning the trust of some of the teachers.

Farm

In Farm, trust building began with helping the cluster's newest teacher to establish cooperative learning groups (Johnson & Johnson, 1989) whose members planted and tended seeds and root cuttings in the classroom. A Farm task force of four teachers then coalesced and decided to pool their resources to write a collective proposal. In workshops during the winter, the task force planned mini-grants around activities that included raising plants, fish, and worms, all couched in a life-environments framework. A summary of the goals Farm teachers and Teachers College staff worked out for these activities appears in Table 1. All Farm teachers participated in luncheon workshops to develop these goals, and all initially agreed to the enrichment curriculum.

Table 1.   Revised goals for farm students

Improve Student Attendance
Activities will be more hands-on and related to things kids can identify with.
Students will experience schoolwork as being more enjoyable.
Students will become more involved in activities and get excited about them.
Students will look forward more to coming to school.
Student attendance will be maintained or improved for the remainder of the year.

Improve Students' Listening, Speaking, Reading, Writing, Observing, Measuring, and Recording Skills
Students will keep journals and complete project reports that become more developed (longer, more complex).
Students will make and record increasingly accurate and detailed observations of things in class (fish behavior, worm behavior, plant growth, etc.).
Students will listen more closely to one another and follow procedures for group work with increasing care.
Students will develop the vocabulary needed to make reports.

Develop and Encourage Respect Among Students and Staff
Students will take care of plants and animals, and their respect for all living things will increase.
Given a semistructured task, students will work better with each other.

Develop Students' Awareness of Careers
Students will become aware of many more careers that are linked to the focus of Farm, life environments, and agriculture.
Students will make the connection between their career ambitions and their high school choices.

The program also engaged a science educator to be a curriculum consultant to the teachers. The consultant involved teachers in "hands-on thinking activities" in a couple of double-period workshops that centered on activities such as examining the parts of different seeds. With those teachers who requested it, the consultant and the project director planned and co-taught enrichment classes. Most students responded very enthusiastically to these activities; their journals recorded observations of plants being fertilized, growing "baby leaves," getting bugs, developing beans, being eaten by a rat, and other such events. "Why can't we do this in our regular science class?" was a representative comment from one student. Nonetheless, activities were implemented in only three of the eight Farm teachers' enrichment classes, and hands-on activities were never introduced into any of the regular–subject-matter classes. The lessons there were almost uniformly "chalk and talk" discussions based on readings from textbooks or from sources that students were to find outside of class, or recitations based on the previous night's homework, followed by the student's beginning that night's homework assignment in class. These lessons required virtually no preparation by the teachers other than writing assignments on the board, responsibility for the bulk of the "prep" for class having been shifted to the students in the form of homework, which teachers corrected and used as a principal component in calculating students' grades.

Reasons for Nonimplementation   There appeared to be several reasons why such alternative activities did not take hold, even though they had been generated by teachers working within Farm's own life-environments framework. One was that a combination of required school tasks, especially unceasing record keeping and coverage for absent teachers, as well as outside demands—second jobs, families, graduate studies, and teacher licensing exams—competed strongly for teachers' time both during and after school hours. A second reason was that some of the teachers felt that only an extensive block of time—for example, 4 weeks in the summer—would suffice to support alternative curriculum development; and teachers who did not feel this way resented the idea that they alone would participate in more limited, though still compensated, workshops. Related to this was a third, more general obstacle: a couple of the teachers blocked discussion of curriculum, the SSN, and non-SSPP matters as well, through constant complaining about the behavior of students in their classrooms. As these teachers tended to be not only those least likely to implement enrichment activities, but also those who gave the most failing grades to students, they were perceived by both Teachers College staff and their own colleagues as being hostile to both the school and the students. To overcome this, we coached the teacher-coordinator in writing an agenda for the weekly meetings and in keeping the discussions focused on agenda topics, and we did observe some increase in the productivity of the meetings over the course of the year.

As early as March, half of the teachers were anticipating that students would be "cutting out as soon as the weather warms up," and we observed that some of the teachers themselves seemed to be burning out. The teams responded to the progressively fading interest in teaching and learning by planning field trips. Within budget constraints, Teachers College, through the SSPP, supported any trip compatible with project purposes. A visit to a nature preserve and wildlife farm in Pennsylvania and a strawberry-picking trip to upstate New York were among the most-enjoyed educational activities of the year.

Progress   Then, literally in the last week of school, an opportunity arose for 1991–1992. Two of the three Farm teachers who had been most openly resistant to participating in the curriculum innovation decided to take early retirement, while the third decided to switch to a cluster with fewer students at risk. The graduation of the eighth grade also allowed time when other teachers in the school could cover classes and the teachers who were to remain in Farm for the following year could participate in a half-day SSPP curriculum workshop. Ideas that had been much talked about and experimented with on a limited basis during the year now began to be committed to paper in concrete plans that the teachers were justifiably proud of. Teachers felt that they had generated sufficient material to sustain the Farm enrichment for a year, especially as they had the flexibility of either taking turns with a unit or repeating it until they felt it was successful. The teachers also anticipated that the basic concepts around which Farm had evolved—the growth and development of plants and animals, recycling, pollution, and environmental crisis—would be extended into their regular classes.

Project staff, having heard from the teachers that students did not seem to know what school was all about, had identified a paperback for middle school students, *Scholastic's A + Junior Guide to Studying* (Colligan, 1987) that includes chapters on "How to Organize Yourself on the Home Front," and "How to Organize Yourself at School," for example. It was obviously written more for a middle-class population than the students of Amerigo, but its high expectations for students could be balanced against its assumptions about how much control students can exercise over their learning environments. SSPP was able to purchase a copy of the guide for every Farm student. Teachers decided to use the book for the first month of school in 1991–1992, and to involve parents in working through it with their children and discussing the issues addressed within it. What had seemed to us like a year of wandering in the wilderness now took on the aspect of the developmental, get-your-foot-in-the-door year that old hands had told us about at the outset.

Mi Casa

The program's work with Mi Casa will be described more briefly than that with Farm, although Teachers College devoted equal amounts of time and resources to the two clusters. As with Farm, the first SSPP event for Mi Casa was a luncheon for parents of 8th-grade students applying to high schools; this meeting was conducted in Spanish. Whereas the driving force in Farm was the teacher-coordinator, whose initiative and own interest in gardening had sparked the formation of the cluster, Mi Casa did not have a central, strong leader. Because there was very little communication during the whole fall semester between the small cliques of the teachers in the cluster, the first SSPP workshops with the Mi Casa staff were focused on team building. Again, as in Farm, just four of the teachers applied for mini-grants, but they wrote the proposals individually, rather than as a task force or on behalf of the team as a whole. Reflecting our influence, as much as the interests of the teachers themselves, the Mi Casa mini-grants all emphasized career education in one form or another. A principal conclusion from our evaluation survey of middle school and high school students had been that Latino students did not see as strong a connection between education and work as did other, mostly African American, students surveyed (Grannis & Torres-Guzman, 1990). This finding informed the thrust of SSPP's work with Mi Casa.

One Mi Casa teacher developed an after-school physical science labo ratory class for 8th-grade students in which they applied concepts taught in their regular class to materials like the batteries, wires, switches, and bells used to make electric circuit systems for question-and-answer boards. This was complemented by career education activities such as cooperative learning exercises that involved exploring different science professions, the duties carried out in those professions, and the tools used in them. Two other teachers each purchased materials like picture dictionaries and easy-to-read science magazines to facilitate English-language acquisition through career education. A fourth Mi Casa teacher founded a "Don Quixote Club" to strengthen Spanish language skills through discussions of film versions of classic Spanish and Latin American stories.

Other Activities   Though not as extensively as in Farm, the coordinator co-taught with the Mi Casa mini-grant teachers as needed. The coordinator also collaborated with the teacher of a self-contained Mi Casa 6th-grade class to teach interviewing skills to the students, who then interviewed visitors to the classroom about their careers. This project served as a model for the larger team's planning and carrying out, in the late spring, the first Bilingual Career Fair at the school. The fair brought a variety of Latino professionals to the school, where they made presentations and answered students' questions in small-group discussions. Students dressed and comported themselves very seriously for this occasion, and some students said afterwards that the fair was "the best thing the school has ever done for us." A variety of trips at the end of the year also stressed both bilingual and career education.

Barriers   The activities described notwithstanding, discipline, more than any other issue, preoccupied Mi Casa teachers in their meetings over the course of the year—even more so than in the Farm cluster meetings. The SSN, which included the Mi Casa teacher-coordinator, was meant to be, in part, a response to just this issue, but the SSPP staff and cluster teachers in Mi Casa never succeeded in taking an individual case to the point at which the SSN process could be invoked. However, the Mi Casa teachers did not punish students as severely with failing grades for inadequate classwork and homework as did the majority of the Farm teachers. There were also substantially fewer suspensions of Mi Casa students than of Farm students—between the beginning of September and the end of April, 18 Farm students and 7 Mi Casa students were suspended. Most of these suspensions were for fighting, breaking school rules, or exhibiting disrespectful behavior.

The SSPP staff members in Mi Casa did not plan for 1991–1992 in the way that those in Farm and the SSN planned ahead. Suspicion that the university personnel would not return if state funding for the program were discontinued; uncertainty about 1991–1992 class sizes and jobs, arising from the city's budget crisis; and the absence of strong cluster leadership all affected the SSPP's efforts in Mi Casa, which culminated with the career fair and the end-of-year trips, rather than with looking forward to the year to follow.

STUDENT ATTENDANCE AND GRADES

Obtaining the Data

The original SSPP proposal called for profiling students' attendance and grades. What had been disturbing about the Dropout Prevention Initiative was not simply that the attendance and courses-passed outcomes were found to be low, which might have been expected, at least in the start-up years, but that this information had not affected the subsequent development of the program. The original SSPP proposal called for purchasing a project computer and school-management software to generate student profiles, but the reduced budget forced SSPP to rely on the resources that Teachers College and the school already had on hand. The school had just been equipped for New York State's Automate-The-School system, through which attendance data for each school in the system are sent each day to a central computer and subsequently printed out back at each school. Well before school staff themselves had learned how to make such special requests, we started asking the attendance secretary to print out the Farm and Mi Casa students' attendance records for periods of 7 weeks or so. At first, we just distributed copies of the printouts directly to each official class teacher; later, we hired a research assistant for data management who started entering the data into a spreadsheet file on his own computer. This gave our program the capacity to create printouts that the ATS system could not. The first such printouts were given to teachers in late February. They showed clearly the total number of days in each quarter, the number of days each student was present, and the resulting percentage attendance. Other information on the printout included each student's percentage attendance during the previous school year and the number of years he or she was overage for the current grade. Such tables allowed the teachers and SSPP staff to compare attendance during different phases of the school year with that from the year before, which for most of the students in this particular class had been 6th grade in elementary school.

Initially, teachers were uninterested in receiving these data: "Farm and Mi Casa don't have an attendance problem," we were told, "the problem is in JET." By the third time we shared the data, however, while the average percentage attendance in Mi Casa had held in the high eighties, the average for Farm had fallen to the low eighties. Our hypothesis was that for some students attendance fell off in the wake of academic failure, if not because of other problems in the school or at home. At this point, when Farm teachers were queried individually, two of those whose classes had the lowest attendance turned out to have communicated with a number of the parents and could give a rundown on every student in their class, including some who seemed at this time to be turning around. Other teachers, including two more whose classes had especially low attendance, did not see it as their responsibility to get in touch with parents, even though they tended to think of the home situations and attitudes of the students as the main reasons why kids stayed out of school. Teachers often said that students were not motivated to do their work, but no teacher spontaneously suggested that this would change if the nature of the schoolwork itself was changed. Concurrently, some of the teachers had become particularly involved in the hands-on activities in the SSPP workshops, but only a couple connected this to the attendance question.

Using the Data

Teachers College staff also entered students' grades into the data file mentioned above. The first profile distributed to cluster faculty gave each student's grades in each subject for the first two (out of four) marking periods of the year. A memorandum accompanying the profile explained it to the teachers and went on to note that Teachers College staff had been matching up the grades with the attendance data and were particularly wondering why some students with virtually perfect attendance during the fall semester were failing two or more courses at the middle of the year. This resulted in quite a discussion, and seemed to reveal to the teachers how little ivory tower professors know about schools! These kids are in school 100% of the time, the teachers said, because it's the only safe place to be, not because they want to learn. When the director followed up with questions about the individual children involved, he heard more about how they were not motivated to do their work, how some were immature, others scored too low on standardized tests to be able to do the work, and so forth. A couple of these "immature, unmotivated" children were even seen crying when they received their last report card. But at least half of the teachers expressed the point of view that students' attendance and grades were beyond their control or responsibility.

In Mi Casa, the attendance and grades of the students were higher, but when we discussed attendance in a Mi Casa staff meeting, the explanations still focused solely on the students. What parts the school, the home, and the students themselves play in school failure is a question that will be answered very differently in various schools. But the idea behind a goal-driven SSPP program is that teachers and their collaborators have to note how students are doing and try to find out what interventions might begin to make a difference.

The issue of failing grades became even more salient at the end of the year. An analysis of the performance of 7th-grade Farm students had showed that at least 30% of their grades over the course of the year in language arts, social studies, mathematics, science, second language, and remedial reading had been failing grades of 60 or lower. Indeed, 41% of the grades in language arts, 50% in mathematics, and 61% in social studies were failing grades. By contrast, in Mi Casa there was only one subject, social studies, in which 30% or more of the grades for 7th-grade students were failing. Still, 20% of Mi Casa 7th-grade students were not promoted to the 8th-grade, most often on the grounds of not having the requisite three passing grades in major subjects at the end of year, while 33% of Farm's 7th-grade students were not promoted to the 8th-grade. Grades for 8th-grade students tended to be higher in both Farm and Mi Casa, and virtually all 8th graders were either promoted or, in a dozen cases, recommended for transfer to high school without graduating.

In another Amerigo cluster that the SSPP had not worked with—named, ironically, "Law and Justice"—48% of the 7th-grade students were retained. We had first noticed that grades and attendance did not correlate at Amerigo, or, more simply, that there was a high failure rate at Amerigo even though the school had emerged from the DPI evaluation consistently showing an attendance gain through the efforts of the DPI/AIDP staff, but not showing a commensurate gain in the rate of students' passing courses. Even knowing this, however, and coming in prepared to work with the teachers to engage the students more in their classes, we accomplished virtually nothing in our program's first year to stem the tide of failing grades. This will come as no surprise to those who have already learned that it is necessary to build trust between teachers and their partners, and that the fruit of this trust may take several years to ripen.

Another factor was that there were no sanctions at Amerigo for what might be considered the failures of teachers themselves. The principal, who enjoyed strong district support, was more focused on maintaining discipline in the school than on the achievement of students whose past test performance seemed to justify failure in advance. The principal was, however, very supportive of SSPP, and toward the end of the year began to spell out to his faculty a new position that was evolving through his talks with SSPP staff: "Instruction is the solution to the discipline problem." The principal was bolstered in this by two visits from the incoming district superintendent, who in 1991–1992 would replace the superintendent who had brought SSPP into Amerigo. After touring the school and reviewing the school profile, this new player declared that on future visits he expected to see instruction with measurable outcomes taking place in all classrooms at all times. The immediate effect of this was chilling, even for SSPP staff, whom the new superintendent perceived as coddling the students through the SSN. In the long run, however, the shift of priorities in the district might benefit the students.

SCHOOL-BASED MANAGEMENT

How has school-based management (SBM)/shared decision making (SDM) figured in the development of this partnership? It does not oversimplify things very much to say that SBM and our program affected each other very little until close to the end of the year. Explaining the reasons for this and what might have been lost or gained in the process, however, is nonetheless interesting and instructive.

The possibility of locating an SSPP project in one of the New York City SBM/SDM schools was a feature of the original proposal, and we planned to relate to SBM from the start. Teachers College staff and the newly appointed Teacher Consortium facilitator for SBM planned a joint presentation at an all-school staff meeting the week before students returned in early September 1990. However, by the time the facilitator had finished introducing himself and describing the process he would enact, literally three quarters of the teachers had left the cafeteria for their rooms, leaving behind mostly new teachers who did not yet realize that they had this freedom. Teachers College staff elected to cut their presentation short and proceed in other ways. As was reportedly the case in many other schools throughout the city, it took several months for SBM to be organized at Amerigo. Sixty teachers wanted to be included in the core SBM committee, while the facilitator urged staff to cut this down to a maximum of 18. By late November, a core of 25 members had been elected and had adopted a set of rules for conducting their affairs. The core committee met approximately every 2 weeks throughout the year, but in diminishing numbers by the middle of the spring semester. It established eight subcommittees: Communications, Parent Involvement, School Climate, Schoolwide Restructuring Project, Student Services, Reading, Mathematics, and Academic Policy. Of these, the Student Services Committee best reflected the principal structural influence that SSPP had on SBM at Amerigo during the year. The committee was recommended by members of the core who were simultaneously involved in the creation of the SSN.

Limited Accomplishments

Most of the committees accomplished very little during the year. Student Service resolved to extend the peer mediation/conflict resolution project developed through SSPP to the school at large. School Climate pressed the principal to tighten up on discipline in the school, and a series of meetings toward the end of the year clarified disciplinary procedures. The one committee that undertook a major new initiative of its own was the Academic Policy Committee, which formulated a set of criteria for students' grade promotion, an issue that became very controversial in the school after the Chancellor, in an effort to discourage retention, urged that students who were overage in the 7th grade be promoted to 8th grade at mid-year. The high number of students retained in 7th grade at the end of 1990–1991 was in part a declaration of near defiance of the Chancellor's policy. However, it was also anticipated that students held back would indeed be promoted before mid-year of 1991–1992 if they demonstrated an ability and willingness to succeed in school. This entered into our recommending that Farm teachers explicitly discuss school success with their 7th-grade students during the first month of the school year. We thought that perhaps the teachers would become invested in this themselves, and their expectations for the students and standards for themselves would be elevated in the process.

In January of the 1990–1991 year, the SSPP coordinator and the SBM facilitator together planned and carried out together an all-day team-building workshop with the Mi Casa staff. SSPP coordinated with the SBM facilitator and the school principal and assistant principals in taking primary responsibility for planning—along with the SSN, Farm, and Mi Casa—the winter and spring Chapter 1 staff-development days. Later, Teachers College staff helped SBM core representatives design an instrument to survey school staff on the school's needs for the Chapter 1 Schoolwide Project Plan for 1991–1992. In the eyes of the teacher who was the principal author of the resulting plan, Teachers College had influenced it significantly. Only a fraction of the school staff responded, but the two most important needs identified by the respondents were the need to implement student-centered curriculum practices and the need to intervene early in the school year to prevent academic failure. Some members of the SBM core staff perceived the SSPP model of systemic staff and curriculum development as the wave of the future in the school and the city. Other core staff, however, saw SSPP as encroaching on the teachers' domain.

From the very beginning of the year, there was talk about "factions" in the SBM team, and representatives of each of these factions perceived what has happened very differently. In the eyes of some, especially the union chapter chairperson, the principal had packed the SBM core committee with sycophants, and used SBM to escape responsibility for carrying out his own duties. From the perspective of others, including the principal, the requirement that the SBM core include union representatives empowered the "blockers" in the school when there was an opportunity to solve problems together. All parties volunteered that SBM had not yet hit the stride that had been attained under the Community School Improvement Plan (CSIP), when major changes took place in the school with less political conflict.

General Observations

First, it is obvious that "restructuring" commenced at Amerigo before SBM/SDM was enacted. The precedent and the environment created by the minischools was part of what allowed our program to work as systemically as it did. SBM, then, in this school and others, has been variously overlaid on structures that may or may not already have contained some of the elements and processes that SBM itself seeks to promote. Furthermore, SBM may or may not enhance these processes. At Amerigo, it seems so far to have had unintended and, at least in some instances, regressive effects. One key aspect of what has happened may be that SBM has refocused political attention and action at the whole-school level, whereas the restructuring into mini-schools had started to decentralize decision making. Related to this are the political implications of the requirement that certain constituencies be represented in the SBM core, rather than the school's leadership evolving in some other, less formal way. Whether or not parent-responsive and learner-centered changes are more likely under a more-centralized approach remains an open question.

Another variable in the situation is the approach that the SBM facilitator takes. At Amerigo, the facilitator presented at a meeting—the one that so many staff walked out on—what amounted to a formula to solve any problem by instituting the three roles of convener, recorder, and reflector. This scheme has been widely employed in New York schools' SBM/SDM efforts and was re-enunciated on various occasions at Amerigo—for example, in a workshop on the process that unfortunately did not allow time for the assembled groups to solve the hypothetical problem they were working on. Thus, the three-roles routine has not been very successful in the context of change at Amerigo. This is coupled with the fact that the SBM core committee at the school did not have a chairperson, which led some to characterize it as a "headless horseman." Our initial experience with the principal of Amerigo was that he was not eager to deal with many problems, so the vacuum at the center of power became even broader. Perhaps a different mode of facilitation and leadership from the beginning would have resulted in a different outcome for

SBM at Amerigo. However, the principal may have simply been trying to give SBM a chance, through a more laid-back style of leadership. By the end of the year, however, the principal, now being pressured by the new superintendent, was taking a much stronger stance on his priorities for the school. He declared to his faculty that he and his administration would drive the school and that the SBM core committee was welcome to share in the driving "from the back seat of the car." Whether Teachers College and SSPP would sit in the front or the back was not made explicit in this talk, but the principal did praise the partnership and announce as good news that we were determined to return to the school in the fall with or without the support of funding by the state.

LESSONS OF THE PARTNERSHIP

Starting a university–school partnership is difficult. There is a long history of school personnel feeling used and condescended to by universities (Cooper, 1988; Sirotnik & Goodlad, 1988). Even when university personnel intend to work collaboratively, there are structural factors that strain the relationship. University personnel, at least in the field of education, are likely to have teachers or prospective teachers and administrators in their own classes, and in this way alone, if not also from reading, to have more information about current practice in schools other than the partner school. Staff of the partner school, however, are not free to move on and off their campus in the way that university personnel can. School staff necessarily have more first-hand knowledge of their own school and its students, and more immediate responsibility for the children it serves. If a "partnership" refers only to the university and the school pooling their resources for students, then it can easily be welcomed by school staff. But if it challenges the way things have been done in a school, or even worse, the reasons for the way things have been done, then it is likely to result in serious problems—both in the view of the university staff, who will interpret these problems as the result of teachers' resistance, and in the eyes of the teachers themselves, whose sense of profession has been violated. A similar observation applies to the school staff's challenging university personnel's ways.

In some respects, achieving the goals Teachers College and the Amerigo School have set through SSPP calls for things that are unnatural. The situation echoes what Baryshnikov has said about dance—that it calls for making highly unnatural movements and positions of the body appear to be natural. And being unnatural, school reform is going to be uncomfortable. At the same time that it is incumbent upon the university, as an outside party with access to special resources, to support, empower, and dignify school personnel, it is also an outsider's role to foster discomfort with the discrepancy between the goals for students and the way things actually are. Again, to the extent that the school can hold the university accountable for its part in meeting these goals, the discomfort will be mutual. This is a tension inherent in a university–school partnership, and it is heightened in a high-risk school.

POSTSCRIPT

The preceding account was written at the end of the 1990–1991 school year. It is important to convey the mix of optimism and realism that SSPP staff felt at that juncture, rather than to write solely from hindsight. The 1991–1992 school year was exceedingly sobering for all involved in our partnership. At the very least, we have learned how long it really takes to make progress in a school–university partnership.

As with all of the SSPP projects in 1991–1992, state funding for the Teachers College/Amerigo project was cut to one third of that for the previous year. Because attendance rates and the numbers of courses passed were lower for Farm students than for Mi Casa students, SSPP concentrated its resources on Farm. Without the support that the project had provided the year before, the career education thrust of Mi Casa did not continue. The reduced budget also meant that the SSPP could not employ the Project Associate who had worked with school staff the first year to create the SSN. This loss seemed to be turned into a gain when a Farm teacher was selected by school staff to be the SSN coordinator. The principal allowed this teacher to exchange several hours a week of clerical work for SSN responsibilities. However, the teacher received very little cooperation with regard to making home visits from regular counseling staff, or even from his fellow teachers, who did not have the time to write up student cases for referral to the SSN, or even to discuss them in staff meetings that for the most part were centered more on administrative issues. This teacher, then, came to focus on students with problems in his own classes, made appointments with parents during his SSN hours, and made home visits after school—all while the SSN as such languished.

A significant part of the reduced SSPP budget was used to employ a parent from the community as a School–Community Liaison for the Farm team. This reflected our realization in the first year that communication with parents and mediation between parents and school staff required special expertise (see Evans, Okifuji, & Thomas, Chap. 2, this volume; Siobhan & Ramos, 1990). The entire SSPP staff this year consisted of this liaison, a graduate student who helped in classrooms and collected project data, another graduate student who worked with the teachers on curriculum development, and the Project Director. The selection of the liaison was made jointly by the Farm coordinator and the Project Director. The person selected was fluent in both Spanish and English and was a parent in a different, alternative elementary school in the district. Her experience there with a welcoming school environment and with parents' participation in classrooms was expected to be of great benefit to parents' involvement in Farm. She did indeed turn out to be very effective in communicating with staff and parents and with students directly, and she was frequently called on to interpret and moderate in crises. But these were episodes in which she basically reacted to situations, rather than fundamentally changing them.

To meet the teachers more on their own ground, the liaison offered to come to each of the eight Farm classes, one at a time, to work with the teachers and students on compositions that would then be shared with the parents of each class in culminating luncheons. In February, a teacher volunteered her homeroom class to be the first. The liaison showed the class the concluding minutes of the Martin Luther King "I Have a Dream" address—the first time that most of the students had seen this speech—and then helped each student, over the ensuing 2 weeks, to write up his or her own dream. About half of the parents came, the class and the parents watched the Martin Luther King speech together, and all of the students read their compositions. Parents, students, and the teacher all enjoyed this event tremendously. Over the remainder of the year, however, only two other teachers volunteered their classes for a similar activity. As one teacher put it, parents were already causing trouble enough just coming in to complain about their children's low grades; if she could avoid having then come in for a special event, she was going to, "Period!"

Several classes did read the study skills book at the beginning of the school year, and responded very positively to it as being written in a style and about problems that the students could identify with. Some other classes, however, did not even open the book, and none of the classes used it as a guide for actually working on the problems of personal organization and study skills that the book addressed. Both the liaison's composition initiative and the use of this book are good examples of what happens when an outside party, even in "partnership," tries to proceed with an idea that did not originate with teachers themselves.

The Farm curriculum, however, belonged to the teachers from the beginning, and all looked forward to continuing with activities that had been started the first year. But even this hope was dealt a severe blow when the school was vandalized over the summer and all of the materials purchased by SSPP—grow boxes, soil, aquaria, and the like—were destroyed or scattered. In fact, the teachers' failure to respond more enthusiastically to the $A+$ book has to be seen partly in the context of this demoralizing event. Of course, vandalism, which happened to the school twice during the course of this project, may be symptomatic of students or the community themselves not feeling a sense of ownership of the school or of responsibility for protecting it. The incident reinforced SSPP staff's perception that it was the school environment itself that most needed to be improved, while at the same time making this more difficult to achieve.

It was not until December that morale was restored sufficiently for teachers to begin to purchase, again with SSPP funds, materials to replace the ones that had been destroyed. This was accomplished by spring, and the classes of five of the eight teachers—two more than in the previous year—variously grew plants, started up a fish-breeding operation, observed an ant colony, and in other ways pursued the life-environments theme. In late spring, these teachers worked closely with SSPP staff to revise and expand a *Farm Curriculum Guide* with lessons and activities in four units: Plant Life, Food Production, Oceanography, and Rain Forests.

At this time, it became clearer than ever that even the most committed teachers could not simply develop curricula and try new classroom strategies on the run, even with substantial assistance. They needed the summer workshop that they had wanted the year before, and SSPP staff again developed a proposal with them, this time to consolidate the work of the first 2 years. Several foundations indicated that they could not fund a project in one school alone, and it thus came down to the partners themselves—Teachers College, the school, and the district—needing to support the workshop. When the Teachers College staff volunteered, the district and the school SBM/SDM committee were persuaded to support curriculum development by four teachers during 2 weeks in July. The workshop was highly productive; in combining hands-on activities with cooperative learning and higher-level skills development, the units embodied all that the SSPP had been striving for. At the same time, the units were built squarely on the teachers' own ideas. The teachers even recommended that parents be involved in classroom projects similar to the ones undertaken by the SSPP school–community liaison during the year, and, furthermore, that parents be commissioned to organize a Farm science fair.

One question that must be asked is why teachers' participation in the project intensified during the last weeks of school in both years. Stipends for overtime were available throughout the year, so that is not the answer. What should be noted is that students' attendance was way down in late spring, not only because the weather had turned warmer, but also because books were collected several weeks before the end of school. Although some might consider this a cynical conclusion, the reality may be that class sizes are in fact far too large, especially when so many of the students need their teachers' attention so much. This acts in concert with the generally low morale and lack of support that teachers in this school have felt. Curriculum work was also constantly interrupted by crises of one kind or another. The new superintendent never reappeared at the school after his initial visit, and SBM/SDM stumbled along much as it had the year before. The overall tone of the school, in most people's opinions, had worsened. Whether the enthusiasm of the Farm teachers could be sustained in the fall and winter depended on the school environment being much more supportive than it had been in the past.

In the short run, the payoff for students may have arisen much less from the staff and curriculum development approach of the Teachers College program than from the directly student-centered tutoring and mentoring that most SSPP projects have emphasized (see the Prologue). A project really needs to be broad enough to include both student support and a more long-range and comprehensive strategy of staff development. Seeing risk as the joint product of both student- and school-related factors means that any effort to reduce risk must concentrate on both. This was the initial thrust of the Teachers College SSPP project as it was originally proposed, but the school and the university will have to be quite equally involved in its reconceptualization.

5

An Inclusion Model to Reduce At-Risk Status Among Middle School Students
The Syracuse Experience

LUANNA H. MEYER,
DILAFRUZ R. WILLIAMS,
BERJ HAROOTUNIAN,
AND ALAN STEINBERG

From August 1987 through February 1988, what was to become the Syracuse SSPP Program began as a collaborative planning Task Force that included teachers, parents, school counselors, administrators, and university professors. The goal of a series of working meetings of the Task Force during these months was to develop a framework for activities designed to prevent school dropout. The process for developing that framework involved gathering information and input from a variety of professionals and resource persons on what was known about school dropout, what had already been tried or was in place in our area, and what particular models or approaches seemed to best fit our needs.

We wish to acknowledge the contributions of Deborah Appleman, Saouma Boujaoude, Paul Casavant, David Cole, Nirmala Erevelles, Nancy Sweeney, and Pat Tinto at various stages of the development of this chapter, and thank the participating teachers and principals of the Syracuse City School District Middle Schools.

Resources for this task included a follow-up study done locally by Casavant (1987), who had interviewed a large sample of young people who had left school without graduating. As others have written, students have a variety of reasons for dropping out, many of which schools have little control over, including poverty, teenage pregnancy, and marriage. Other reasons, however, illustrate Natriello's words: "Everyone agrees that the way young people experience school is the most frequently cited reason for quitting school" (Natriello, 1987, p. 5). Subsequently, we decided that rather than emphasizing the various demographic and background variables that we could not change, our focus would be on trying to change the way that young people experience school.

We also decided to select middle school as the focus of our efforts. We intuitively felt that middle school represented a crossroads. Middle school is structurally very different from elementary school, and our "constituent group" of professionals and parents felt that young people entered middle school with a spirit of starting over and an urgent new sense of their developing personal identities as they approached adolescence. We wanted to build on this sense of newness and enthusiasm and attempt school change that would in turn alter teens' perceptions of the school experience. Second, we wanted our program to focus on prevention as well as intervention. Even as we selected our target group of students, consisting of those who were absent 20% or more of the time and/ or were failing at least one subject by the end of the first marking period, we hoped to also have a broader impact, to affect any student who might be at risk of school alienation and dropout, regardless of whether he or she met these specific criteria. And, finally, the importance of our efforts was supported by the evidence that middle school did represent a time of critical needs as well as unique opportunities.

VULNERABILITY DURING THE MIDDLE SCHOOL YEARS

> Young adolescents today make fateful choices, fateful for them and for our nation. The period of life from ages 10 to 15 represents for many young people their last best chance to choose a path toward productive and fulfilling lives. (Carnegie Council on Adolescent Development, 1989, p. 20)

In 1989, the Carnegie Corporation of New York released *Turning Points: Preparing American Youth for the 21st Century*, a report calling for major changes in the structure of middle schools in this country. The report, written by a task force of representatives from the fields of education, research, government, health, and community, drew upon commissioned papers, interviews with experts in relevant fields, visits to exemplary programs, and upon meetings with teachers, principals, health professionals, and leaders of youth-serving community organizations to generate recommendations for educational reforms to enable today's young adolescents to ". . . avoid a diminished future" (p. 8). Specifically, the Task Force called for reforms that would improve the educational experience for all middle-grade students, but would most benefit those at risk of being left behind.

Academic challenges are already significant by the middle school years. Jenkins, Jewell, Leicester, Jenkins, and Troutner (1990) reported that the typical classroom contains students whose skills vary across an average of 5.4 different grade equivalents. In 1985, the National Assessment of Educational Progress study reported that only 11% of 13-year-olds were able to read well enough to understand relatively complicated written information, and fewer than one in five 8th graders were able to write adequate or better essays (National Assessment of Educational Progress, 1985). "Most distressing," continues the Carnegie report, "is the fact that the critical reasoning skills of many American young adolescents are extremely deficient" (Carnegie Council on Adolescent Development, 1989, p. 27).

The educational response at the middle school level to these acknowledged needs and circumstances has been mixed (George, 1983; George & Oldaker, 1985/1986). Eccles and Midgley (1990) have argued that there is a serious mismatch between middle school instruction and the cognitive, emotional, and interpersonal needs of the early adolescent. At the very time when young people are experiencing tremendous biological changes, they must abruptly make the transition from small, neighborhood elementary schools comprising self-contained classrooms with one teacher each to a large, regionalized middle school where they change classes throughout the day and must adjust to several teachers whom they see infrequently.

While the change from a "junior high" to a "middle school" model was conceptualized as a way of easing this transition for students, the actual organization and structure of schools in many regions appears to have remained unchanged. It is easy to imagine some students spending their entire middle school careers isolated from friendships or any close relationships with teachers (Hirsch & Dubois, 1989; Simmons & Blyth, 1987). This situation clearly creates the conditions that can lead to further school alienation, lack of achievement motivation, and difficulties in forming positive interpersonal relationships. In contrast, there is some evidence that various efforts that have the effect of "breaking down" the larger school into smaller cohorts of teachers and students (e.g., house structures, teaming, and cooperative-learning instructional groupings) have overall positive effects upon the personal and social development of young adolescents and their sense of belonging in the school setting (Ashton & Webb, 1986; Lipsitz, 1984; MacIver & Epstein, 1991; see also

Chap. 8, this volume). One logical emphasis in school reform might therefore be to foster caring communities in which students felt they belonged and were supported by peers and teachers (Berman, 1990; Meyer & Henry, 1993; Williams, 1993).

The Shift from Deficit to Support Models

The concept of creating a caring community in which all students were valued as members, however, seemed a contradiction to most remedial models that have dominated thinking in past years. Historically, efforts to address problems such as school alienation, under-achievement, and dropout have focused on the individual student, rather than the school organization, as the major contributor to problems and the proper target of solutions to those problems. These efforts have been theoretically grounded in a deficit model of cause and a remedial model of intervention. The deficit–remedial model assumes that the student at risk presents a complex of motivational and/or academic deficits, which may include the influence of a dysfunctional family, the absence of family support, and even an openly negative parental attitude toward school (Maccoby & Martin, 1983). Hence, intervention has emphasized the remediation of such deficits. To help meet individual student needs, remedial pull-out approaches have predominated in school programs; these have ranged from individualized tutoring to attendance in an alternative academic track or even a separate school.

While these approaches seem to focus on meeting individual child needs, we also saw them as a rather singular solution to a complex problem. First, remedial and pull-out interventions with clearly targeted students are based on certain assumptions about the presumed deficits of a diverse group of children and youth. One assumption is that the major determinants of at-risk status lie within the child and the child's culture and family. There can be little doubt that factors such as poverty and family structure will affect a child's performance in school, but the way that the school responds to those challenges may be as significant as their existence in the first place. Much has been written regarding the diversity and complexity of the very different circumstances of those labeled "at risk." Pull-out programs that deliver a standard remedial tutorial service directed to academic needs may err fundamentally if they do not also reflect students' individual sociopersonal clinical characteristics in their approach.

Another problem lies within a core belief that ties together alternative programs. Smaller alternative programs that are tailored to meet individual student needs through more intensive, remedial instruction are designed to guarantee success experiences and, in turn, higher academic self-esteem. This seems a seductive solution: the goal of providing academic success experiences in the context of smaller class sizes and close teacher attention has a certain intuitive appeal. Yet, theories of motivation would caution us that success in such "protected" settings in groupings that contain only "labeled" students is unlikely to have a lasting impact on student self-esteem. It would be easy for the child to devalue achievements in such settings, and overall self-concept is not ultimately changed by time-limited and devalued success experiences. Students can do well in such alternative programs without altering in the slightest their basic beliefs that they cannot succeed in, and are in fact not wanted in, the mainstream student culture.

There may be other side effects as well. Given that the purpose of the alternative program is to provide an open agenda to remediate student deficits—and the students who attend such programs typically carry many formal and informal labels, ranging from diagnoses of learning disabilities to terms such as "chronic truant," "behavior problem," and even "at-risk"—attendance in such a program carries a stigma that further isolates the student from the school and community mainstream. By creating and maintaining the expectation that students with special needs of one sort or another are the responsibility of someone else, who will teach somewhere else, regular school personnel are given justification for believing that the student should adapt to *them*, rather than accepting some responsibility to better accommodate diverse learning styles in the typical classroom. Finally, alternative programs create a new grouping arrangement with largely uninvestigated consequences. Grouping students together because they share a problem may increase their camaraderie and mutual support, but can also have other, unwanted effects: negative peer modeling may escalate, teachers may lose sight of age-appropriate expectations, and positive peer models and influences upon behavior and academic performance may be drastically reduced.

Principles

Our intention was to create a fresh start, and we decided that certain principles had to be reflected in whatever practices we developed: 1) our concern was for the way students experience school—prevention as well as intervention—so the school experience had to become our focus; 2) we wanted all students to feel that they were valued and supported members of the school community, so our intervention could not rely on traditional pull-out models; 3) we did not want students to become further stigmatized by new "labels" such as *at risk*, so activities had to occur in the context of the general classroom and typical instruction; and 4) we assumed that students who did meet our criteria for being at risk did indeed have significant academic and sociopersonal needs, so we did need to create a within-class support structure to meet those needs.

THE SYRACUSE CITY SCHOOL DISTRICT CONTEXT

Syracuse City School District policies support full inclusion of the entire student population in the general-education school, and district practices include a range of academic enrichment and remedial support educational activities and programs to make full inclusion work. Approximately 22,500 students are enrolled in the City School District; about 50% are African American, Native American, or Puerto Rican or other Latino nationalities, and smaller numbers are Asians, Pacific Islanders, or native Alaskans. There are also smaller numbers of students from other immigrant groups and children of foreign nationals whose parents are working and studying in the area.

The District's commitment to full inclusion extends to all students, even those with the most severe disabilities, who are enrolled in their local schools and attend general education classes for at least some portion of the school day. The District's special education programs for students with autism and other severe disabilities in the general classroom have long been well known and, as exemplars of inclusion and mainstreaming, are often visited by interested educators and administrators (Meyer & Putnam, 1988). In fact, the film *Regular Lives*—shown nationally on Public Television in 1988—featured Syracuse City School District programs (Biklen, 1988). Thus, a strong values base that emphasized the inclusion of all children in general education schools and classrooms already existed within the community.

Organizationally, the middle schools employ a team approach in which a subset of the total school population are assigned to classes taught by a core of four to five subject-area teachers (Math, English, Social Studies, Science, and sometimes Reading). An advisor–advisee program provides students with an opportunity to establish a closer relationship with at least one member of the school staff. Each of the six middle schools maintains an active partnership with at least one prominent area business that supports activities to enhance the quality of educational opportunities offered to students. Various organizers of other district activities have also collaborated with SSPP. For example, a Strategic Planning process involves action teams charged with defining the district's vision of an educational future for its students. The Director of the Middle Schools chaired the Action Team on student outcomes, and many of the individuals involved in SSPP (including both city and university personnel) served as participants on one of the Action Teams. The recommendations put forward by the Multicultural Awareness Action Team included an emphasis on staff development to increase teacher skill in various instructional strategies supported by SSPP (such as cooperative learning). As these Action Teams were broadly representative of district constituents, their recommendations carried weight and credibility. This process was also consistent with the announcement by the New York State Education Department that each district across the state would be required to develop a set of goals for itself and its students; these efforts are reflective of a national movement encouraging clear statements of goals aimed at improving the quality of education, addressing the growing demographic diversity of schools, and functioning within the constraints of the present economic situation.

The City District's school population represents considerable academic and socioeconomic variability. Five of the City's six middle schools are AIDP eligible, and an average of 18% of the middle-school population of 3,200 students are receiving special education services (higher than the national average). The chronic truancy rate (the percentage of students absent more than 20% of the time) at the six schools ranged from a low of 4.1% to a high of 13.8% during the 1989–1990 school year. In that year, we identified approximately 80 students as being at risk for school dropout based on the dual criteria of an absentee rate of 20% or more and/or passing grades in fewer than five courses at mid-year. Students from non–European-American ethnic backgrounds were disproportionately represented in this group.

Consequently, the direction for our collaboration seemed clear: our activities would be a joint effort by selected middle-school personnel and Syracuse University faculty to develop and implement exemplars of instructional and peer-support activities that would be delivered to students at risk within the general education classroom. The inclusive approach that was planned in response to these needs is described below.

AN INCLUSIVE APPROACH TO DROPOUT PREVENTION

In keeping with our commitment to avoid labeling students or sending them to a labeled program, it was determined that students would not be "pulled-out," nor would they be identified in any formal way by the teachers or administrators. Instead, the focus of the intervention was the goal of modifying the school experience for students judged to be at risk. Such modifications could address a variety of aspects of school life—academic, social, and extracurricular. Consistent with concerns that students maintain relationships with peers who can provide positive models of behavior and academic performance, our project emphasized primary prevention approaches representing instructional modifications to better meet the needs of a diverse, heterogeneous classroom of learners. The project components were:

1. *Academic engagement*   To increase student engagement, staff development activities were designed to enable teachers to become skilled in the use of a wider variety of instructional approaches. This included a major focus on cooperative learning and multicultural curricular adaptations in particular.

2. *Peer support*   To increase socioemotional supports for students, individual teachers participating in project activities were assisted in the purposeful design of peer support networks. Cooperative-learning instructional groups became the context of activities over an entire marking period in each class. These "longitudinal" group contexts provided students at risk with systematic opportunities to develop positive interaction patterns—including friendships—with peers in their group who had been carefully selected as potential supports and friends based upon personal, social, and cultural characteristics.

3. *Individualized opportunities for support*   In some instances, specific student needs were addressed in extracurricular activities. For example, three "Breakfast Club" groups were organized in 1990–1991 to meet once weekly with a graduate student Health Education major; these groups focused on nutrition and diet and consisted of students who were significantly overweight, including students in the at-risk group.

Selected aspects of these program components are summarized below.

Academic Engagement:
The Cooperative Learning Component

Friesen and Wieler (1988) examine cooperative learning as one of three recent educational movements (along with multicultural education and peace education) that they regard as natural developments of the progressive education tradition in North America. They comment:

> Research shows that societies everywhere value respect for others and equality as quality of life indicators. Thus, philosophical considerations, social science research and social values combine to present a social obligation and therefore a pedagogical mandate. In other words, the school as a primary agent of socialization has the responsibility to create enlightened, well-adjusted, respectful members of society. Without this understanding of the role of the school in society, multicultural education, cooperative learning and peace studies would not exist. (p. 50)

Cooperative learning was originally developed as a strategy to assist schools as systems and children as individuals to thrive in the environment created by mandatory bussing aimed at achieving racial integration. Structurally, cooperative learning involves organizing students into small learning groups that are heterogeneous by design on dimensions of race, gender, ability, disabling condition, and achievement, and that are guided through a learning process that requires students to cooperate with one another in order to master academic content. Interestingly, the value of cooperation is also being increasingly recognized in the criterion adult world of work. Thus, while individual achievement continues to be critical, and competition can be viewed as a motivational strategy to encourage students to achieve to their fullest potential, cooperation is viewed as both a process to enhance achievement and an outcome of value in and of itself, with direct relevance to the needs of the real world.

After nearly 20 years of research, cooperative learning proponents claim that the method enhances academic achievement, intergroup relationships between students with and without disabilities, positive self-esteem, positive peer support, internal locus of control, positive group/classroom management, altruism, and perspective-taking skills (Bossert, 1988; Johnson & Johnson, 1985; Lew, Mesch, Johnson, & Johnson, 1986; Odynak, 1985). This is also consistent with Wentzel's (1991) review of theoretical and empirical work, which concludes that student social responsibility is both a valued outcome for its own sake and is instrumental in the acquisition of knowledge, the development of cognitive skills, and the enhancement of motivation to achieve. Particularly because it entails positive peer support and heterogeneous student groupings, cooperative learning seemed to be a natural educational reform to promote feelings of connectedness among students at risk of dropping out.

Our goal was to refocus at least some of the instructional activities at the middle-school level from an individualistic and competitive goal structure to a cooperative goal structure, and thus provide direct, in-classroom support for participation by *all* students in each learning activity. Throughout the project, teachers were recruited on an individual, voluntary basis to participate in various inservice and technical-assistance activities to enable them to master cooperative learning as an instructional strategy. During the 1988–1990 school years, we provided extensive training in the use of the Johnson model (Johnson & Johnson, 1989) to 25 teachers who volunteered for the project and were nominated by their principals. The training included several all-day and half-day workshops on instructional adaptations through the use of cooperative learning, with consultants trained in the Johnson model. Ongoing bi-monthly meetings were also held with faculty members from Syracuse University who were selected for their content expertise. These meetings enabled teachers to develop and design their own lesson plans and unit adaptations of required New York state curricula in English, reading, social studies, physical education, science, and mathematics. In addition, these small-group meetings were intended to promote camaraderie as teachers and university faculty shared information and discussed with one another ideas related to the implementation and use of cooperative learning.

Yet, after the first 2 years of participation by approximately 25 teachers, certain basic practices and student behaviors continued to make it unlikely that those students at greatest risk would be in a position to benefit from instructional changes such as the use of cooperative learning in the typical classroom. Many of our students at risk were so isolated from others that they had developed successful strategies to avoid classroom participation on even those days when they did attend class. Teachers needed to become more directly involved in structuring student participation. Thus, during the 1990–1991 school year, we intentionally designed cooperative learning groups to place potential friends and peer support networks around each student at risk; this process was visible to teachers who designed the groups, but not to students, who were all organized into similar, heterogeneous groupings.

The Peer Support Network Component

There are various guidelines for the formation of cooperative learning groups, relating primarily to the goal of achieving heterogeneity. Without altering our commitment to that goal, we decided to work more directly with the teachers to ensure that a peer support network would be accessible to students regarded as being at risk. Thus, various predictor variables were utilized to identify those students at risk, and project staff met with individual participating teachers to deliberately structure, around each of these students, a cooperative learning group that could potentially function as a peer support network.

Figure 1 shows a form that teachers can use to structure peer support networks. We would recommend that the first step be for the grade-level team to select a class period during which all students are enrolled in one of the core academic subject areas. The team would then plan the base peer-support groups, which should be structured around each student at risk, but in a manner that is invisible to the students themselves. The first step should be for the team to identify those students with the greatest support needs and fill in one of the four slots in each cluster with the name of one of these target students. We used the project's dual criteria of an absence rate of 20% or more and/or passing grades in fewer than five courses at the end of the first marking period to identify these students.

Interestingly, we have been unable to locate any empirically based literature on the design of positive peer supports for students at risk. To compensate, we have been guided by our own background and clinical experiences in structuring student–peer interactions, inclusive schooling for students with disabilities, and special education for students with emotional disturbance. Thus, our criteria for constructing these net-

CLASS GROUPINGS

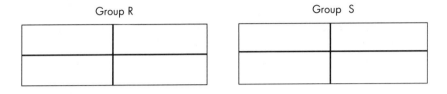

Group R   Group S

Group T   Group U

Group W   Group X

Group Y   Group Z

Figure 1. A form to assist in structuring peer support networks.

works was necessarily clinical and experiential. The literature on students at risk suggests that these individuals have friends who are a negative influence on their school achievement and motivation (see Evans & Matthews, 1992). Our own interviews with teachers suggest instead that many of the students most at risk are socially isolated, and some might well be labeled as clinically depressed. These students have virtually *no* school behavior—they are often absent, and when they do attend school, they keep to themselves and do not participate in classroom interactions. A smaller sub-sample are characterized by aggressive, acting-out behavior and friendships with peers who are similarly acting out.

Teachers in our program participated in a general training session on using cooperative learning to encourage positive peer supports, and an experienced teacher provided a model-class scripted example of how to gather the necessary student information for constructing such groups. Students were asked to complete the primary portion of information on an individual index card themselves, including their name, age, grade, gender, race, favorite activities outside school, and a content-specific preference list (e.g., in English class, the students were asked to indicate what they regarded as their major strengths/interests related to English). After this practice session, teachers then gathered this background information from students in their own classes to prepare for the individual consultation sessions that would help them design the cooperative learning groups. This occurred at mid-year, and teachers were by then quite knowledgeable regarding their students' school interests and peer-interaction patterns. Based on our data, we developed a partially validated School Self-Rating that is highly predictive of at-risk status, which we were able to use by October to identify likely student needs, allowing us to form the groups early in the school year, without waiting for the semester grades that would signify actual failure (Meyer, Harootunian, & Williams, 1991; see also Meyer & Henry, 1993, for a copy of the scale).

Without exception, teachers were enthusiastic in their choices for peer networks. For the first year that this approach was used, several general "rules" were followed in assembling groups of four students. Each group was to be heterogeneous with regard to race, gender, and ability/achievement level (e.g., African American and European American; male and female; one "high," one "low," and two "average" achievers). With rare exception, only one student at risk would be included in any single group. Each cooperative learning group included at least one student who was generally on task in group activities. At least one, and, if possible, two of the four group members were selected based on teacher judgment that he or she might be a potential friend for the student at risk, and these students had to have similar interests and academic ability (though their achievement levels were, in fact, quite different). Thus, rather than selecting "star" students as potential friends, we attempted to identify students who were very much like the student at risk, with one important exception—the potential friends were regarded by the teacher as positive influences. Finally, personalities were taken into consideration in order to avoid potentially explosive or otherwise negative group combinations, such as putting together "macho" boys and timid girls or two volatile students. Table 1 illustrates the criteria for group formation that were developed at the end of the first year of the program.

These groupings of students stay together for their class cooperative learning activities for at least a 10-week marking period. In some instances, group combinations did not work, and modifications were made. "Debriefing" sessions were held between the first author of this chapter and most teacher participants to discuss their impressions and review student records. Various individual-student data (e.g., on achievement and attendance) from throughout the year are available to help investigators discover the extent to which students were engaged and academically successful. Overall, we found that attendance and participation by target students improved, and students became (according to teacher reports) increasingly more engaged in the cooperative learning activities in particular. However, attendance and participation improvements were notable primarily in those classes in which these procedures and networks were in place. As this was not the case for at least some of the classes attended by the students, our overall impact on grade-level performance was not dramatic. A final serious flaw in our approach especially affected students with the most significant absentee records or school alienation behaviors, those who were particularly withdrawn from peer interactions and classroom group activities. These young people simply came to school so seldom that they did not have the opportunity to experience the peer support networks. And, when they did come, they often refused to sit with their groups and participate as a member; these situations are described in more detail below. While this was only a problem with fewer than one or two students per grade-level team, this most-needy student population will require more structure and individual attention in order to even participate in the inclusive opportunities available to them.

TEACHERS' PERSPECTIVES

Our effort to reduce the incidence of at-risk status emphasized the delivery of enhanced academic and peer support components by the classroom teacher; the teachers themselves implemented the intervention. For the majority of teachers who participated, project components represented an educational innovation—a new way of organizing instruction,

Table 1.   Criteria for constructing peer support networks

General Criteria for Groups

Each group in the class period should be heterogeneous with respect to:
  Gender
  Ethnicity (e.g., African American, Native American, EuroAmerican)
  Achievement levels in the subject area
  Academic ability
  Preferred in-class activities (e.g., writing versus speaking)

Specific Criteria for Peer Support Networking

With rare exceptions, no more than one "at-risk" student per group

If a student receiving English as a Second Language services is in the group, try to also include another student who is bilingual (same first language) but more fluent in English

Avoid potentially explosive or otherwise negative group combinations (e.g., two volatile students who would set one another off, a "macho" boy with "victims," too many off-task students within the group)

Try to plant one "worker" and/or a "diplomat/peace-keeper" in each of the groups

Building Specific Peer Supports

For each group, select at least one and possibly two students who might be a potential friend for the student at risk. These matches should:
  Be good influences/models
  Have similar interests/hobbies
  Be of similar academic ability (although doing better academically and/or attending school more regularly)
  Seem to be a good personality match with the at-risk child (How to judge? Use your observations/best hunches).

From Meyer, L.H., & Henry, L.A. (1993). Cooperative classroom management: Student needs and fairness in the regular classroom. In Putnam, J.W. (Ed.), *Cooperative learning and strategies for inclusion: Celebrating diversity in the classroom* (p. 116). Baltimore: Paul H. Brookes Publishing Co., reprinted by permission.

grouping students, and adapting materials to fit student needs. How did teacher participants perceive this process and its impact on students? Teachers' perspectives on their implementation and the outcomes as they experienced them are important evaluation data for several reasons:

First, practitioners are in a position to report on the dynamics of implementing an innovative practice. For example, teachers can delineate the nature and degree of resistance they may have encountered from students, other staff, and parents; they can also describe their own strategies for addressing that resistance and their perceptions of what worked and what failed to have a positive impact.

Second, teacher feedback is needed to assist in making adaptations based on student characteristics, building characteristics, content-specific and grade-level needs, and individual teacher style and preferences. Third, information from teachers about instructional and management "successes" and "failures" in the classroom can not only help to generate hypotheses for potentially fruitful future work, but can also allow for more accurate predictions of outcomes for individual children. Gaining these teacher perspectives was particularly important to us, as ours was an effort to not only enhance the academic performance of students but also to affect other related motivational and social-interaction variables not easily measured through traditional assessments.

A qualitative study of teacher perspectives on the process and effects of the cooperative learning component was undertaken; teachers were selected for participation based on a stratified sampling procedure to allow for maximum coverage of subject areas, schools, grade levels, and gender/race, and on integrity of frequency and degree of implementation of cooperative learning activities (i.e., those teachers interviewed were also those teachers who showed acceptable levels of fidelity in implementation, as supported by both direct observation by project personnel in the classrooms and process data on classroom activities collected over the course of the year). The six teachers in the sample taught English, Math, Physical Education, Reading, Science, and Social Studies; one of the five female teachers was African American and five of the six teachers were European American. Four of the six middle schools were represented; four teachers taught grade 8, one taught grade 7, and one taught both 7th and 8th grades.

Following standard procedures for qualitative study, the interviews were semi-structured to allow for in-depth exploration. When necessary, follow-up questions were asked for clarification. Confidentiality was assured, and each audio-recorded interview lasted 60–100 minutes; the interviews were later transcribed and checked for accuracy with the teachers themselves present. For each theme area, patterns across responses were identified. Each theme is described briefly, along with direct quotations from teachers where appropriate, to highlight points and illustrate representative comments (for more information and a report involving an additional school district, see Williams, Meyer, & Harootunian, 1992).

Teachers' Perspectives on Valued Outcomes

Overall, teachers expressed a number of examples of the importance of cooperative learning to their students. These ranged from enhancing academic skills to the development of important social skills and networks of peer/social support. As one teacher reported telling her students:

> In real life, you work with a lot of different kinds of people, you learn to adjust to different situations. . . . In cooperative learning you work with others; groups change often, and that gives you an opportunity to learn to work with different classmates.

Similarly, another teacher stated:

> Very seldom in a job will you sit in your own cubicle doing your own work. You will be working with a number of other people on a project or you will need to work with another agency that your company might deal with . . . and you are going to need to cooperate with these people. If you don't learn the skills, then you are not going to go very far.

Another teacher emphasized that communication skills were a critical need among the group he referred to as the "difficult kids," who put each other down and did not know how to disagree without saying things like "No, you dummy, that's wrong" or "That's stupid." His first step was to discuss communication skills with the students, including how to disagree with one another; as an important part of cooperative learning, he asked the students to suggest ways to disagree "without putting each other down." And altruism was promoted: "It is nice helping people . . . working with people. . . . Can you think of something that you have learned all by yourself? With no guidance? No help?" The teachers reported that they wanted students to think about the social dimensions of their lives as they learned and emphasized the positive aspects of empathy and mutual support.

Teachers also shared information on the academic benefits of cooperative learning with their students, telling them, "You get better at something when you help each other learn. . . . You succeed better together than by yourselves," and "Discovery and problem solving can best be accomplished when you work with others." Finally, teachers reported sharing some utilitarian goals with their students, including those of reaching more of them through small-group support and increasing their motivation by making learning fun. Clearly, these teachers were comfortable with school as a setting in which students are not only to master academic skills, but also develop critical social skills and experience the benefits of social support as they grow and learn.

Teachers' Reports of Student Responses

Without exception, teachers reported considerable difficulty introducing cooperative learning and reaching the point at which students participated with enthusiasm. (Teachers have told us again and again that they do not themselves feel confident using cooperative learning until well into their second year of experience with the procedure. It may be relevant, however, that most students in these classes have had no prior exposure to cooperative learning; things may go more smoothly if students are more familiar and comfortable with the strategy.) All six teachers reported hesitation and open resistance from students at the beginning. Students simply did not like to be placed in groups, and were initially "turned off." As one teacher said, at the beginning of the year cooperative learning elicited "Battles . . . fights, screaming, referrals, kids running out of the room, refusing to work with so and so. It was horrible." The teachers believed that middle school students were particularly resistant because of a tight "clique" structure—getting students to move out of their cliques and share activities with others was not an easy task. Some students isolated themselves and adamantly refused to move their seats, preferring to do their work on their own. In fact, a percentage of our at-risk group were students who—if they attended school at all—would refuse to sit with other students and typically selected an individual desk away from classmates.

According to the teachers, resistance arose for several reasons. Many students simply seemed to hate the idea of having to sit next to someone with whom they had had no previous interaction. In the academic areas of Social Studies, Reading, English, Mathematics, and Science, the resistance was least likely to come from the students with high ability. Instead, the students who had academic and emotional difficulties seemed most resistant. The situation was exactly the opposite in Physical Education, during which students with high ability openly protested about being "held back" by students whose motor and sports skills were less developed. Teachers reported that the "difficult" students taunted them by expressing the idea that the teachers used cooperative learning only to make their jobs easier, or because they "did not wish to do any work." Finally, students were also apprehensive about the social contact required during group activities. Students enter the 7th grade from different elementary schools—typically more tightly focused on a single neighborhood, in contrast to a middle school, which usually serves many different neighborhoods. Hence, the middle school represents, for most students, the first significant contact they have had with others from those different neighborhoods. Racial intolerance was often initially evident, and racial slurs were not uncommon. Yet the teachers persisted, and, as one teacher put it, "after nine months of keeping at it and not giving up, there are only two little groans all day."

Without exception, learning to work cooperatively was a long-term, evolutionary process:

> As students began to break down barriers, they realized that so and so wasn't as bad as they had thought . . . and they began to give respect to

each other. They also realized that someone whom they thought to be dumb wasn't after all without strengths. . . . If this person could not do one thing, he or she could do something else and do it well. Students began to develop and build respect for the strengths of others. For example, when they did three dimensional projects in English, which involved writing, acting, drawing, they tried to pool their resources—if one could not write, perhaps he or she could draw—since they knew that each one had at least certain strengths.

So even though in the beginning it was a bit forced, once the students began to trust me and to know me, they were willing to try to work in groups. In fact, they developed self-esteem and pride when they recognized what their group members could do instead of refusing to have someone in their group because of the preconceptions that he or she was no good. This, I believe, is a positive approach in teaching. . . . learning to respect others for what they can do, rather than merely concentrating on academics.

Teachers reported confronting resistance by telling their students to "give it a chance"—a strategy that they felt generally worked as students adjusted to a new way of doing things over time. The exceptions to this gradual adjustment involved genuine personality clashes within a group.

Teachers' Stories

The teachers were in agreement about what they believed worked and did not work. Successes were generated through carefully planned, creative lessons and activities; particular topics that seemed well suited to cooperative learning; activities that involved several dimensions of different talents being used simultaneously (thus allowing different students to "shine" in turn); allowing students to switch roles; and assigning tasks that involved hands-on, challenging problem solving. Failure stories, however, centered on student characteristics: isolation of one student from the group because of seriously discrepant academic skills (being "left behind"); personality clashes within a group; headstrong behavior by a student; particular students who would manage to get their group off-task and were disruptive in school regardless of the nature of the particular activity or instructional structure. Overall, the success stories point to the potential for greatly increased school engagement for many students who have not previously responded to more traditional instructional approaches. At the same time, the "failures" highlight the continued need for additional socioemotional and academic supports for students with the most extensive difficulties.

Successes   The teachers reported various success stories that related to instructional and curricular issues, but here we summarize only those that related to student needs. For one teacher, success was most focused on inclusion—having those students who initially refused to join groups, who stomped out of the class in anger, and who were always disruptive change over time to become a part of the classroom community, to be accepted by peers, and to come to feel that he or she had something to contribute to the group:

> There was this kid Josh . . . refused the first two months. He was down in the office all the time when we would do cooperative learning because he would refuse to sit down and be part of a group. . . . Sometimes, instead of a referral, I would let him work on his own.

According to the teacher, one day, during a cooperative learning activity that involved writing a fairy tale, the other students liked what Josh had written. Some of the students started to tell him to "do this" and "do that" with the story, and "that began to turn him around. So at least he would come in and he would sit in a group after that." This teacher believed that encouragement from his peers was crucial for Josh and students like him, who are always in trouble at school because they cannot cope with the academic material. She also told of another boy with a history similar to Josh's—a boy who had been just as adamant about refusing to engage in cooperative learning, or any other type of instructional activity for that matter. During a cooperative learning unit that centered on a book called *The Friends*, the teacher felt that Thomas "was able to identify with the problem of the girl in the book." Students took the roles of different characters from the story and acted them out in skits:

> And one of the kids said [to Thomas], "You should be this character." "No, no, I just want to go to sleep," and he put his head down on the desk. . . . [The students persisted]: "You know you would be great doing this." And so finally, he decided he would do it, and so he got on stage and he did the skit and he was wonderful. . . . And the kids said, "He was great, he was great!" That turned him around.

This teacher believed that the most beneficial feature of cooperative learning was that it

> helps every level of kids . . . the kid who is super and would produce super work anyway gets the benefit of being able to teach others, and I think that always helps a gifted kid. And I think that the average kid gets the benefit of the gifted and all their ideas and creativity and abstract thought.

She believed that through cooperative learning, the abstract and concrete thinkers come together, and there is real "welding." Students begin to realize that if they cannot do one thing, they can do other things; groups can achieve things that no single individual can do alone. Students also learn to be patient, to respect the individual contributions of each person, and to build upon one another's strengths.

The teachers felt that when cooperative learning worked, it made them realize how many more students they could reach than they had been able to using more traditional instructional methods. During the group work, the students were supporting one another's learning, solving problems, communicating, brainstorming, and building on one another's strengths. And the teacher could work with each small group in turn and concentrate more on individual students than had been possible during direct instruction in large classes. Clearly, the teachers who had become more comfortable with use of cooperative learning as an alternative instructional style believed that it enabled them to reach a broader group of students and at the same time meet individual needs through the closer contact involved.

Failures   The teachers all focused on problems with particular students in their stories about instances in which cooperative learning did not work. Generally, these stories involved students who engaged in open conflict with one another and students who were individually disruptive to the group's task orientation. For example:

> I had two boys that simply could not be together. I said, "Well, try it out." The way they worked it out was they ended up in a fist-fight in the classroom and had to be removed. My trying to put them into cooperative groups did not work. They told me it wouldn't work, they decided it wouldn't work, and they made it not work. When they came back to class, I put them in different groups because it was very obvious that it wasn't working. . . . Even when I put them in different groups, it wasn't working.

and:

> I had other groups where, again, because of personality problems, students were unable to work with one another . . . . [There was one girl who] had a lot of self-image problems, a lot of negativity, and really needed some serious counseling. She would come in and undermine the whole group and destroy what was going on. She has a strong personality and the students did not know how to deal with her . . . I was not able to resolve it. . . . It didn't matter which group I put her in.

Although none of the teachers reported giving up on their efforts, three of them admitted that by the end of the year they had still not succeeded with certain students who were so far behind academically and had such serious emotional problems that classmates regarded it as impossible to include them in groups. These teachers were bothered by this failure of inclusion.

One teacher would not acknowledge any attempt at cooperative learning as a failure; as she said, "Even though it is rough sometimes at certain points, in the end it always worked out . . . It was [my] planning just how much they would be able to do in a day and then realizing that asking the students to section off work in a particular way just didn't work. . . . I learned a lot." Her worst stories dealt with how, in looking back, she realized she should have done things differently. If something hadn't worked, it was because she had not anticipated and prepared for a particular problem, and she believed she would be able to do so in such a situation in the future.

HIGHER EDUCATION AND TEACHER EDUCATION

The SSPP initiative was intended to be a series of joint efforts by both school systems and universities to address the needs of students at risk and their families. At Syracuse University, we decided to take a more critical look at the extent to which our teacher-education programs "walked the talk" in how we approached the needs of students at risk (see also Chaps. 11 and 12, this volume). One question that might have justifiably been asked by practitioners is: What are the universities and colleges doing, in their own teacher education programs, to ensure that the next generation of teachers will be better equipped to address the needs of these young people? Indeed, school administrators and the teachers themselves also responded to criticisms of practice by pointing out that each of them had been trained by the very institution of higher education with whom they were now working—in programs like ours at Syracuse, in fact!

Teacher Certification Requirements

SSPP did require that the university and college partners attend to at least one dimension of their own programs as part of the partnership: the proposal guidelines included reference to providing evidence that each of the teacher-education universities and colleges would incorporate attention to the student at risk into their training programs (see Chap. 12, this volume). And along with New York State's 200+ teacher-education programs, we were also responding to required changes in teacher certification that allowed additional attention to be paid to diversity issues (see New York State Education Department, 1992). The new elementary and secondary programs that had to be in place in order for any graduates after August 1993 to be eligible for provisional teacher certification did not call for meeting the needs of a broader range of students by addressing various adaptations in a program's core methods coursework. Instead, programs were able to address required issues such as multiculturalism, disabilities, and other aspects of diversity in the curriculum through "add-on" approaches such as offering one new course or single-course components. Required revisions of teacher certification programs did not even explicitly address the possibility of joint degree programs with special education, for example, which represents a significant service and even a system component through which many students at risk pass at one time or another in their lives. Even if these students would not receive special education services under present policies, there might be benefits if they could do so. But because access to such services requires diagnostic labels and even separate, segregated schooling, the cost is often seen as too great and the label as too stigmatizing for students who are already alienated from the system.

Inclusive Teacher Education and Students at Risk

How might a university's teacher-education programs address the needs of students at risk with regard to the knowledge and skills acquired by students preparing to be tomorrow's teachers? This section briefly highlights the changes made by Syracuse University's School of Education in three of its teacher education programs.

The Inclusive Program   While many university teacher-education programs (including those at Syracuse and many other universities involved in SSPP) have historically offered dual certification programs, what was different about the Syracuse program was that this was no longer one alternative offered simultaneously with single-certification options. A decision was made that Syracuse graduates should enter the teaching profession with a major commitment to—and a basic repertoire of teaching methods for—addressing the needs of the broad range of students found in today's classrooms, from those we refer to as typical to those whom we label with terms such as *gifted and talented, at risk, ESL, Chapter 1, disabled, or culturally diverse*. It was determined that this commitment would be expressed through a merged program in elementary and special education, and that this would be the only undergraduate-level option available leading to recommendation for certification in these two areas. And in response to those who challenged this arrangement with a concern that some students would not want to enroll in such a program because they preferred to teach "typical" students, the faculty reply was that there was no such thing as a typical classroom in today's schools. Tomorrow's educators must graduate with a deep commitment to all children, and if a prospective teacher is not ready to make that commitment, he or she would be better served by attending another program. For a private university that is highly dependent upon tuition derived from undergraduate enrollment, this was not a values-based commitment to be taken lightly, or one without potential negative consequences. Since that time, however, the Syracuse University Inclusive Elementary and Special Education Teacher Education Program has attracted considerable attention and praise, both in New York and nationally (National Association of State Boards of Education, 1993).

Syracuse's Inclusive Program, coordinated by Luanna Meyer, who was also the Co-Director of the Syracuse SSPP program throughout the period described in this volume, includes a number of features that represent integral commitments to diversity and to addressing student needs through both "add-on" requirements and revisions of professional core and liberal arts sequence requirements:

Two dedicated multicultural education courses, one early in the program and one taken in the last semester, paired with student teaching, require focused attention on issues of diversity in educational values and practices.

Two multicultural courses—one in the Social Sciences and one in the Humanities—were included as parts of the liberal arts cluster requirements.

The new requirement for a concentration in an academic field of study in the arts or sciences was addressed through negotiated 24 + to 30 + credit "specializations," which represented agreements with the academic major areas that students would be eligible for graduate study in that area. These new specializations included many traditional majors, such as history and English, but also included interdisciplinary concentrations in, for example, Social Sciences Perspectives on Childhood, and Nonviolent Conflict and Change. What was also interesting about this process was that it involved the education department working far more closely with members of many liberal arts and sciences fields than ever before.

Core professional education coursework was completely revised to include team-taught and merged courses on content that had been taught separately in Elementary and Special Education. For example, the introductory and educational psychology courses, as well as methods courses in language arts, reading, mathematics, science, and social studies, now address issues of entitlements and specific instructional and curricular adaptations to accommodate diverse student needs.

Some dedicated coursework specifically focused on meeting individualized needs was retained, but, along with faculty co-planning across elementary and special education and coordination of field placements, was integrated into the professional-methods semester.

Professional education coursework content was to reflect the most promising educational practices, but we also committed ourselves to using the same kinds of innovative practices we wanted our students to use when they became educators. Thus, university professors were challenged to team-teach, rely less on "chalk and talk" lectures and discussion sessions, incorporate group assignments and grades into their course requirements, implement cooperative-learning techniques in all courses in which they were appropriate, incorporate technology such as instructional software packages into lessons, adapt authentic alternative assessments (such as portfolio student-teaching evaluations) to replace more traditional student evaluation practices, and generally revamp and revise the way they taught at the university level.

It was decided that every student in the program would progress through a sequence of six field placements (during 3 of their 4 years of study) in the most inclusive school programs that could be found and a sophomore-year–long respite placement with a child with disabilities (not a school placement) designed to give future teachers the family perspective.

Ongoing program evaluation and revisions were instituted; these were based on the experiences of faculty and students across the first 4 implementation years.

A complete description of the program and its components is available in Meyer, Mager, and Sarno (1994), and the history of the change process in the School of Education that led to this program is available in Meyer and Biklen (1993).

Secondary Program and Middle School Sequence   Less dramatic and less systemic were the changes implemented in the school's Secondary Education Program and the design of a six- to eight-credit course sequence leading to add-on certification (along with either elementary or secondary certification) in teaching at the middle school level. The Secondary Program, for example, is also an undergraduate option, but, as is the case at many universities, continues to focus on upper-division coursework in professional education in combination with an academic major in the liberal arts and sciences. One reason for this pathway is that many students start as academic majors and decide later that they will use that major by teaching at the secondary level. Even if students intend throughout their academic career to become teachers, the practice of secondary education—particularly with those who wish to teach at the high school level—is to emphasize disciplinary preparation rather than pedagogical training. This pattern represented a very real constraint for the secondary education programs. Students are enrolled in the School of Education for a relatively brief period, perhaps only 1–2 years, and all required coursework must be completed within that time frame.

Thus, it seemed impossible to pursue a joint Secondary Education–Special Education degree program within these time constraints. Furthermore, many secondary education faculty members and teachers were not as convinced that personnel should be prepared for the full range of student needs. Ideologically, schools are no longer "tracked." In practice, however, tracking occurs in many ways—from the very structure of a system leading to different diplomas (Regents vs. General) to individual student decisions about subject-area choice, career paths, and increasingly diverse academic levels by the time students reach the teenage years. The School of Education at Syracuse thus maintained its undergraduate program in Secondary Education leading to recommendation for provisional certification at that level. The necessity of providing training on meeting diverse student needs—such as those of students who are gifted and talented, at risk, or who have a disability—was addressed through a broad commitment to incorporating the necessary components throughout the program as part of the mainstream coursework. But it remains difficult to document whether such incorporation actually occurs, especially when the instructing faculty members themselves may lack the technical expertise to incorporate strategies to accommodate students with diverse learning needs into their own curriculum. One new *required* course in curricular and instructional adaptations was included in the program—and since its inception has been consistently rated highly by students—but this does not seem to be enough. As a result, the program faculty are considering further changes in the Secondary Program as of this writing. One obstacle, however, is that the K–12 certification in Special Education has not been "broken down" into elementary and secondary certification; it would be logistically impossible to include pre-K–6 requirements for special education in a merged program in secondary education. The state-level administrative action of splitting special education certification would greatly facilitate the ability of schools of education to create merged secondary programs that could better prepare teachers to enter a profession committed to meeting diverse student needs.

Our middle school story is at one level more hopeful and at another less so. Certification to teach grades 7–9 has historically been structured as an "add-on" component to either elementary (K–6) or secondary (9–12) certification programs. When the new requirements in New York State, including those for this middle school component, were developed, the Syracuse SSPP program took on the task of creating a new course sequence that would both reflect those state requirements and incorporate our middle school efforts targeting students at risk and inclusion at the middle-school level. Syracuse City School District personnel—through the ongoing participation of the Director of Middle Schools, Alan Steinberg, and the involvement of various district personnel connected with various aspects of middle schooling—were consulted throughout this process. In fact, Steinberg, who also served as Co-Director of SSPP, co-designed and co-taught the first offering of middle school coursework with a faculty member (Meyer) at Syracuse University. When the formal course proposals for a six-credit sequence and an optional two-credit practical requirement (for those who were not inservice teachers at the middle school level) were developed, district personnel were again involved in reviewing and revising the proposals before they were submitted to the appropriate university and state bodies.

We also approached this coursework in middle schooling in a manner designed to incorporate what we had learned about how teachers should think and feel about meeting student needs. Our first course, entitled "Meeting the Needs of Middle School Students," includes required content on early adolescent psychology/learner characteristics as well as models of ways of addressing the needs of early adolescents. But in an effort to put teachers "inside the heads" of these young people, exploration of the early adolescent begins by reading works of fiction popular with teenagers and discussing themes from those stories that seem to represent how young people experience their world. Next, students are asked to construct their own theory of one aspect of learner characteristics, and base their theory not solely on previously read literature, but on a series of interviews with children, parents, and teachers. Models of ways of addressing student needs are explored with the help of invited speakers who are administering and teaching those models, and in their interactions with these practitioners, prospective teachers must again critique and challenge their own assumptions and those in the literature. The second course in the sequence, entitled "Curriculum and Methods for Middle School," is heavily based on responsive practices in middle schooling, and requires that the students in the course engage in processes such as team projects that themselves reflect such practices. But a continuing challenge of this sequence is that it is an add-on: The students taking the courses are undoubtedly heavily influenced by the certification program (either elementary, secondary, or special education) that is their "home base."

CONCLUDING COMMENTS

Throughout our activities in the schools, we have been guided by a dynamic sharing between university personnel and practitioners. The teacher voices provide insight into the evolution of cooperative behavior among students, strategies teachers use to encourage students to support one another in cooperative learning activities, and the kinds of activities that facilitate the attainment of both academic and social goals to meet student needs. Recent dropout-prevention theories reiterate the idea of "school membership" that "occurs through social bonding which is generated by attachment, commitment, involvement, and belief in the institution" (Wehlage, Rutter, Smith, Lesko, & Fernandez, 1989, p. 176). The teachers' descriptions of their successes and failures further reinforce the need to modify the school experience to reach the ever-increasing numbers of students who fail to respond to the impersonal, large-group, direct-instructional model that once seemed the inevitable consequence of a system of education that placed one teacher in charge of perhaps 30 students at a time. Furthermore, these stories emphasize the importance of the intervention of peers as critical to change for students who offer strong resistance.

The teachers' experiences provided the groundwork for more structure in forming the groups and monitoring individual participation. As a result, our work showed a steady increase in participation, engagement, academic improvement, and even the development of positive peer relationships for a significant number of students at risk. However, our data also reveal a small core of young people with significant problems who require something more than modified instruction, the offer of peer support, and even individual attention from concerned school staff. We are disturbed by the relatively large number of such children who have serious personal and apparent clinical needs that have thus far gone unmet during their school careers. We suspect that dropout-prevention programs have underestimated the extent of certain individual needs.

If, as Evans and DiBenedetto (1990) suggest, there are multiple pathways to school dropout, and, as Evans and Matthews (1992) describe, each of these calls for different intervention approaches, our efforts must be both preventive and interventionist. Furthermore, interventions should be more "clinical," in the sense that they should take an individualized look at the child's sociopersonal needs and attempt to meet those needs, in addition to addressing academic remediation issues. Our approach to preventing school dropout must become multivariate in perspective and far more responsive to the empirical data on the needs of individual children.

Attempts to "fix the child" should not detract attention from the clear need to restructure schools and schooling to better accommodate today's diverse population of students. Traditional school organizational patterns and the typical Eurocentric and college-oriented curricula may no longer be suitable for an educational system serving such a diverse population. A high incidence of school failure may be the consequence of the enrollment of high percentages of youngsters whose culture and learning styles are "discontinuous" with those that underly teaching strategies and materials designed for a different age and different circumstances. Students who are at risk of dropping out without a high school diploma are disproportionately children of poverty and of color. Grant and Secada (1990) note the growing discontinuity between the demographics of today's teachers (increasingly white, middle-class, older, and female) and today's school children (increasingly from non–Euro-

American ethnic and cultural groups and, of course, including as many boys as girls). They stress the urgency of addressing this discontinuity in the restructuring of our schools and the recruitment and training of tomorrow's teachers. In her recent study based on interviews with students of low and those of middle-class socioeconomic status, Brantlinger (1991) reported troubling major differences in the perceptions of these students regarding how they were treated by the very same teachers in virtually identical situations. Whether or not these perceptions are entirely accurate, the remarkable and clear patterns in the students' reports of how they *felt* about events suggest that—at least in these children's minds—school is not always fair.

Today's school must become more capable of truly celebrating diversity. Teachers, curricula, and administrative practices within our schools can affect this process at many levels. Higher education must also take a far more serious look at its own roles and responsibilities in producing the next generation of teachers. Will these graduates enter their profession with both the values and the skills necessary to commit themselves to meeting the needs of all students? And in cases in which the challenges presented by students—whether they are labeled as being at risk or as having a disability—surpass a teacher's abilities, can the school provide collaborative and consultative services to the teacher, classroom, and students that do not result in isolation, stigmatization, and exclusion? As long as educational groupings and outcomes continue to reflect a racial and cultural caste system in this country, schools will be suspect as participants in a system that segregates and tracks. Instead, our schools must become what they were intended to be—the provider of equal opportunities to all those who will be tomorrow's citizens, with or without a high school diploma.

6

A Middle School Perspective on School Change

MARVIN COHEN

The Bank Street SSPP Program was a collaboration between two urban middle schools and the Graduate School of Bank Street College of Education. Over a 4-year period, we were able to focus on bringing about school changes in order to design and implement educational innovations tailored to the unique needs of middle school students. At the same time, the project provided College personnel with the field-based experience necessary to initiate an early-adolescent degree program in teacher education. The precise plans and processes in each school varied based on particular needs as perceived by those involved: indeed, every innovation was adapted to the circumstances and complexities of particular buildings, staff, and children. Yet, throughout our efforts, we found that an essential key to supporting school change in a systemic manner is a change in educators' beliefs and attitudes about teaching and learning. And, of course, in order for this to occur, a constellation of bureaucratic and cultural supports must first be in place. What follows is a description of the dynamic of our School–University Partnership in the support of the mutual goal of redefining the school experience for children who might otherwise drop out even before they reach the high school years.

BACKGROUND: MIDDLE SCHOOL AND SCHOOL REFORM

Little attention has thus far been paid to junior high school and to the developmental significance of the early adolescent period. Too often,

An earlier version of this chapter appeared as Cohen, M. (1993, May).

111

junior high school students experience failure in school programs that address them as if they were either older elementary or younger high school children, rather than early adolescents with their own unique developmental needs. This is not a new idea: Hall (1904) long ago summarized research on the nature of adolescence, supporting the need for responsive school models for this unique group of students. And even before the turn of the century, the National Education Association (NEA) established several national committees to examine the goals of secondary education and to rethink the role of grades 7 and 8 in particular (see Armstrong, Henson, & Savage, 1993; Stinnett & Henson, 1982). These grades had historically been viewed as a time to review content from grades K–6 prior to entering high school. The NEA committee reports emphasized the need to create "real junior high schools," in separate buildings, with various curricular initiatives that recognized individual differences, and activities designed specifically for students of this age (NEA Research Bulletin, 1923, cited in Henson, 1993, pp. 393–394). The middle school movement emerged in response, but the reality is that neither junior high nor middle schools have clearly established unique educational models and instructional practices that differ from those of other levels in order to meet the unique needs of this age range (Henson, 1986). Programs that serve these children and their schools seldom offer instruction and activities tailored to early adolescent needs (Winn, Regan, & Gibson, 1991). Entering adolescence poses great challenges: drugs, teen pregnancy, and school failure are all problems that face young people as never before, yet schools have failed to successfully address these problems. When we began our efforts, programs in New York City designed to address such needs were not focused at the middle school level. For example, the city was engaged in a variety of programmatic initiatives for students in grades 9–12 to address the escalating dropout rates. Yet, our experience at Bank Street told us that it was much too late to begin such an effort. The Ypsilanti studies (Berrueta-Clement, Schweinhart, Barnett, Epstein, & Weikart, 1984), as well as other recent research, were clear about the impact of programs that addressed dropping out even before the child entered middle school, including efforts as early as the preschool and elementary school years (Comer, 1984; Levin, 1986). The missing component seemed to be the middle school.

At the time we began our initiative, *Turning Points* (Carnegie Council on Adolescent Development, 1989), the landmark Carnegie report on the school needs of early adolescents, had not yet been released. The dearth of literature made it clear to us that this critical time in the child's life, when children are not quite yet adolescents, needed to be addressed. In their own development, teens' autonomy and social interaction are central concerns, yet school continues with a highly structured, homogeneous and passive-student academic model. Rather than providing opportunities for learning in social contexts in which identity and self-esteem can grow, schools tend to function as large anonymous places where learning could best be characterized as passive, where teachers distribute knowledge for absorption by children (Romberg, 1986). In addition, course content and organization continue to be based on a white, middle-class perspective. Meyers and Rowan (1983) argue that schools are organized in a standard way, with elements of control and bureaucracy, decoupled from instruction, that are meant to inspire a "logic of confidence"—reassurance to the white middle class that the schools remain as the white middle class experienced them when they were growing up, and that the education system is therefore working properly. Schools are also structurally more alike than different, and seem to reflect the historical search for "one best system" that can serve all children (Tyack, 1974).

In contrast, we saw the need to support diversity in schools. Our schools were big—one of the schools described in this chapter served 1,400 students—and uniform in design. There did seem to be a growing recognition of the need for small, diverse units that personalize schools for children who experience too much anonymity and each of whom comes to school with a broad range of needs, but little action was being taken when our program began. The literature is also clear about the limited effectiveness of top-down and centrally designed mandates for educational change that do not reflect the unique and complex characteristics and circumstances of specific schools and school personnel (Deal & Nutt, 1983; Popkewitz, 1983). Efforts at change have demonstrated that even when there is a high degree of fidelity to a reform, centrally designed models are instituted differently at different sites. New programs are not likely to be assimilated in the ways that their creators originally intended. It is more likely that the labels and procedures of a reform, and not the substance, will be adopted. It is also true that while an innovation may be validated in one particular setting, the real-world schools and classrooms in which changes are expected to be implemented represent a range of complex and varying environments that will affect implementation in unknown ways. In summary, mandated new programs get less than a fair chance to succeed.

THE CONCEPTUAL MODEL

To focus our efforts on the middle school age group, and in the belief that theory and practice must inform one another in order for either to be valuable, the Bank Street College of Intermediate School Collaborative, later renamed the Center for Minority Achievement, was born. This program predated the Stay-in-School Partnership Project initiative, and began by identifying schools with leadership and staff who had stated a willingness and ability to change and an interest in sharing expertise—theirs and ours—about children at risk. Our program began with four basic premises:

1. The most effective and long-lasting reform must be site-specific.
2. Effective reform cannot be imposed, but requires collaborative and collegial work based on mutual trust built up over time.
3. Dropout prevention begins before high school and cannot be effective as an isolated "one or two hit" project.
4. Dropout prevention consists of everything aimed at enriching the professional and educational experiences of all persons in the schools that involves administration, staff, students, or parents. (Cohen, Gaines, & Monroe, 1989)

We wanted to work with schools that already included our target population, but saw the challenge of serving them better and the potential benefits of sharing the experiences and results of personnel at these schools with others. Of the five schools that established a working relationship with the Center for Minority Achievement, two of the three Central Harlem schools in the borough of Manhattan became the focus of our SSPP program. Both of these schools had more than 95% "minority" student populations, and both served families from low socioeconomic backgrounds. Funds available from the New York State Education Department through SSPP provided a critical infusion of financial support that allowed us to dramatically increase our level of activity and establish a limited research component. Although SSPP, arriving in our third year of activity, covered only two of our five schools, it enriched our work at the other three by allowing us to maintain a stable staff and financial credibility that attracted corporate support.

Teacher Involvement

Teachers' views and beliefs play an important role in their instructional behavior (De Franco, 1987). What is transmitted to students is a function of everyday practices and values in the schools (Dalton, 1988). We therefore felt that it was these beliefs about teaching and learning that had to be changed if schools were to become more effective. As noted above, innovations are typically developed by outsiders, and teachers are expected to adopt those innovations in their schools and classrooms. In our experience, teachers prefer to respond to innovations through an "add-on" approach rather than by fundamentally redesigning their programs. The process of adoption of new ideas is generally voluntary at the building level, so only those teachers who are interested in an innovation are engaged in the implementation process. Again, these teachers tend to approach innovations as an addition to their collection of programs, rather than a reorganization of existing practices; of course, a full redesign would be further complicated by the fact that not all teachers at a given school were even participating in a particular innovation.

One approach to this individual variability in implementation has been to support a uniform approach, encouraging close fidelity to the original model. Rather than taking this perspective, we decided to encourage decentralized and varied enactment of programs that were themselves the results of thoughtful practitioners reflecting on the cognitive and emotional needs of early adolescents. Teachers would be empowered to design and enact the programs. Our role would be to ask the tough questions and supply new information. We felt that through this process of reflection on practice, teachers would construct new cultural meanings as well as rethink their existing beliefs about teaching and learning. Thus, adopting or adapting any innovation could not be accomplished as an "add-on," but would by definition require a fundamental reevaluation of existing overall instructional practices.

Teaching needs to occur in a manner that will empower children to productively challenge the world in which they live as well as the social order in which they are growing up. This supports not only good education, but also a broader role for the schools as agents of social change, in the tradition of George Counts (1969). We were not subscribing to the idea of innovations as strict adoptions of uniform, centrally dictated models, and so did not view our role as one of correcting lapses in quality control through such actions as securing better textbooks or improving the recruitment of teachers. We felt there was a need for basic design changes in the way learning occurred (Romberg, 1986). We wanted to challenge the passive model of learning that prevailed in schools, to enable children to not only have the opportunity to master the existing body of knowledge in a field, but also to view themselves as potential creators of new knowledge. Just as constructed knowledge is more powerful than that which is absorbed, so too are teacher-constructed programs and meanings more powerful in bringing about lasting change. In short, we felt that ownership would guarantee support.

We were trying to support teachers in an effort to build a model of professional development that would lead to lifelong learning and therefore best serve teachers and children in the long run. We felt that the best way to provide direct service to children was to educate teachers and give them the opportunity to reflect on their practice. We wanted new programs to grow from the interactions of teachers and principals, who would strive to address the unique needs of their settings and students. This process seemed to have the potential to engender ownership in order to give the program a life beyond our presence in a particular school. Ultimately, even if our school teams constructed a "new" idea that turned out to actually be well-established in a series of published research articles, we believed that this discovery process would not be a waste of time. Instead, it would encourage a sense of ownership and make the professional team far more receptive to studying the published literature (which we would share) for specific implementation approaches for something that they had themselves identified as being important.

All of this was consistent with the College personnel's own experiences in graduate-level teacher education. Central to Bank Street's Teacher Education program was the "conference group," a weekly meeting of six to nine pre- or inservice teachers who were given an opportunity to speak with each other about issues of their own choice. It was an opportunity to reflect on their practice with the benefit of one another's support and insight, as well as the guidance and expertise of a senior graduate faculty member. There were monthly site visits and biweekly individual conferences. The goals included discussing new techniques, but also, more importantly, learning to ask the kinds of questions that would inform the teacher's practice and become part of their lifelong professions as educators. The result was a model of personal professional growth that encouraged educators to think about their work long after they had completed the conference-group experience.

We wanted to adapt this approach and provide opportunities for teachers to reflect on teaching and learning. We felt that teachers, not outside consultants, are the ones who can change children's lives. Barbara Biber perhaps best described Bank Street's approach in a 1973 speech:

> This combination of methods—highly developed person-to-person interaction plus systematic analytic procedures—represents our conviction that basic change will not occur or last through distribution of learning tools and techniques or through dissemination of ideas unless attitudes, perceptions, and commitment of school people at the grass roots are part of a fundamental change process. This takes time, lots of time, and deep involvement of those who undertake—presume may be a better word—to be change agents in an established system. (Biber, 1973)

We felt that the College's model of working with small groups of professionals would provide the teachers with the opportunity to air their views, add to their experience, rethink practice, and then create new models. The challenge was to construct the small groups and then provide members with the necessary time together in their professional day. The hope was that this dialogue would continue after SSPP personnel had left the school.

Administrative Involvement

Our model for working with principals was less clear. We began our work committed to a belief in the pivotal role of the principal in school success. The principal has the opportunity to bring about change by influencing both bureaucratic and cultural factors. Monroe (1985) found clear agreement in the literature on the importance of the principal to school effectiveness. Goodlad (in Monroe, 1985) also pointed out that most of the school principals he studies lack the skills and abilities required for enacting educational improvements. The principal must coordinate many small actions to bring about larger changes (Firestone & Wilson, 1985). Even at the most micro level, the principal's role was critical: teacher groups could not collaborate with one another unless the schedule developed for the school (by the administration) allowed time and space for such collaboration. Yet, Olivera and Armistead (Monroe, 1985) found that principals' needs for professional development go unnoticed for the most part.

We determined early on that despite their stated concern and commitment, principals were generally not willing to be available for meetings outside their buildings. This is true in many urban areas, where the principal feels a very real need to be in the building to support students and staff at all times. And in an urban area such as New York City, a meeting scheduled after dismissal at any other building is likely to be complicated by nonschool factors (transportation) as well as unpredictable school needs that will, at the last minute, require the principal to stay late at the school. We therefore selected a process of formal and informal mentoring relationships supplemented by twice-yearly luncheons attended by teachers and principals. As a result, we were able to address a broad range of individual needs, from staffing, to scheduling, to how to observe and support teachers. The result was a rich and productive dialogue that greatly enhanced our own ability to work in the schools.

In all cases, the participants were allowed to define their own needs and thus focus on the areas that they felt were most important. The plans and processes varied from school to school. The Graduate School brought with it the expertise and experience of its entire faculty, as well as an eagerness to learn about how an urban middle school worked. The administrators and teachers brought their expertise as practitioners who served students who, because of their low socioeconomic status, were seen as being at high risk for school failure and for dropping out. We agreed to learn from each other, and thus we hoped to create programs that could outlive the collaboration and/or infusion of special funds from the SSPP grant program.

Since we wanted teachers and administrators to invent programs, we needed a fairly sophisticated funder—one who understood the importance of the process we were trying to create and who would trust us to work with school personnel who would develop worthwhile programs for children. Many federal and state-funded grant programs are highly directive, and dictate that a preapproved approach must be implemented. Such a program would have been totally contradictory to our process and our previous findings about how to successfully engage schools in meaningful change. We needed funders who understood that the best "direct service" to children was teacher development, because children spend 5 hours each school day with their teachers. When we applied to the New York State Education Department for state funding, we saw it as a necessary evil and were apprehensive about possible bureaucratic restrictions from a government agency. Instead, we found a bureau that philosophically, as well as financially, nurtured and supported our work—and respected the combined expertise and experience of Bank Street and its partner schools to develop a model for drop out prevention that was likely to endure.

THE PROCESS OF CHANGE

The Schools—Two Profiles

The two schools we worked with in Central Harlem had various things in common:

- They both served children from low income homes, with a variety of sociological needs.
- A passive model of instruction prevailed in both schools; children spent most of their time sitting in rows listening to a teacher who dispensed knowledge.
- Both the schools' administrations were anxious for new ideas and support in implementing them.
- Teachers did not dream; they thought about school in traditional terms and definitions and respected the traditional boundaries of structure and instruction. Too often, myths defined the limits of teachers' imaginations.
- Teachers did not see variation in instruction as an alternate way to help students be successful. They seemed to feel that if they could fix the children, the schools would be fine.
- Most important, teachers in both schools were interested in trying new things.

While the schools shared these features, they also differed in several ways. School A served approximately 1,400 students in grades 6 through

8 and was organized into several subschools that had existed since the school opened in 1975. All teachers who participated in project-related activities were licensed, and most were experienced. The administration was initially staffed by a principal who was described as "visionary and charismatic." We had begun our activities by inviting three principals of neighborhood intermediate schools to a luncheon at the College, and this principal was the only one who came (and he was late). The purpose of the meeting was to determine if we could work together and learn from one another; it turned out to be an exciting meeting that went on for 2 hours and resulted in an invitation to meet the staff of one of his subschools to discuss our possibly working together. This principal was later succeeded, during the project period, by a new principal who, as an interim acting principal, espoused the goal of simply maintaining order during the transition of leadership.

Our second site, School B, was not yet a school. It was an alternative site enrolling children in pre-kindergarten through grade 8, with an enrollment that grew from 250 to 700 during the 4 years of the project. Children who were identified for enrollment at School B had been unsuccessful at other schools in the district. Seventy percent of the staff were hired on a temporary, per-diem (unlicensed) basis, and all the teachers who worked with our program were unlicensed. This building principal was new and actively seeking support; she openly requested help with curriculum and staff-development activities for her (largely untrained) teachers. Consequently, she met frequently with our Center's Director about staffing, programming, and basic building management. She also was quite clear about the need to make her own professional and personal development a top priority. We could appreciate how difficult her situation was: She was constantly "fighting fires" and did not even have her own office. We worked with her because she seemed to want to learn.

Each school chose to work with us in different ways and with different stated goals. One thing was consistent, however—both of the principals agreed to make our work a priority. They were willing to schedule teachers for common preparation periods and to entertain any suggestions that came from their staff as a result of our meetings. In both schools, they were willing to provide bureaucratic support for our work. The meetings we had with the principals were welcomed by them as opportunities to engage in dialogue and transcend their own isolation. The resistance to change did not come from the principals. In fact, the principals were more than willing to provide bureaucratic "power tools" (Clark & Astuto, 1988)—to bend rules, shortcut paperwork, and even find small amounts of money. They themselves did not seem to have the time to do the work we were doing; they were too consumed with administra-

tive matters. There were either no underlying structures in their buildings or they were being used to foster instructional reform. The principals
did, however, welcome our instructional support and created the necessary opportunities for us to work with individual teachers or with fluid
groups. These fluid groups would then generate a core with a goal they
wanted to pursue or a theme they wanted to develop, and a teacher representing the initiative would schedule a meeting with the principal, to
which we would also go in order to help sell the idea.

Project Goals

Teachers needed a chance to talk about children, to engage in a professional dialogue, and to try out new ideas with colleagues. Until they did,
they found it difficult to progress beyond what they perceived as existing
barriers. The resistance and barriers to change lay with the teachers and
the myths that permeated their schools and limited their willingness to
try new things. Pedagogy that challenged norms—the way things were
generally done (e.g., taking neighborhood field trips as part of a thematic
unit)—was rejected as not allowable. What the college was able to do
was provide an opportunity for new information to enter the system—a
system that had difficulty looking beyond its present policies and circumstances. The principals did their part by scheduling common preparation
periods and flexibly interpreting rules. We from the college did our part
by clearly stating our long-term commitment and valuing the work of the
schools.

Our work in each school varied, depending upon the specific needs
of the site. However, our goals were explicit and consistent:

- To enhance student self-concept, academic achievement, and at-
  tendance
- To build parent support for the student and the school
- To support the empowerment of teachers and schools

In order for us to achieve our stated goals, we knew that there would
need to be dramatic changes in the schools, teachers' attitudes and beliefs, and the basic teaching–learning dynamics being employed. We also
knew that we were beginning a long-term relationship with the participating schools and wanted to create structures and processes that
would encourage teachers and administrators to think and plan together
for children in a way that would support our goals even long after we
had left.

The Working Relationship

We wanted to work with teachers in groups, but neither of the schools
initially provided us with this opportunity. The principals did not have

clear visions of how we might work with them or their staff. Instead, we were a resource offered to large groups of teachers to be used in some "site specific" way. Thus, we were not particularly aggressive in pursuit of our agenda, for three reasons:

LIBRARY

1. We were trying to build a relationship with the principal and teachers. If he or she wanted us to work with individuals, then that would be the way we would begin. There was ambivalence toward a college coming into the school with "the answer." Teachers also had enough things to do without another meeting that did not have a specific short-term goal from their own perspectives.
2. School-based management was not yet a part of the culture of the City's schools. It was 1986, three chancellors before an official endorsement of shared decision making and school-based management. Such ideas were only known in isolated pockets around the city. The culture of the schools still supported teachers operating in isolation under the watchful eye of "the Board" and principal. Even where there were mini-schools (School A), they had not yet begun to rethink curricula. Instead, teachers collected programs in an attempt to enrich, rather than rethink, curricula.
3. We began with no budget. The dean of the college supported us on a shoestring, with the rest of our time (about 80%) being voluntary. We had made long-term commitments, but needed to keep it flexible. We also needed time to raise money to get the project on its feet. We did not have substantial ongoing funding until 2 years into these efforts, when the SSPP initiative began.

Our intervention with teachers took the form of small-group meetings, curriculum workshops, and individual meetings with teachers about their classrooms. We allowed teachers to select topics. This permitted us to enter their classrooms and their world of work in a way that was safest for them. As a result, we could build on their strengths and move them beyond their traditional paradigms. We looked together at children and used the children's needs and interests as a way of discussing curriculum and change in the classroom. The result was slow progress with very strong advocates among the staff and administration. We came regularly and followed up; we built loyalty:

> Teachers had a professional experience, and they got to see that people cared and came in here and really did what they said they were going to do. Teachers in general don't lack for lip service from a variety of sources. But few promises are actually implemented. . . . I will tell a textbook salesman, "Not right now," but I'll always squeeze in someone from CMA [the Center for Minority Affairs]. (Teacher Survey, School A)

Major Program Activities

Teacher Meetings   Those who became part of groups began with biweekly meetings with a member of the Graduate School Faculty. These were usually supplemented by our visits to classrooms or individual meetings with teachers on an as-needed basis. A faculty member would help plan a lesson and then come to the classroom as an aide, or as a master teacher working with the regular teacher, or not at all, depending on the needs and comfort level of the teacher involved. Teachers identified common interests and their own strengths and weaknesses. We then planned workshops around their interests and applauded their strengths:

> My frustrations were minimized by the quiet assurance from Bank Street that what I was going through was perfectly normal and expected [of a new teacher]. Therefore, my frustration did not transfer to my students. Instead, I was able to encourage them to believe in themselves and work better. (Teacher Survey, School B)

For the experienced teacher, participation in these groups provided a chance to interact with other professionals and to continue to grow. For the new teacher, it was a chance to benefit from the experience of other teachers and the college faculty.

Teachers were reminded how similar to these adolescents they had been at that age. They were asked to think about why the children were behaving the way they were. They were not allowed to accept pat sociological answers (poverty, drugs, and family structure) as excuses for not continuing to try to educate their students. Rather, we asked them to look at what went on in their classrooms and to determine if they could alter the child's experiences there to support positive interactions and focus on success, instead of reinforcing their students' anticipation of failure. We asked them to think of alternative instructional and behavioral strategies and to see the link between behavior and instruction. Teachers thus became resources for each other in the development of alternatives.

Our process with the teachers themselves modeled what we wanted to happen in their classrooms with students. We couldn't just tell teachers what to do, any more than you could ask a child to memorize a skill or algorithm and expect him or her to read, write, compute, and think creatively. Instead, as we built trust, we would ask teachers to relearn things they had learned in their adolescence. But this time the process was different; they were not passive. They constructed new knowledge about teaching and learning and thus came to believe that children could do the same in the usual academic content areas. Teachers' attitudes changed.

Workshops   Workshops grew out of the needs and interests of teachers and administrators. The topics varied and included content and affective areas such as self-esteem. Most important, workshops provided opportunities for teachers to ask a faculty member to join them in the classroom to do a demonstration lesson or to just help out. We wanted teachers to see how they could change their methods within the constraints of their own classrooms. All curriculum workshops were available to the entire school community and emphasized the value of heterogeneous groups, cooperative learning, and the use of culturally diverse material. Teachers were asked to expect the most of children and were then helped to understand how children could be supported in meeting this expectation.

Intervisitations Teachers were encouraged to visit other public and private school classrooms. We suggested that they go in pairs as a form of "triangulation" and to support dialogue in their schools when they brought their descriptions of the experience back to the group meetings for discussion.

Teacher Incentive Grants (TIGs) Small grants of up to $300 were given to teachers who requested them to support a new program initiative. Some examples of what these grants went toward were math materials based on one of the workshops, paperback novels to support a pilot literature-based reading program, and a trip to a Spanish restaurant for a foreign language class.

Luncheons Food has always been an important part of our world. Teachers frequently gave up their lunch periods for program meetings, so, as often as time and budget permitted, we provided food. This made teachers feel special! They felt they were being treated as professionals. We also held luncheons twice a year at the college for all participants. At these luncheon meetings, teachers and administrators heard about what the other schools were doing. They spoke freely and realized that they were part of a larger effort that included other schools like their own. They began to share, plan, and expand curriculum ideas. It was at these events that people overcame their sense of isolation and began to see what was possible, rather than only noticing their limitations.

Brokered Services We also brokered services to the schools. In the 2 years before SSPP, brokered services were an inexpensive way to have an impact and gain credibility within the schools. Some powerful examples of brokered services provided on a limited budget included:

1. *Time to Read* We were approached by Time, Inc. (now Time Warner, Inc., an early supporter of the Center) to help them locate a school to participate in a one-on-one tutoring program at their corporate headquarters. They had previously had problems connecting with a school that could reliably implement the program. We made the right match.
2. *Alpha Phi Alpha Tutoring* Alpha Phi Alpha is a national black fraternity that has a service requirement. We were able to bring them into

a school and provide the staff development and orientation that the undergraduates needed to be effective with the children.

3. *The Harlem Hospital Volunteers*   This program matched a teacher's interest with a community resource directly across the street from the school. Middle school students worked as volunteers from noon to 3 P.M. once per week. The experience was integrated by the teacher into the "careers and writing" curriculum.

These were all low-cost ways to be effective and to demonstrate commitment. All of these activities required nurturing to get them started and make them part of the schools. Administrative support and perseverance were necessary. None of these programs would have been put in place if not for the persistence of the Center's staff, yet they all remained in place after we left.

Many of these activities required coverage of teachers' normal duties during the school day. On a few occasions, teachers covered for each other. On most occasions, the principals somehow arranged for coverage, despite tight budgets—another measure of their commitment to our work together that the teachers appreciated.

Mentoring of Principals   Principals were not willing to be available regularly for group meetings outside of their buildings. However, the principal of School B was new, and clear about her desire for professional development. The project director therefore assumed responsibility for serving as her mentor, and eventually for mentoring her two assistant principals as well. The director and principal reorganized her office, discussed programming decisions, and made joint observations of teachers; There was complete trust between them. We also met with principals at least biweekly about our work in their buildings, using these meetings to advocate on behalf of teachers and children, as well as to help the principals develop a broader vision. In School A, the principal had an alternative vision for childrens' work, but was unfortunately moved to the district office and replaced by an interim acting principal who viewed program maintenance as his primary duty.

Teachers were generally supported in their desire to try things they might not have considered previously. They used the newspaper to teach reading and social studies, did cooking and canning, showed the children pictures of colonial children at play and then allowed them to play the same games and make their own toys. The teachers participated in workshops on a broad range of topics that they selected. They were then encouraged in their efforts to engage children in similar activities. We supported their work with money (in the form of TIGs) for supplies and by taking faculty members up on their offers to allow us to come into their classrooms to help or to do a demonstration lesson. We continued our individual work and began lunchtime seminars. We became part of the schools, and teachers came to know us and what we were doing.

Consequently, the principals knew they could trust us and had entered into mentor relationships of varying degrees with the then director, who provided an opportunity for the principal to safely reflect on practice. There was new information entering the system that forced school personnel to rethink their beliefs, and we had become part of the building and therefore could help them try out their new ideas.

IMPACT

The impact of our work varied based on several factors, not the least of which was the on-site leadership. What did happen most consistently was that teachers came to believe that it was possible to be effective with children at risk. Instead of blaming sociological factors for children failing in schools, they began to invent programs that supported success despite those factors. The manifestation of this idea can be summed up as follows:

1. Teachers were creating programs, rather than collecting programs developed by others. They began by considering the children and then created programs to meet their needs. They no longer accepted every offer to participate in a program, but rather sought out opportunities that specifically supported their curriculum.
2. The programs that were created were aimed at increasing student choices, included cooperative learning, and reflected the current research on what was effective in middle schools. "Book clubs" in one class allowed children to select novels from a teacher-edited list that related to the social studies curriculum, while in another class, the teacher made a first effort at small, heterogeneous discussion groups.
3. Programs that were created during our work with the schools remained in place even after we had formally stopped working with the teachers involved. These programs had become a part of the teachers' generic approach to teaching. There was a sense of ownership that allowed programs to persist and grow after we had gone.
4. Teachers were working together and talking to each other in ways that supported program development beyond the initial group. The teachers were becoming advocates for a new kind of teaching in their buildings, and teachers doing staff development in a subject such as cooperative learning would have greater credibility than university personnel because they were not from the "ivory tower."

Our impact on principals was less clear, although their cooperation was essential to any progress we made. At School A, a charismatic principal was moved to the district office just as our funding increased. The new principal was appointed as an "interim acting principal" and never exercised full leadership, although he remained in this position for 3 years. At School B, although the principal subscribed to our approach to curriculum and teaching and responded well to inquiries about pedagogical decisions, she had difficulty managing bureaucratic functions and relations with the district office. Mini-schools were attempted by fiat and never took hold. In September, 1989, three classes of children were without classrooms for 2 weeks. Teachers' and students' schedules changed three times during the opening weeks of school. One year the schedule changed daily for the first week of school while a new master schedule was being drawn up. It eventually changed two more times and again on October 5, 1989, when New York City's fiscal crises rained down on the school, causing staff cuts.

Our advantage was the development of teacher leaders. Where this was possible, it had the effect of increasing the potential pool of leaders and allowing us to identify and cultivate that pool. Once empowered by the principal, based on our advocacy, these teacher leaders took responsibility for the day-to-day implementation of programs developed collaboratively by teachers and Bank Street staff.

The real impact on the schools of this kind of patient, site-determined work is most easily seen in what one then nonparticipating teacher said informally before a site visit by the State Education Department. He was proudly showing off his successful results from a stock market game sponsored by a Wall Street brokerage firm and telling me how great the kids were when they visited the firm on Wall Street. I told him I wished I could claim credit for his success. He responded, "You should. Really! It's the spillover. When you're working in a place where everyone around you is doing something extra and taking part in a program that is exciting, then you feel you want to do more." These successes are not occurring every day, and each effort is being filtered through a web of local social meanings (Popkewitz, 1983), but where teachers have scheduled forums that allow them to rethink their practice on behalf of children, there is continual growth. It is in these meetings that teachers can challenge old beliefs and develop new ones.

WHAT WE HAVE LEARNED

When my predecessor was asked, "What have you learned from your work with the Center?" She responded, "Patience." Perhaps this is the greatest and most difficult lesson. We were in School A for 5 years and School B for 4 years and saw varying degrees of change. All of the participating teachers in these schools were committed to serving children better, which often results in a collection of unrelated programs that may make things more interesting, but does not provide an alternative to the passive learning that is already frustrating so many children. While interesting content is certainly a necessary and commendable goal, it is not in itself sufficient to bring about change.

What is necessary is a commitment to a new teaching and learning dynamic—one that empowers teachers to provide children with interesting and relevant opportunities to learn. We cannot be satisfied with students who only learn to store knowledge and never to create new knowledge. What we learned is that for this change to occur, many factors are necessary, but none is sufficient by itself. The most important of these are discussed below.

Teachers Need Time to Talk Together   Groups go through a *pre-change* stage, which I describe as the initial period during which teachers meet to define meanings and determine shared values. Through these discussions, teachers begin to confront the inconsistencies, if any exist, between their goals and their behavior in the classroom. Too often, teachers say they want their children to be able to solve problems creatively, or learn to love literature—but when we ask how they support these goals in their classrooms, they can only point to textbook pages in math and reading.

During this period, teachers benefit from observations of colleagues and from participation in workshops. Both provide teachers with new ideas and methods, but there are other equally important benefits. The opportunity to observe their colleagues also gives teachers a new understanding of their own work in the classroom and specific examples to discuss with each other. They can then begin to resolve discrepancies between their goals and their practice. Workshops give teachers a common basis for discussions during which beliefs and attitudes change and develop. These new beliefs and attitudes then become part of the larger "web of social meanings" (Popkewitz, 1983) that shape the entire culture of the school.

Most importantly, during this period, the programs and curricula developed are based on knowledge constructed by the teachers themselves. This model, supported by the last 20 years of research in cognitive science, then becomes a model for the entire teaching and learning process in the school.

Administrative Support Is Essential   The principal, assistant principal, or other person in charge has to offer his or her support. He or she need not be the instructional leader, the team leader, or even present at every meeting, but the group that has decided to rethink a program must know that they should approach the administrator in charge for help working around or bending the rules. They must know that they can suggest some fairly unconventional ideas and have them receive serious consideration, or at least a fair hearing. The administrative attitude that needs to be in place was best exemplified by one principal who said, "If it is good for the children, then let's give it a try." Because the prevailing myth is likely to be that there is always administrative resistance to change, teachers need to be shown that the administration is willing to empower them. This can be demonstrated in part by providing bureaucratic "power tools" (Clark & Astuto, 1988). Important power tools that a principal can provide for teachers trying new things include common preparation periods for the team, release time to visit other schools and attend workshops, and access to clerical support.

As part of this administrative support, financial resources also need to be reallocated. Initially, small amounts of money can go a long way. We have found that our TIG program—providing $300 mini-grants for teachers to pursue pet projects—has been a strong stimulus to teachers who would like to try interdisciplinary teaching that requires art materials or a trip. These funds can also pay for conference attendance or materials not available in the school.

If there is administrative resistance to change, the first step must be to win over the building administration and involve them in the collaboration from the start. In a partnership, this responsibility will likely fall on the college or university. Without this administrative support, benign or active, progress will be difficult.

Schools Must Support Variety and Innovation   Teachers working together in small groups with the support of the administration are likely to come up with a variety of ideas that they wish to implement. They also need to build bonds based on a shared value system and shared meanings. When this happens, the creation of mini-schools seems to be an appropriate next step. The experience of the Center for Minority Affairs in these and other schools is that the mini-school provides a manageable unit for innovation because the teachers' shared belief system provides a foundation for such a unit, as well as a manageable unit of implementation. Implementation on a schoolwide basis in a building of 700–1,400 children can involve anywhere from 23 to 50 or more teachers. This makes reaching a consensus and developing shared values much more difficult. These smaller units seem to support the teachers in the continuation of their ongoing professional development, as well as providing a flexibility that allows innovation. Teams can thus plan and allocate resources based on an identifiable group of children (120–250), rather than a more anonymous schoolwide population.

Within a building, the role of the principal then becomes that of nurturer of individual subcultures and teacher leaders. The instructional innovations will come from the teams; it will be the principal's job to provide the resources and to support innovations that best serve children.

However, the locus of change will be at the mini-school level. This allows teachers the time and place to talk together and build new social meanings and a new, supportive culture.

Design Changes Must Be Allowed   Although the center has tried to focus on curriculum, this remains the area of greatest resistance. Teachers and principals are most willing to make structural or quality control changes—improvements in existing pedagogy. Quality control changes refine the existing pedagogy, but don't challenge the basic assumptions of most schools. Design changes, changes that challenge the basic teaching–learning equation, meet the greatest resistance, even when agreement with the need for innovation is espoused.

Teachers made structural changes, such as establishing mini-schools or having students work in groups, as long as the children were all pursuing a teacher-determined answer or product. Teachers were interested in cooperative learning and peer tutoring, but seemed unready to trust children with the opportunity to construct knowledge in classrooms with 30 or more students. We developed strategies to combat this problem that involved providing teachers with useful information and activities through workshops and visits to public and private school classrooms where other teachers were doing things differently. Such visits to other classrooms, followed by meetings with the host teachers and a college faculty member, were especially powerful. Teachers then self-edited the visits and made choices that challenged existing norms. All of these steps grew out of the group meetings, and the process was finally discussed with the group again. Most of these activities are oriented toward a reflective process that allows for the development of new beliefs.

There Needs To Be Adequate Research   Research is not a frill. Although many of the answers to the problems of middle schools have already been found and are waiting to be disseminated, there are still many questions that need to be answered if schools are to serve all children better and site-based management is to be more than just another educational fad. Assessment, grouping, parental involvement, and collaboration are but a few areas that need more study. Our efforts were originally conceived as an outreach project, with research being a secondary consideration. The limited availability of funds aggravated this fact and allowed us to put formal research on the back burner for much of the initial phase of the program. Only the infusion of State Education Department (SED) monies and the attendant reporting requirements allowed us to justify a half-time research assistant position. As a result, our own learning, as well as the insights we can offer the education community, have been limited.

Governmental Support Must also Be Flexible and Nurturing
Perhaps our greatest surprise was the nature of our relationship with the SED, which turned out to be collaborative. They worked with us and

supported our efforts through phone calls and site visits. They were aware of the enormity of the challenge we had undertaken and wanted us to be successful. Rather than being bureaucratic and inhibiting innovation, they were flexible and supportive. They adjusted reporting requirements to suit the needs of the individual SSPP programs, and therefore supported site-based planning in the schools. They have also supported statewide conferences that serve the projects' needs and have asked us for help in designing each event. As a result, these conferences are not consumed by the discussion of administrative issues; they instead become part of the process of supporting change in the schools. They are a sorely needed conduit for information that those of us in the academic community working in schools need in order to help facilitate our work with the schools.

THE NEED FOR FURTHER RESEARCH

The question for the 1990s is, "How can schools, colleges, universities, and businesses communicate and share what they know works in a way that supports teachers' creation of new and better solutions?" The answer must be one that can outlive any funded project: it must include permanent and varied relationships and lifelong learning for all involved. Short-term relationships solve nothing. Collaborations need to be ongoing and fluid. Money is important, but trust and shared meaning comes from being on site and working together for many years. The answers will not vary from school to school, but rather within a school, on a minischool-by-minischool basis.

Another question that faces every collaborator is how to set goals and reasonable time parameters. We all want schools fixed instantly, but what is a *reasonable* time frame, and what are reasonable results, quantified in a reasonable way? Given the need for long-term relationships and the associated long-term costs, multi-school projects may not be the answer. We may need instead to create models that support other schools and universities in the development of their own collaborations.

As we enter a period of scarcer resources, our commitment will be tested. The schools must challenge themselves, as the academic community must question and rethink ways in which dissemination is carried out. What do we model if we do no more than *tell* the schools how to improve?

CONCLUDING COMMENTS

The meetings and workshops we had with the people from Bank Street were useful in that we could share and exchange ideas and suggestions about teaching, subject matter, and techniques. I was able to recognize

where my strengths and weaknesses lie and to begin to work towards those
areas which needed improvement. As a result of what Bank Street started,
the teachers at our school were able to continue meeting, sharing, and ex-
changing ideas among each other. (Teacher, School B)

School reform is a function of a constellation of factors that support
changes in teachers' beliefs about children and learning. These are often
thought of as independent of each other, or not considered at all. Individual initiatives persist, and usually involve either quality-control adjustments or small-scale design changes. In this form, they are not likely to
take on a life of their own and become part of a new culture that supports
lifelong learning for children and school personnel. Systemic reform is
very difficult in a culture of discrete innovations. It is now time for educators and administrators to provide opportunities for instructional change
to continue within the schools and subschool units. Where there is an
underlying foundation or framework to support this process, there will
be forums for questioning the status quo and for discussion and discovery
that lead to lifelong learning. Thus, teachers will be able to construct beliefs that serve children.

The role of the college or university in this situation is to help teachers learn to learn together. Teachers need to constantly receive new information and they need to get it in a variety of ways. Only then will they
have the raw materials necessary to create programs that can work in
their settings.

Most teachers' present beliefs perpetuate the view of schools as
places where learning is passive and childrens' work is to absorb existing
knowledge. Although teachers often use language associated with active
learning and innovative programs, their practice reflects a "web of social
meanings" (Popkewitz, 1983) that prevents change and supports the status quo—a factory model of school. At best, the children learn to be
19th-century factory workers in a 21st-century information age that
needs workers who can create, not simply store, knowledge.

If you visit one of our partnership schools today, it may not be physically different from other urban schools that you have seen or heard
about. The difference is in the dreams of the teachers and what they now
see as being possible.

III

THE HIGH SCHOOL YEARS

7

The University Visit
A Mosaic of Futures

JEFFREY BEAUDRY,
WILLIAM SANDERS,
MARY GIBBONS,
AND AMY COFFEY

St. John's University is a private, urban, Catholic university. Our SSPP program was entitled Project LEARN (Link Education and Retention Now) and involved a partnership with three urban high schools in the New York City borough of Queens. Like other SSPP programs, our dropout-prevention efforts involved a variety of activities, but among the most successful was a series of visits to the St. John's campus by the high school students in the program. It was felt that systematic exposure to the university campus helped these high school students at risk begin to form an understanding of career possibilities, and better engaged them in their academic work.

On reflection, the value of the university visit is not without some irony, in that high school students at risk may not be likely candidates to attend college at all. Much of the prevailing wisdom supports the notion that socioeconomic status and home-environment factors are more influential than school in affecting the future of students at risk and that dropping out of school perpetuates these disadvantages (Coleman et al., 1966). "Students who drop out of high school are destined for minimal employment opportunities, are less likely to prepare for a career, and have a higher probability of drawing upon the social welfare resources" (Levin, 1989, p. 48). College-bound, academically proficient students would be *expected* to visit a number of universities, but concerning students at risk of dropping out, what effect could a series of university campus visits possibly have on their futures? It would take years to formulate a truly definitive answer to this question. We will focus on the more immediate process of engaging and motivating students who have been labeled "at risk" and who have not as yet come to value the connection between school and career.

The purpose of this chapter will be to describe some of the practical and theoretical issues that arose during 3 years of experience in planning and coordinating campus visits. We will look at the intricacies of the campus visits, from both the high school students' perspectives and those of the sponsors and organizers on the university campus. Specifically, our objectives will be to: 1) discuss Project LEARN in general; 2) describe the conceptual framework of the nonschool curriculum component of the partnership; 3) describe practical issues, programmatic activities, and evaluation concerns related to the visits; and 4) suggest possible changes and make recommendations for improving campus visits.

BACKGROUND

Project LEARN did not seek to change the structure of the high schools; rather, the project planners sought mechanisms to increase engagement and to motivate students to become involved in school activities. Three high schools from southeastern Queens were selected for the school–university partnership based on the criterion of having significant numbers of students at risk. As with the other SSPP programs, students so labeled had two or more of the following characteristics: a failing grade-point average; failing grades in three or more subjects; a high rate of absenteeism; retention in a grade; excessive work hours; and being perceived as having, or demonstrating, discipline problems.

In each high school, students were selected for the program by a team that consisted of some combination of the principal, assistant principal, counselor, teachers, and special program staff. As expected, the selection process for the program varied from school to school. In two of the high schools, the major criteria for selection were the number of subjects failed and low grade-point average. As Grannis notes in Chapter 4 of this volume, it is ironic that students from these schools were less likely to have problems with absenteeism. However, for the third high school, a much greater number of students selected for Project LEARN had been absent at least 30 days in the previous school year.

Project LEARN included a wide range of interventions: 1) staff-development seminars, workshops, and courses for school counselors in topics such as group counseling, multicultural education, and learning

styles; 2) one-on-one coaching and academic tutoring provided by college tutors; 3) on-campus visitation programs including academic and
co-curricular components; 4) multicultural career education lessons to
be field tested at the high school sites; and 5) a graduate course in curriculum development for the student at risk offered at one of the high
schools. Over a 3-year period, the components that were implemented
with the most consistency and success were academic tutoring and the
campus visits. In two high schools, the academic tutoring was a pull-out
program enlisting the help of undergraduate and graduate students from
the School of Education as tutors, similar to those in the program described by Devine in the prologue. The selected high school students
were expected to attend two 1-hour tutoring sessions a week. There were
a total of 20 tutoring sessions per semester; students attending at least 10
sessions per semester were publicly cited for their participation. The tutoring component was not altered in design during the life of the program, but after the first year, the campus visits underwent considerable
change. This is discussed in more detail later in the chapter. Since the
campus visits represent a unique and challenging mode of intervention,
and there seems to be little critical analysis available, we concentrate here
on this particular aspect of Project LEARN.

GENERAL EVALUATION

Evaluation studies of the St. John's University Project LEARN effort were
done on a regular basis, and results have been presented at a number of
conferences (Beaudry & Sanders, 1990, 1991). Analysis of these results
has focused on the following outcomes: 1) change in grade-point average, 2) change in the number of subjects failed, 3) change in the number of days absent, and 4) change in self-esteem as measured by the
Coopersmith Self-Esteem Inventory (Coopersmith, 1986). Changes in these
four variables have been extremely difficult to accomplish. However,
there was a tendency for the students in our program to improve in number of subjects failed and in attendance rate. A significant increase in
grade-point average occurred less frequently. For the first 2 years of our
program, an average of 25% of the students surpassed the criterion of
fewer than 20 days absent. In addition, an average of 33% of the students
showed a reduction in the number of subjects failed. One of the most
encouraging findings for Project LEARN has been the consistent negative
correlation ($r = -0.4$) between the number of tutoring sessions attended and number of days absent. Apparently, the tutoring program offered a motivational, as well as an academic, basis for the students to participate in a school-related activity. Based on student and tutor feedback,
the motivation may be related to informal interactions. Students' atten-

dance at tutoring sessions may also be attributed to the tutors' positive role modeling, combining academic and social influences.

As for the measure of self-esteem, the results were less encouraging, but were tempered by the realization that students at risk generally have low self-esteem. In each of the 3 years, students completing surveys showed no significant changes on the *Coopersmith Self-Esteem Inventory* when given at the beginning and again at the end of the school year. The overall mean scores as well as the subscales for home and school were low compared to those of normative groups of average students of similar age.

Formative evaluation results suggest that the high point of our partnership was the campus visit program. From the start, these visits were highly regarded by both high school and university students and staff. The students felt that the campus visits motivated them to consider attending college; in a student survey, this item received a rating of 4.2 on a 5-point Likert scale, and was consistently rated as the most popular aspect of Project LEARN. As discussed below, the visits were not without their problems, which were not always identifiable through inventories or surveys. But the Project LEARN staff and university faculty concurred with the very positive opinion expressed by the students, thus prompting further development and evaluation of the campus visits.

CONCEPTUAL FRAMEWORK: THE OUT-OF-SCHOOL CURRICULUM

As far back as the Great Depression of the 1930s, social programs such as the Civilian Conservation Corps have focused on the needs of men, women, and children as they struggle to cope with massive societal problems. In the 1960s, there were numerous programs such as Upward Bound and Outward Bound that were based on similar program designs, blending out-of-school experiences with meeting the practical and educational needs of targeted disadvantaged groups. Education in school and nonschool settings was discussed in the 1984 Yearbook of the National Society for the Study of Education, in which Fantini and Sinclair (1985) emphasized that "the formal school setting is not the only place in which children and youth learn and are taught" (p.xi). Other educational resources include the family (see Chap. 2, this volume), religious institutions, museums, the work place, the media, and peers.

In discussing the stages of linking school and nonschool environments, Fantini (1985) categorized the history of education as progressing through these stages: 1) shared model—based on the rural, agricultural economy; 2) comprehensive/delegative model—based on the urban and industrial economy; and 3) coordinative and facilitative model—based on the information-based economy. What this means is that schools must subscribe to a broader definition of curriculum, one that includes school–

community partnerships that will allow students to take a more active role in sharing responsibility for their learning.

> This approach is in the spirit of Cremin's (1980) suggestion that we think about curriculum "relationally," and in the spirit of all serious curriculum theory that stresses the need to consider the nature of the learners, the milieu from which they come, and the society for which they are being educated. (Cohen & Lukinsky, 1985, p. 148)

In the context of Project LEARN, the university is a nonschool environment for these students, as it represents a time and place away from the high school campus. The value of nonschool curricula (Dewey & Gardner, 1983; Fantini & Sinclair, 1985) as a means of engaging students has been one of the fundamental assumptions of experiential education. The guest speaker, the demonstration, and the field trip have long been used to supplement the usual school experience. Off-campus trips have been discussed specifically in terms of their value in teaching through a social group (Klepper, 1987; Marlowe & Sartor, 1983; Steiner, 1987).

Schubert and Steel(1983)emphasized the necessity of conducting research on a wide range of out-of-school curricula. Following up on this thesis, Melnick (1988) investigated the ways in which teachers acquire and use knowledge of the out-of-school environments of students' lives to enhance the school curriculum and their own teaching. One of the themes was that knowledge of the students' out-of-school lives engendered shared awareness and celebration by student and teacher of each other as human beings. A more tangible theme was that teachers and students who share their out-of-school experiences by mutual invitation and through interpersonal communication develop a greater identification with school-related activities.

Both in-school and out-of-school factors were addressed by Wehlage and Rutter (1987), who found that especially effective programs emphasized experiential learning strategies that included combinations of individual and group-learning projects. Grannis (1991) reported on a 3-year Dropout Prevention Initiative in New York City, one of the few successes of which arose not from school-based counseling services or academically oriented programs, but from the use of "seed money" grants to local businesses to hire participating students. Although students were paid minimum wage for their work, the program's success seemed to be related to the students' out-of-school experiences (see also Grannis, Chap. 4, this volume).

Museums are typical settings in which schools use the out-of-school curriculum in pursuing their educational aims (e.g., exchange visits, after-school activities, and continuing education for teachers). Field trips may be as diverse as visits to work places (a bank, a factory, a hospital), or the more contemporary example of a "tough love" trip to a prison. While there seems to be little in-depth research conducted on the value of these ubiquitous school activities, Pitman and Romberg (1985) say that field trips, especially visits to museums, must go far beyond "sightseeing" tours. Mere presence at the museum, or at a university, is not sufficient to ensure that the student actually participates in the visit or exchange. Visits, whether to museums or university campuses, must be made sensitive to the child's experience through an attempt to link these experiences to the child's out-of-school world, and by the provision of a structured, highly participative experience. The notion that the campus provides a *mosaic* of possible futures is intended to be the deeper, long-term message delivered to the visiting high school students. The mosaic of the university must be examined closely by visiting students, as it is composed of individual student's experiences gathered into meaningful social, academic, and career patterns.

MODELS FOR DROPOUT PREVENTION

The search for long-term, comprehensive strategies to prevent students from dropping out of school has prompted a variety of theories to explain the impact of psychological, educational, and socioeconomic factors on students' academic persistence, self-concept, and career-mindedness. From the beginning of Project LEARN, the campus visits and other experiences prompted us to shift our focus from the frustration/self-esteem model, which emphasizes academic achievement as measured through grades and other school outcomes, to the participation/identification model of dropout prevention, which emphasizes the process of schooling. The frustration/self-esteem model has frequently been invoked to explain schools' influences on disruptive behavior and juvenile delinquency. The participation/identification model, conversely, emphasizes the importance of a student's bonding with school. When such bonding fails to occur, the likelihood of problem behavior, including leaving school before graduation, is increased. As students participate more in a variety of school-related activities, their sense of identification or "belongingness" is strengthened and, in turn, they begin to value school-related success.

While the two models are not totally distinct, the participation/identification approach underscores the need for intervention efforts like university campus visits that promote students' involvement both inside and outside of the classroom. In addition, the participation/identification model includes a developmental dimension. The hierarchical stages of development include: 1) participation in classroom activity during the early grades; 2) student-initiated questions in class and increased time spent outside of class on homework; 3) participation in noncoursework, school-related activities; and 4) student participation in the governance of the school. From our perspective, the tutoring component addresses classroom participation and academic persistence, while the campus visits are an example of our engaging the students in organized extracurricular activities.

Of concern to the participation/identification model would be process-oriented measures of participation such as classroom behavior and time spent on extracurricular activities. Other measures might begin to affect the home environment, the quality of study time, and parental support of intellectual development. These process measures are more time-consuming, but reflect the importance of "participation" variables that mediate the decision to drop out. For Project LEARN, participation in the university visit might be seen as an extracurricular activity that provides a measure of students' identification with school. In other words, students who engage in school-related activities will have a basis for valuing the goals of school.

VISITING THE UNIVERSITY CAMPUS

Evolutionary Planning

The purpose of university visits was consistent over the 3 years of our program—the partnership focused on the interaction of people, contexts, and ideas—but the method of planning and the content of the visits continually evolved. Visits to campuses have been a widely used recruitment tool aimed at academically proficient, college-bound high school students. However, Project LEARN set out to foster an understanding of career possibilities and to forge the necessary link to higher education for students at risk through repeated exposure to our university campus. The success that we had was due to flexible planning and a commitment to long-term extracurricular participation by the students.

Two approaches for planning campus visits were used in our program, a survey approach and a model emphasizing structured, experiential activities. The survey/inventory model was used during the first year. Students were surveyed prior to coming to campus, and their responses were grouped according to their interests. When they arrived on campus, they were informed of the match between their selection on the survey form and a relevant on-campus site. Students were then expected to break into groups and go to their selected sites, but they did not always move according to plan. The problem with this approach was that the students' choices on paper did not match their immediate interests when it came down to splitting them into groups. Peer pressure, coupled with the "tourist" attitudes of the visitors, apparently changed the students' minds, and they tended to gravitate toward the most popular choices. The visits were well-designed, but were too much like sightseeing—they lacked involvement.

Our planning staff concurred that the visits were interesting but did not include the necessary depth of participation. High school coordinators suggested that a classroom experience might be a more effective method of orienting students to the reality of college life. Our revised planning model for these visits evolved from this revelation. The goal of the visits was to maximize the hands-on participation and involvement of the students. These adjustments were key factors in the development of our final visit design. Developing this structure was not without problems, since we had to make arrangements with both the university student groups and faculty members. A great part of our success was due to the flexibility of the planning group in seeking alternative solutions, such as changing lunch arrangements to include student responsibility for seating and meal selection. In addition, different university presenters have been matched with high schools and have tailored their classroom experiences based on the students' developmental levels and interests.

Specifics of the University Visit

Below, we probe some of the practical, as well as the psychological, sociological, and institutional dimensions of campus visits. The basic design of the visits involved bringing high school students to the university campus for 3 half-day visits. Busses arrived on-campus at 9:30 A.M. and returned the students to their high school by 1:30 P.M. The social and extracurricular activities of the first visit focused on the various clubs, athletic teams, sororities, and fraternities on campus. It was vital to let the students know that there are clubs and activities to match the interests of every student at the university. For example, the Caribbean Club at St. John's is not only a center for social activities, but also performs services for the community. In addition, the selection of clubs to visit was patterned on the theme of multicultural education. This was important not only because it reflected a significant aspect of the mission of our university, but also because more than 50% of the high school students who visited the campus were from African American, Caribbean, or Latino backgrounds. At various times, students had been invited to events such as Carifest, International Night, and a St. John's University Redmen exhibition basketball game. It appears that students will come on campus with the support of teachers and staff, but are less willing to do so on their own and after school hours. For these forays on their own, the campus was still not a comfortable environment. Even with these mixed results, it is important to keep experimenting with different venues for the students in order to encourage their involvement.

The second visit focused on a look at career opportunities. Two popular and outstanding career-exploration sites have been the TV Center and the school newspaper. Initially, a visit to the TV Center meant that students received a guided tour, reflecting a "look but don't touch" approach. But over the course of the program, we made major revisions to this visit; in 1992, students were invited for the first time to participate as guests on the student television magazine show, the St. John's *Redmen Magazine*. For these video productions, each school chose the type of program it preferred. One selection was an Oprah Winfrey–type show, which the students titled "Springfield Garden Speaks Out." Another high school called its production "Take One With John Adams." Two undergraduate communication majors were instrumental in making this production possible. They assigned students to different technical roles necessary for television productions, such as cameraperson, audio technician, stage manager, or host or panel members.

The reliance on faculty expertise and experiential participation is even more essential for the third, "academic" visit, which involves students attending an actual college class. Two professors from the School of Education invited Project LEARN students to their classes, which dealt with multicultural education and human relations. Participation was facilitated by one professor who used "Coat of Arms," a values clarification activity, as the class project. Another professor from the Criminal Justice department staged a mock trial in which the students were presented with a hypothetical crime and were involved in settling the case. One of the sessions prompted a visiting high school student to question the professor, "Do you really teach like this all the time, or are you putting on a show for us?" In fact, these teachers were selected specifically because of their creative teaching styles and experiential teaching strategies. This question was especially poignant because students at risk may perceive such visits as showcases rather than typical classes. The answer to the student's question was "Yes, we really do teach like this."

The arrangements for lunch in our program came to take on a life of their own; lunchtime became a finely crafted sociodramatic event, one of the most intricate of the day's happenings. Having lunch and "hanging out" in the cafeteria are familiar activities for students of any grade. At first, our goal was simply to provide the students with a meal. Space was reserved for the high school students, and they were grouped in block seating. Not only were the students uncomfortable being separated in this way, but planning for separate seating proved to be very difficult. We also tried to secure dining reservations and offer box lunches, but this was criticized by both students and staff as being too formal. Ultimately, lunch represented an event at which the high school students could be most like their college counterparts. The visitors wanted to be anonymous, to break up into small, table-sized groups, and yet stay near their friends and guides. Eventually, the students simply received luncheon vouchers; they were allowed to blend in and sit wherever they wanted. Interestingly, despite their bravado in claiming to want to be on their own, the students continued to cluster with their tutors, possibly demonstrating the ambivalence of adolescence.

Students who attended these campus visits left with tangible, as well as intangible, benefits. On the first visit, the athletic department gave out baseball caps and the Project LEARN team distributed tee-shirts and posters. The tee-shirts and caps were seen in the school as visible signs of participation in the university–high school partnership. The intangible effects were evident in the students' attitudes toward the visits, which were seen as "cool" and "better than going to class." In fact, some of our best advertising came from students who had participated in the program the previous year.

It is important to note that when asked to rank-order the campus visits according to preference, students picked the second visit, dealing with career opportunities, as their top choice. This was followed by the academic visit and, finally, the orientation day. Apparently, the visits helped to make the connection between school and career. We have not been able to assess the extent of such changes in a long-range follow-up, but we believe that as a result of the visits, students may have a more concrete understanding of what having a career really means.

Issues and Problems

By definition, the group of young men and women involved in Project LEARN were very difficult to motivate. However, what has been gratifying is the fact that these students seemed to look forward to the on-campus visits and, most of all, to the contact with university students. When indicating their favorite aspect of the visit, over 50% of the participants identified the university students, while 33% identified the university faculty. This fact illustrates the positive contribution of the Project LEARN tutors, who doubled as campus guides, and of the general student body of the university campus.

Because the university staff were themselves multiethnic, the high school students were able to better identify with them. As they became more comfortable on campus, the high school students were able to shed their street images, their feigned boredom, their attitudes that this place didn't matter, and that they didn't need college. The "us versus them" mentality that many of the high school students displayed dissolved as the university came to be recognized as a participative environment, and not a threatening place.

In addition to the highly structured, planned events described above, students had some coincidental encounters with friends that produced surprising results. One student ran into someone from his neighborhood and was shocked to find him going to college. After the initial surprise, the high school student was overheard saying, "Well, if he can do it, we can do it, too." This is one example of the positive influence of peer relationships.

Negative peer pressure, consisting of loud and humiliating comments, occurred on the first visit, but was controllable during subsequent visits. One of the solutions that helped to neutralize negative peer pressure was the elimination of the survey as the basis for planning the visits. The initial design of the campus visits may have inadvertently prompted the students to remain distant, uninterested, and uninvolved. The conflict was between the students' private, pencil-and-paper choices, and the pressures against maintaining those choices in the company of friends. When gathered together with peers, some students were reluctant to admit that they had indicated an interest in art, computers, or pharmacy, and opted instead to visit the gym or TV center with their school friends. Our original approach proved to be unsatisfactory because students seemed to be unable to break away from their high school persona. At the beginning of the second year, based on suggestions from the high school coordinators, we made changes that addressed these subtle problems of peer interaction.

It was our intention to present opportunities for students to step back somewhat from their peers. To some extent, the social pressure that they usually face seemed to be removed when they came to St. John's University. Some students even asked for applications and information. The visits provided glimpses of the social and academic reality of campus life, and for a brief moment some students may have felt, "I am in college, I can go to college, I want to go to college."

It seems that students involved in such a program become genuinely enthusiastic about the visits, which may carry over into changed attitudes toward school. We believe that these types of visits help keep students at risk in school, which was the primary purpose of Project LEARN. We have data that suggest that students who participated came to class better prepared, and many also attended tutoring sessions. But the visits should not necessarily be held out as an incentive or a reward. However, we do recommend that students attend at least half of the tutoring sessions in order to qualify for the second and third campus visits. In our program, we also recognized the students who accomplished this goal with an end-of-year luncheon. Many SSPP programs have reported that teachers themselves sometimes resist university visits and other enrichment activities for poorly achieving students, usually based on the argument that these students do not deserve to be rewarded. When the SUNY-Binghamton partnership, for example, began to conduct campus visits for high school students, a number of the adolescents commented that it was the first time they had ever been allowed to participate in a field trip. It is, therefore, necessary to persuade teachers that these are enrichment activities, not simply fun trips that serve as reinforcers for specific accomplishments.

Lessons Learned

One of the major lessons of these visits is that it is necessary to be flexible in planning structured, experiential activities. Another is that back-up plans are a must; alternatives should be identified and prepared for, because working with volunteers can be risky. We have found that despite advance scheduling and commitments, clubs, groups, and individual volunteers have sometimes canceled at the last minute.

Another critical component is the participation of university professors. In our program, professors were chosen because their backgrounds were similar to the students', thus allowing them to serve as positive, ethnically matched role models.

Developing a core group of undergraduate and graduate students to participate in the visits is also essential. Our core group of students worked as tutors in Project LEARN, and some of them were also involved in other projects (notably the Teacher Opportunity Corps) and activities in the School of Education. These students acted as campus guides for the visiting high school students, and they sometimes coordinated the involvement of campus groups, such as the Organization of Latin American Students. Due to the small student-to-staff ratio of 3:1, opportunities for peer contact between the college and high school students were maximized. The college students were given a basic guideline: listen to the high school students without prejudging them, so that honest peer, or near-peer, interaction is encouraged.

Another benefit of the campus visits is their cost effectiveness. Overall, the visits do not entail a large expenditure. In our program, incentives such as tee-shirts, hats, and posters were given to each participant, depending on the nature of the visit. In return, each school coordinated and paid for bus transportation. The actual cost of the campus visits, including lunch, averaged less than $7.00 per person. These expenses could be underwritten by donations, funding, or gifts-in-kind from universities, schools, or businesses.

Finally, evaluation has been a critical component of Project LEARN. We have already described some of the successes and failures of formal outcome measures and of using surveys for planning visits, and there are other important evaluation techniques that helped to inform decision making and planning in our program, such as a university faculty member who was enlisted to assess and evaluate program goals, and end-of-year reports that included statistical analyses. In terms of access to records and data accuracy, the collection and evaluation of statistics on students at risk is difficult. By their very nature, those who drop-out or are close to doing so leave only a faint trail of untaken tests, unmet appointments, and transfers between schools. In practical terms, consistency of data on GPA, course failures, and absences among such students is very difficult to maintain. The only remedy is to make this a priority for everyone participating in a project.

In our opinion, surveying student interests may help identify popular activities, but should not be used as a method of sorting groups. Instead, the use of follow-up surveys with fixed and open-ended items to assess activities at the end of each visit are more helpful. Items that inquire about the specific activities, as well as the relationship of the visits to the tutoring program and high school life, should be included. Another means of evaluation is the use of focus groups, which can serve as important sources of information for program development. Fostering trust at organizational meetings of the high school and university staff allows for criticism and problem solving. Without the candor of the high school coordinators, we might have struggled far more in reaching a workable and useful visit design. Focus-group interviews with university staff were tape recorded, transcribed, and used to investigate some of the concepts underlying the visits and to clarify points for this chapter. Finally, informal feedback from students, staff, and faculty continually revealed the subtle effects of the visits, while more systematic and thorough evaluation and research studies could be used to investigate the connection between career and school.

CONCLUDING COMMENTS

If you are a high school principal, should you pick up the phone and call the nearest university and schedule visits for your students at risk? Or, if you are a university administrator, should you call a principal and suggest campus visits as an alternative strategy for motivating such students? Clearly, the answer to both questions is "yes." School–university partnerships are delicate, but potentially highly productive relationships. Be forewarned by our experiences: campus visits are not a magic answer to the dropout problem. They can be effective only if you have a commitment to maintaining consistent institutional missions and values, as well as an investment of both human and financial resources.

Admittedly, it is difficult to measure the impact that a brief campus visit may have on high school students. Our university–high school partnership was always in the process of revision and change. Suggestions for improvement include offering courses for high school students on campus, as LaGuardia Community College has for almost 20 years, and another alternative model is discussed, in the next chapter, by Norman Shapiro. Another idea is to get parents involved by bringing them to the university for seminars or workshops on such topics as effective parenting, computer skills, and adult literacy.

We have begun to develop a dynamic relationship between the university and local high schools. We have observed connections between the visits and the tutoring, and we hope that students who participate in both the tutoring activities and the campus visits understand that they can graduate from high school and that it is possible for them to attend college as well. Programs for students at risk require more than just financial investments. What are also needed are long-term extracurricular activities like those we have described. It is our belief that, although they are brief, these visits to our university's "landscape of learning" (Greene, 1978) have given a sense of vision, pride, and possibility to all those high school students who have participated.

8

School–University Houses
Support for the Restructuring of Secondary Schools

NORMAN P. SHAPIRO AND RHODA PEARL PELTZER

Eight years ago, armed with SSPP funding, a small group of faculty and staff from City College's School of Education set out to solve the dropout problem. Our initial approach was to offer an enrichment program of courses one day a week at the college—a program that we called the Mini-College, which was designed to improve attendance, attitudes, and achievement of the high school students who participated.

THE EARLY WORK: THE MINI-COLLEGE

The assumptions behind the Mini-College were: first, that it was particularly important for students at risk to visit a college campus and meet African American and Latino students like themselves who were achieving in college, and second, because students considered to be at risk generally described their high school classes as "boring," that it was neces-

We would like to acknowledge our appreciation to Nancy Mohr, Debbie Meier, and Eric Nadelstern, directors of wonderful schools who helped us frame our initial vision for Liberty and Varsity Houses. We would also like to thank those administrators, teachers, and staff who still struggle to make that vision a reality.

The work described in this chapter covers an 8-year period, from the early years of the Stay-in-School Partnership Project, when we first experimented with the Mini-College, to our work in the mid-1990s on school restructuring. While we retained a constancy of purpose and direction during this time, we also made many changes in the way we approached our work. This retrospective describes those changes.

sary to rekindle their enthusiasm for learning through interesting and exciting courses. Freed from the many constraints under which most high schools operate, the Mini-College could offer courses that we thought students would enjoy—courses such as astronomy, anthropology, computer math, nursing, journalism, planes-rockets and space flight, adolescent psychology, poetry and creative writing, acting, architecture, photography and video production, New York law, swimming, parenting, leadership, cooking, anatomy, and African dance, all of which were offered during the first year of the program.

We did not offer remedial courses, feeling that not only were these done and overdone at the high school, but also that the students were more likely to acquire basic skills through course content that they found exciting. Teachers were selected based on their ability to reach and interest minority adolescents. City College students served as in-class teaching assistants and mentors, modeling appropriate student behaviors, and also met with students during lunch and occasionally after school and on weekends. We wanted high school students to be actively involved in their learning, so we asked instructors to keep lecturing to a minimum. Students participated in a lot of hands-on activities and often worked in cooperative groups. Whenever possible, Mini-College courses were designed to produce specific outcomes (e.g., a newspaper, a radio show), and at an end-of-term showcase students were given the opportunity to exhibit their work.

With a number of small changes along the way, we offered the Mini-College for 4 years. While we found that students were very positive about their experience (some even attending Mini-College classes more often than their high school classes) and that high school teachers were equally enthusiastic, we were consistently unable to improve students' high school attendance or achievement. Students did, however, consistently rate the Mini-College very positively, and most reported positive changes in their attitudes toward themselves, toward learning and education, and toward high school. In retrospect, although the Mini-College did not succeed in improving high school attendance and achievement, we were convinced that the program had been worthwhile.

Each year, we struggled for possible explanations to account for the program's lack of impact on high school attendance and achievement. One possible explanation may have been the fact that our project, along with the others throughout the state, chose to work with students who were classified by their schools as being most at risk for school failure and dropout. They were students who had already been identified by their high schools as irregular attenders or "LTAs" (long-term absences). All participated in special programs for students at risk within their high schools. The Mini-College may simply not have been a powerful enough treatment to have an impact on these students, many of whom needed intensive counseling and social-services support. We wondered whether the Mini-College might be a better program for students who were coming to school regularly, but who still failed to graduate, than it was for the students most at risk. The large number of students at risk who have acceptable high school attendance records but yet do not graduate represents a population too often ignored by programs such as the Stay-in-School Partnership. Many high school teachers question programs that pour money into services for students who show up only intermittently. They argue that available resources should be directed to students who are making the effort to succeed in high school but who, for a wide variety of reasons, ultimately drop out.

Although the Mini-College was a meaningful and interesting experience for students at risk, Mini-College classes were held on only 1 day a week for 12 weeks each semester, for a total of 24 days a year. During the remaining 156 days of the school year, students were still attending their regular high schools, schools which were at least partly responsible for putting these students at risk in the first place. Would it be possible to develop a program that would provide the Mini-College and other support services to students and, at the same time, work to improve the high schools from which the students came?

CHANGING PERSPECTIVES: CREATING COLLABORATIVE HOUSES IN THE HIGH SCHOOLS

In the fourth year of our work, we decided that rather than provide the Mini-College and other services to high school students at risk in isolation, these services needed to be contextualized and provided as part of a more integrated effort. At about the same time, high schools in New York City began to experiment with houses—smaller groupings of students within the high school. Houses were intended to encourage students to identify more closely with their school and to feel less alienated and isolated. While houses were mandated by the High School Division, each high school was left to determine how their houses were to be created and what they would look like. In most instances, high schools resisted any real restructuring of their schools into truly separate entities and simply took the path of least resistance by creating houses pretty much in name only.

But we believed that, when structured properly, houses could be beneficial for students at risk. Because of our interest in the growing national effort to restructure schools, we decided to work on the design of model houses with the two high schools that had been sending students to our Mini-College. We collaborated with "Uptown High School" on the creation of Varsity House and committed our SSPP grant to support for the house and for direct services to Varsity House students. At the same time, we also received funding from the New York State's Liberty Partnership Program (LPP), a similar, although much larger State initiative, which was designed to replace SSPP. We used our LPP grant to support Liberty House at "Outer Borough High School."

Our goal was not simply to provide support services to students who were attending each of the houses, but to create houses that would incorporate some of the best practices in education. Varsity House and Liberty House would be models for the ultimate restructuring of both high schools. We wanted to change not only the way these large dysfunctional high schools were organized and structured, but also the way that they approached curriculum and instruction. We agreed with those who argued that school reform needed to do more than tinker with surface issues—that it should seek to make fundamental changes in the institution of schooling itself.

The High School Settings

Both Uptown and Outer Borough High Schools are among the most poorly performing in New York State based on student graduation rates and levels of achievement. Each is a very large, overcrowded institution with more than 3,500 students in attendance. Most students are immigrants, and many are recent arrivals, with the majority being Spanish speaking. Uptown and Outer Borough are both zoned, neighborhood schools, schools of last choice for nearly all of the students who attend. Of the 3,500 students who attend each school, only 200–300 graduate each year. Poor attendance and academic achievement on entry (from feeder intermediate and junior high schools) and exit are typical of both schools.

Structurally, these two high schools are like most others in New York City and throughout the country. Built on the factory model, the American high school has resisted change for more than 100 years. As if on an assembly line, students move from one discipline to another, having bits and pieces of knowledge, organized by subject matter, delivered by teachers from the several departments. Every 40 or so minutes a bell rings and the students move on to the next subject. Following this model, teachers see more than 150 students every day and neither know nor care who teaches the other subjects to their students. Such a system can be daunting for gifted students, let alone for students poorly skilled and largely unmotivated.

The Design of the Houses

Because we had worked with Uptown and Outer Borough High Schools for more than 4 years in a variety of successful programs and because we consistently provided each school with additional services and resources, we had gained the trust of teachers and administrators at both schools, and this trust was essential for the creation of the new houses. Part of the strength of both the SSPP and the LPP programs was that colleges and universities became providers, rather than recipients, of resources. Both houses were designed collaboratively and, while the high school retained responsibility for the direct supervision of students and teachers, all aspects of school operation (curriculum, instruction, educational policy, etc.) were collaboratively planned. Differences in the way each house would operate reflected different decisions made at each school site.

What influenced us most in the design process was the work of Ted Sizer (1985, 1992) and of the Coalition of Essential Schools (1988). Three schools in New York City—Central Park East Secondary School, University Heights High School, and International High School —provided exemplary models of what we hoped our houses would be like. In fact, during the semester prior to the opening of the two houses we worked with teachers after school in preparation for their houses, and at one point early in the process, teachers and administrators from the widely acclaimed Central Park East Secondary School worked with house teachers on a weekly basis, describing in detail how their schools approached teaching and learning. Many of our ideas came from what we learned about Central Park East and schools like it.

Dedicated Teachers and Dedicated Space   Varsity House would start small and build slowly. It would begin with a single 9th-grade class and add a class each year through 12th grade. Liberty House, with greater state support to start out with, would begin with students at all grade levels. Ultimately, the design called for the inclusion of 350–400 students in each of the houses. One important characteristic that would distinguish our houses from the other so-called houses in the school was the fact that 9th and 10th graders would take all of their courses in the house with "dedicated" teachers who, likewise, would work exclusively within them. In effect, at least for grades 9 and 10, these houses would be small schools within the larger schools. Because students needed to fulfill other requirements and to retake failed courses, after 2 years they would have to move out of the fully self-contained house structure. While some of their 11th and 12th grade courses would be taken with house teachers, most would be offered outside the house. We urged both schools to provide house offices as well as dedicated classrooms, so that each house would have its own identifiable space.

House Size and Organization   In large, impersonal schools, a sense of identity and a feeling of community are critical, and houses can provide both. With an average class size of 34 in the typical New York City high school, teachers who teach 5 periods each day see between 150 and 170 students. Many teachers know little about their students, and their impersonal teaching styles often reflect this anonymity. One reason students drop out is because teachers don't know them well and because they have not developed a meaningful connection with any of the adults in the building.

Deborah Meier (1987), Diana Oxley (1989, 1994), and others have persuasively argued that smaller is clearly better. Varsity House and Liberty House were designed to, in Cizor's words, "get the numbers down." Teachers at both houses would be responsible for no more than 100–125 students, a significant reduction from the norm. Furthermore, by changing the way in which the instructional program was organized, teachers would see only half of these students on any given day.

Varsity House started out with 9th graders and with one team of teachers in each of the four major academic disciplines—English, social studies, mathematics, and science. Varsity House students would work with these teachers and take electives and physical education classes outside of the house. Liberty House, twice the size of Varsity House, began with two teams of four teachers for 9th and 10th graders, and three additional teachers who would teach a limited number of courses within the house for juniors and seniors. The advantage of having dedicated teachers was that they would come to know their students quite well. Additional time would be provided for teachers to work together, and they would use that time to coordinate curriculum and to case-conference about individual students, both of which were virtually impossible under the traditional organization of the high school.

Noddings (1992) notes that the need for care in our present culture is acute, and the concept of a caring community would be at the heart of the organizational changes initiated by the two houses. Youngsters would feel that they were part of a caring community and that they were being taught by caring adults, which is especially important for poor children and children of color, who often see the larger society as remote and uninterested. The key question for us was how to operationalize the concept of a caring community. Reducing the number of students that teachers see every day and utilizing "dedicated" teachers who would come to know their students were two ways of achieving this. A third would be the institution of what many of the alternative schools in New York City call "family group" or advisory.

As initially designed, family group would involve teachers meeting with groups of students for one period each day in a nonacademic context. This would permit teachers and students to get to know each other and allow them to explore some of the critical issues teenagers face. The family-group teacher was also to become the principal advocate for the students in his or her group during the student's entire stay at the high school. This meant that the family-group teacher would become the primary point of contact for the student and help him or her deal with issues of attendance, cutting, achievement, and personal problems to the extent that those problems did not require professional intervention. The family-group teacher would get to know the student and the student's family and maintain regular contact with the home.

The fourth way in which we sought to create a caring community was through a commitment to hear and respect the voices of teachers and students. Decisions would not be arrived at in a top-down fashion, but rather through consensus among house staff. Student opinion would be sought in classrooms as well as through student advisory committees. Neither teachers nor students would be silenced (Fine, 1991) and both would be supported in seeking the truth. Ultimately, both houses would model democratic school communities and represent alternatives to the traditional, hierarchically structured high school.

We also wanted to extend this ethos of caring to responsibility for the improvement and well-being of the community. As the fabric of urban society continues to unravel, the notion that students need to be involved in community service has grown in importance. The "me" generation of the 1970s and 1980s is gradually being replaced by the "we" generation of the 1990s. Still, most schools do not include community service and many that do simply require a certain number of hours of service that the student must complete independently. In contrast, the LPP grant provided the resources needed to support a community-service program built into the Liberty House schedule. Ninth and tenth grade students would work at child care centers, tutor in schools, help out in hospitals and nursing homes, and become involved in other services to benefit the community. In a caring community, one is not only cared *for*, one must care for others. Community service would provide students that opportunity.

Finally, the caring community would be furthered in the classroom through the utilization of cooperative approaches to learning. To the greatest extent possible, students would work in small cooperative-learning groups. Whereas the traditional classroom fosters competitive learning, in which how well one does is often judged in comparison to others, students who engage in cooperative learning care about and support each others' efforts to succeed (see also Chap. 5, this volume).

Utilization of Time   One of the most precious commodities a school possesses is time. Teachers need common planning time to discuss curriculum and time to talk about the needs, problems, and strengths of individual students. House teachers would be scheduled to teach at the same times, so that they could meet with each other during common free periods. In addition, the days that Liberty House students would be involved in community service would provide teachers with even more common planning time.

Time is important for students as well. The traditional high school has something like eight 40-minute periods over the course of the day. Teachers often complain that students have little time to get deeply involved in any activity. While the 40-minute period may be appropriate for whole-class, lecture-driven forms of instruction, it is not appropriate in classrooms where learners are actively involved in their work. To the greatest extent possible, the houses would work toward etending the 40-minute period, mindful of the constraints imposed by the larger school community. We believed that houses would need to experiment with ways of using time flexibly.

Teaching and Learning   Fundamental to school restructuring is the rethinking of the process of teaching and learning. In a major study of secondary schools, Goodlad (1984) found that the most predominant form of high school teaching, by far, was the lecture, or what he termed "frontal teaching." Some 90% of classes are based on such teaching. While some students can and do learn from lectures, students at schools like Uptown and Outer Borough include large numbers of mostly disengaged learners. They have not done well in their previous schooling and are not particularly interested in or enthusiastic about coming to school. When they do drop in, they do so for social reasons or for want of anything better to do. The curriculum not only seems unattainable but also removed from students' interests and lives. Students often don't buy into what the school is selling and fail to engage with the subject matter.

One reason the lecture is the dominant form of instruction is because most teachers simply teach the way that they themselves have been taught. Another is that teachers feel that the only way to "cover" the curriculum is to lecture. Lecturing is the most efficient way of getting through large amounts of material, and teachers feel the pressure of the scope and sequence of the traditional curriculum. This view likens teaching to telling and knowledge to something that can simply be transmitted from teacher to student. If the lecture is interesting, students will pay attention, and, in paying attention, they will learn the material.

We would seek to convince house teachers of the Coalition of Essential Schools' aphorism that "less is more." We would urge teachers to examine their curriculum and attempt to do less in greater depth. Rather than covering a curriculum, house teachers were invited to identify "essential questions" about their disciplines and frame instruction around these essential questions. Essential questions cut to the heart of the disciplines and provide the framework or scaffolding for course content.

Rather than have teachers standing in the front of the classroom doing all the work, subscribing to the Coalition's metaphor of "student-as-worker" would be encouraged. Students from both houses would be actively engaged in learning. Projects were to be encouraged, as well as other activities that would make learning more active and students more involved. The goal would be to get students not simply to listen to a teacher's lecture but to use their minds well—the first and perhaps most important of the Coalition's common principles. Students in Coalition schools are urged to question authority and think critically, something seldom done in the traditional classroom, where the teacher is more concerned that the student takes notes and regurgitates lecture content. In Varsity and Liberty Houses, the role of the teacher would be more like that of a coach or facilitator, creating the conditions for learning and encouraging learning to take place.

Finally, we wanted our houses to begin to use alternative approaches to assessment. The short-answer, multiple-choice format emphasizes rote learning and the memorization of isolated and often trivial facts. We encouraged assessment through projects and through written and oral presentations in which students would be challenged to use their minds. Teachers would involve their students in projects that would culminate in what Coalition schools call "exhibitions." Students would demonstrate their understanding of course content through the projects that they completed, some individually and others in groups. Much like professional artists who carry samples of their work, students would assemble portfolios containing the work that they completed in high school. These portfolios might be used like transcripts and provide a record of what students had accomplished.

Other Design Issues We believed that teachers from the two houses would work to redesign a number of the other aspects of schooling. Not only would the changes described above be put into effect, but teachers would address a whole host of other needs and develop ways of addressing them. New procedures for involving parents, new forms of grading, ways of involving the business community, planning cocurricular and extracurricular activities, and many other issues related to schooling would be part of their purview.

LATER DEVELOPMENTS: SUPPORTING THE HOUSES WITH STATE GRANTS

Stay-in-School Partnership Project (SSPP) and Liberty Partnership Program (LPP) grants were used to support Varsity House at Uptown High and Liberty House at Outer Borough High respectively. Since the LPP grant was considerably larger, it gave us the capacity to undertake the creation of a larger house at Outer Borough and the ability to provide more services for Outer Borough's students. With our two collaborative houses, we were in a position not only to provide support services for students but also to work to improve the schools themselves.

Over the next several years, grant funds would be used to provide supplemental support services to house students, including: continuation of the Mini-College; a community service program (coordinated by the community-based organization with whom we were collaborating); the participation of college students as instructional assistants, tutors, and mentors; special services and programs for parents; afterschool and summer enrichment activities for students; and additional support personnel (e.g., family assistant, social worker).

While utilizing the grants to support staff and curriculum development was permitted, significant expenditure in these areas was discouraged. Program guidelines, both written and unwritten, reflected the enabling legislation, and that legislation was not aimed at improving schools or teachers. It was about providing direct service to students. For this reason we were never able to institute the kind of staff and curriculum development that we would have liked or the kind of staff and curriculum development, we later learned, that each of the two houses required.

THE HOUSES IN PRACTICE

We created Varsity House and Liberty House because the Mini-College, our original intervention, was not improving the attendance or achievement of students at risk. We believed that houses would improve students' education not only for the one day a week they attended the Mini-College, but for the full 180 days of the school year. Yet, after a number of years, neither house seemed to have fulfilled its promise. Comparisons over the years failed to show differences in attendance or achievement between students who attended our houses and comparable students in other programs in the schools. Does our failure to find differences in attendance or achievement mean that the houses we designed don't work, or that the beliefs and assumptions upon which the houses were based are flawed? We don't think so. In fact, when we look closely at what happened, we find that the problem may have been the general failure to implement the houses in the way in which they were designed.

The Sad Story of Varsity House

Varsity House was a theme-based house for students who were interested in sports and athletics. The vision of the teachers who created it was that the house would ultimately be populated by athletes and other students interested in sports. Varsity House was given office space in the school, developed its own mission statement and set of goals, had "dedicated" teachers who taught all of their classes within the house, and had students attend the Mini-College one day a week. For 2 years, Varsity House staff worked hard and were successful in a number of respects. They developed alternative procedures for communicating with the home and managed to involve large numbers of parents. Varsity House teachers also taught family-group classes and moved from 40-minute periods, which they knew were too short to accomplish significant work, to double periods taught on alternate days. None of these changes were made anywhere else in Uptown High School.

While these steps were indeed accomplishments, Varsity House was never fully implemented. We were unable to convince the administration to provide "dedicated" classrooms in an identifiable part of the building. Although we were able to ensure that teachers were fully "dedicated" to their houses while we were in the school, we often had to remind administrators to schedule Varsity House teachers properly. Scheduling mistakes were often made, with significant consequences. Most important, for a variety of reasons that are discussed below, we were never able to significantly affect classroom instruction. Teachers did not revise their curriculum, nor did they change their pedagogy. Without such changes it is unlikely that attendance or academic achievement can improve. It is simply not enough to group and regroup kids or to alter some of the organizational, structural, and scheduling elements of school. Unless we reform what is going on in the classroom nothing much will be accomplished.

As State resources for SSPP declined, we were able to provide fewer and fewer services to the house. When the SSPP program finally came to an end 2 years after Varsity House began, the college could no longer sustain a presence in the school and the house's principal advocate was gone. So too were the Mini-College and other services provided by the college and supported through SSPP funds. Moreover, changes in school leadership made the original agreements null and void. Once the college left, and once a new principal took the helm at the high school, the house was gradually dismantled.

Family group, intended as a way of bringing teachers and students closer together and of enabling them to communicate in more respectful and caring ways, was the first to go. It is true that creating successful family-group classes was more difficult than we had first imagined. Teachers had virtually no preparation for teaching family group and little intuitive sense of how to do it. The training we provided never seemed to be enough. As a result, students were often unclear about the purposes of family group and tended to cut frequently, especially when we mistakenly scheduled the course at the end of the school day. A year or so after City College's departure, rather than seeking a way to improve family-group classes, the school gave up on them entirely.

Double periods were the next to go, as the school continued to push Varsity House back into the old, time-honored way of defining and scheduling instructional periods. Finally, and perhaps most significantly, the school gave up on the notion of "dedicated" teachers. Students in Varsity House are back in the old factory model, taking courses with different teachers throughout the school. Varsity House is simply another of the in-name-only houses that exist at Uptown High.

The Ongoing Struggle at Liberty House

Liberty House was not designed as a theme-based house. From the beginning, it had its own office space as well as "dedicated" classrooms. It developed its own mission statement and goals, had "dedicated" teachers who taught all of their classes in the house, and had half of its 9th- and 10th-grade students attend the Mini-College one day a week while the other half were involved in community service. Liberty House had greater resources than Varsity House, provided both by the high school and through the LPP grant. While there were three different principals over a 6-year period, state funding and the College presence remained constant during that time. Liberty House teachers taught family-group classes from the beginning and had more support to experiment with alternative approaches to curriculum and instruction. Liberty teachers also became a relatively cohesive group. Like Varsity House at Uptown High School, Liberty House was the only house at Outer Borough that began to resemble its own school.

At Liberty House we succeeded in creating a community of teachers who felt that they were part of their own school within the larger school. They achieved close relationships after many years of work. New teachers seemed to fit in well and were brought along by the group. Teachers met regularly and had a strong say in the policies that governed their house. We have learned that there are many teachers who are not comfortable working in programs that require frequent meetings and collaboration with colleagues. Teachers in traditionally organized high schools are used to working alone and in relative isolation. They rarely talk about specific kids, because they all teach different kids. They don't often talk about their classes because they are not part of a collaborative enterprise. After years spent in relative isolation, teaching within a house demands greater effort, communication, and collegiality. Some teachers thrive on it, while others would rather be left alone.

Part of the reason for the increased cohesiveness among Liberty teachers was the fact that they often felt besieged and put upon by the rest of the school. There was the general sense that the school was dumping on the house; that the administration was placing some of the most difficult students in the house and that the rest of the school would take every opportunity to undo the program. Programming mistakes were frequently made, effectively sabotaging some of the best house plans. House teachers felt these mistakes were made on purpose, and those responsible for the mistakes blamed house teachers for not clearly communicating their needs. House teachers believed that the needs of the larger school always took precedence over the needs of the house, and teachers in the larger school believed that the houses always received special consideration at the expense of the larger school. For example, when students attended the Mini-College or went to community service, house teachers used this time to visit Mini-College classes or community service sites, to meet in order to plan curriculum, and to case-conference. Other teachers saw this as a day off and felt that house teachers were getting away with something.

While we wanted students' voices to be heard and advisory committees to be formed and active, this has yet to be fully accomplished. We also set aside resources for after-school clubs, classes, and activities, yet most house teachers declined to participate, despite the offer of additional compensation. The energy and effort required to teach adolescents at risk two double-periods of an academic subject and a family group can drain even the hardiest of staff. As a result, the kind of active involvement in the life of the school that we hoped to encourage was not achieved.

Community service at Liberty House was to have been another way of operationalizing the caring community. The program initially involved students providing service during the school day. While students enjoyed the program and seemed to get a lot out of it, we ran into trouble pulling kids and teachers out of school one day a week. Not only did we decide to drop community service, we also decided to discontinue the Mini-College. Though both experiences were felt to be enriching, we felt that we simply could not afford to pull kids out of school to attend them. When we made the community-service program a voluntary one on an after-school basis, the numbers of participants diminished significantly. We are still in the process of struggling to find a way of putting a meaningful community service program in place.

Finally, and again most telling, the changes we wanted Liberty House to make in curriculum and instruction were largely foregone. The house remained a part of the larger school, and although there was an assistant principal in charge of the house, supervision of teachers in their disciplines continued to be done by the department chairs. Teachers were free to make changes only within certain boundaries, and these boundaries were defined differently by different departments. Radical change would have been impossible, with supervisors most often citing the state competency tests as reasons for preserving the status quo. Unlike at the Coalition schools that we were using as models, interdisciplinary instruction did not seem feasible at Outer Borough and Uptown High. State competency examinations, the expectations and traditions of the two high schools, and the fact that most house teachers were not trained across disciplines forced us to retain the disciplines pretty much as they were in the larger school. In addition, the teachers themselves were not fully convinced that teaching and learning needed to change. Such change would have required enormous amounts of time and energy, which teachers were not entirely willing to provide, and which the State grant, with its emphasis on direct services to students, might not have provided for.

Liberty House, like Varsity House, looked fine on paper. Yet neither house made the changes in teaching and learning that we felt were critical in educating students at risk. Until those changes are made it is unlikely that measures of attendance and achievement will improve.

SOME CONCLUDING THOUGHTS AND FUTURE DIRECTIONS

We started out with a modest little program that we hoped would improve the attendance and achievement of high school students at risk. We got increasingly involved in the problem and began to look not only at providing direct services to students but at ways of working with schools to develop new approaches and new models that worked. The problem of educating the high school students at risk is a far more difficult one than we first imagined. We see more clearly why schools seem to be failing, why success is so hard to achieve, and why exemplary programs are so few and far between.

We believe that high school students who are at risk exhibited no better attendance or achievement in Varsity House and Liberty House not because the changes we made were ill advised, but rather because we were unable to make all of the changes that we felt were necessary. If we failed, it was due to a failure to fully implement our design. Those who work in schools know that the process of change is difficult if not impossible. Even where change is introduced, the norms of the school work to undo it. In an unpublished 5-year study of Coalition schools, Muncey and McQuillan (1991) suggest that most schools remain impervious to schoolwide restructuring.

We now believe that houses simply do not have sufficient autonomy from the larger school to experiment with radically different approaches. The only way to achieve that autonomy is to create small autonomous schools within the larger school, something which is happening with increasing frequency in New York City. In 1993, nearly 30 small new high schools were born thanks to the support and encouragement of Chancellor Fernandez, the Coalition, and other groups within the city. We are now in the process of working with Uptown High School, Outer Borough High School, and a third high school in Manhattan to transform existing houses into autonomous schools, and we are hoping that Liberty House will be the first autonomous school at Outer Borough.

But even if we succeed in creating autonomous schools, that does not mean that we have succeeded in making such schools work. While we agree that small schools are probably better than large schools, smallness by itself is not enough. We need to find school leaders with energy and vision, teachers who are willing to work collaboratively with their colleagues and assume new roles and responsibilities; a flexible system that permits schools to experiment with different ways of reaching students at risk; and the additional time and money needed to accomplish all of the tasks required for creating and sustaining really fine schools. Until we can get our schools to work properly, providing isolated services to students at risk may not be sufficient. We need to provide those services and, at the same time, to help bring about the changes needed to improve the schools from which our students at risk come.

IV

PARTNERSHIPS AS LEARNING OPPORTUNITIES

9

Partnership Dynamics in Practice

MICHAEL N. BAZIGOS

P ace University's Stay-in-School Part-
nership program sought to improve the English-language proficiency of
some newly arrived Asian immigrant pupils in a junior high school in
New York City's Chinatown. These students were thought to be in jeop-
ardy of prematurely leaving school to pursue the lure of the Chinese-
speaking underground economy: low-paying jobs in factories and res-
taurants, or nefarious gang activity. After 5 years' experience directing
this project, I joined a panel of six colleagues identified by the American
Association for Higher Education as "pioneers" in school–university
partnerships. The themes we sounded will ring familiar to many:

Will my college institutionalize my position?
Universities must demonstrate the value they place on collaboration by
    changing the reward structures.
We need evaluation studies specifically on partnerships.
Directors are most effective when they build political bases around their
    partnerships that are capable of provoking an outcry if an attempt is
    made to disassemble the program.
How can faculty involvement in these projects be sustained?

It quickly became obvious to us that the role of directing school–
university partnerships is a new and innovative one. Partnership directors may be the first-generation leaders of a new group of professionals:
the linkers, the boundary spanners. Implicit in this view is the fact that
partnerships are unique enough to merit their own study, their own liter-

ature, their own methodology. This chapter explores some of the many vectors, both convergent and divergent, that formed the operating space for the partnership activity within Pace University—in fundese, an "IHE," or private institution of higher education—and between the university and our partner "LEAs," or local education agencies, also known as schools. A critical incident illustrative of forces working at cross-purposes is also presented and discussed. Although the case described here is specific, I propose that the dynamics illustrated are universal to the school–college partnership phenomenon in this most recent reformulation of the school-reform movement and will prove instructive to practitioners while providing researchers with a useful model as well. While the focus of this chapter is not on the services provided through SSPP, a brief history and description of the Pace University program precedes the exploration of organizational issues that makes up the body of this narrative, thus providing the reader a context.

Analysis of partnership constellations takes on added import at a time when all concerned sectors, each anxious to make its unique mark, are jumping into the act: government, higher education, and business, with the latter providing the strongest approximation of broad societal validation of the partnership initiative, for better or for worse.

THE PACE PROGRAM

Our original plan called for four of the university's six divisions to assist each other in a coordinated response to one junior high school's problem. The danger was the same throughout our program—that newly immigrated Asian pupils with limited English proficiency (LEP) who stagnated in their English acquisition progress would drop out of senior high school shortly after entering 10th grade. In our third year of activity, it became necessary to extend our efforts to another school in order to ensure program survival, as explained below under "Anatomy of a Conflict." The same configuration of university divisions would now respond to a differently framed problem (now imminent dropout in general, not LEP, was the significant risk factor) that required serving an older population of returning Latino, African American, and African-Caribbean students who had previously dropped out of school.

Pace University's Involvement with the Schools

The four university divisions involved in our program were the Dyson School of Arts and Sciences (Psychology Department), the School of Computer Science and Information Systems, the School of Education, and the Lienhard School of Nursing. The lead entity among these organizational units was the School of Education, which hired the project director, and whose dean provided ultimate executive leadership.

A comprehensive and integrated service plan included: tutoring services with a special emphasis on language for students with limited English proficiency, language-immersion field trips, personal computer instruction with an emphasis on word-processing as a writing-improvement vehicle, critical-thinking training for teachers in School I, health screenings for students, and small-group discussion sessions focusing on bicultural dilemmas led by advanced doctoral students in the School–Community Psychology program. Service delivery was provided primarily after school at School I and during school hours at School II. The primary service delivery site in both settings was the school building, although workshops and other special events were held on the university campus.

School I is a junior high school (Grades 7–9) in lower Manhattan's Chinatown. Identified as being at risk according to two state program criteria (the Attendance Improvement and Dropout Prevention program and the Comprehensive Assessment Report) the school was successfully served by Pace SSPP for a number of years. There was an ever-burgeoning mass of newly arrived students at the school for whom educational and life outlook was growing exceedingly bleak. Over 40% of the 1,400 students had been labelled as having LEP. Many students acted out in class, shared meager resources with a number of siblings, were unsupported educationally and emotionally by their near-absentee parents, and stood a good chance of never becoming literate in English in their lives. Students who dropped out were lost to sweatshops, menial factory employment, or gang membership. The school's population was 87% Asian, 11% Latino, 2% African American, and less than 1% Caucasian.

School II is located on the tough streets of Manhattan's Lower East Side. Also identified as being at risk by the Comprehensive Assessment Report, and funded through the Attendance Improvement/Dropout Prevention Program, the school represents a safe haven for its 600 students, who walk quickly past drug dealers and buyers as close as one block from the school. The significant population served by our program was disproportionately Latino and African American. Because School II is an alternative school designed to attract, retain, and graduate high school dropouts, it abounds in transfer, referral, and walk-in students from the larger comprehensive high schools. The typical student has been retained in grade at least once in the past; 17 years is the mean age among pupils.

MARGINALITY AS A FORCE IN PARTNERSHIPS

All partnership conceptualization must address the notion of marginality. From a strictly interpreted missions stance, colleges are pretty marginal to the daily operations of public schools, which are most immediately concerned with the delivery of instruction to thousands of pupils per building. Schools, in turn, have been pretty marginal to the mission of colleges and universities, which are often most immediately concerned with course delivery to their tuition-paying clientele.

Why, then, a partnership? Morton Deutsch (1973) writes:

> Any attempt to introduce a change into the existing relationship between two parties is more likely to be accepted if each expects some net gain from the change than if either side expects the other side will gain at its expense. (p. 34)

From the school's perspective, the college stands to gain from SSPP. By statutory design (see Chap. 1, this volume), the college is the lead financial entity, since it receives the funds; schools may gain services from the college, but given the fiscal landscape of public education, school leaders would certainly prefer unrestricted funding directly to their own buildings. Also, since the college is the lead entity, university personnel, and not the school principal, are credited with partnership results. Finally, teachers—particularly those for whom the grant offers no stipend—"have the power 'not to do it.' Therefore, bargains, usually implicit, have to be struck. . . . By striking these bargains, people will be encouraged to 'try' the innovation" (Fullan, 1991, p. 2). Many experienced teachers, regardless of stipend, initially viewed SSPP as another "Band-Aid" program that was doomed to fail.

From a skeptical vantage point, however, SSPP offered the college nothing of great value either. This counter-intuitive stance arises from at least three factors. First, a grant narrowly restricted to predetermined community activities holds less allure than an unrestricted gift. It was also anathema to university comptrollers that the enabling SSPP statute required a 15% in-kind match, not including space, and allowed only 6% for indirect expenses. In our case, since most money was flagged for either release time, stipend, or salary, individual university schools, departments, and personnel profited from SSPP, but not central university budgets. Consequently, mercenary interest, a powerful force when properly harnessed, was in this case only tepid from an institutionwide perspective.

Second, although every urban independent university has by now implemented a guerilla recruiting agenda to survive the demographic trough of "baby busters," students at risk of dropout (i.e., SSPP participants) are still seen by most universities as low-yield propositions (see Chap. 7, this volume). Two camps are divided along this issue: proponents who view "access" as a desirable end, and critics who raise concerns of "quality." Extremists in the former camp focus singular attention on the market-sector advantage that accrues to colleges that relax admissions standards to varying degrees. The seductive logic of this argument in an institution that is over 90% tuition-driven, however, is lost on the latter camp, who fear the perceived compromises in academic integrity that would follow an "opening the floodgates" strategy. One faculty member from another institution, who was clearly in the quality camp, noted that "we can only slightly burnish the product we receive from the secondary schools." The issue of diversity suffuses this complex matter, whose parameters are succinctly delineated in this excerpt from a recent Pace University position paper:

> Many of the students [with potential, but who lack appropriate preparation] are not prepared to meet, initially, the demands of Pace's academic programs. Costly interventions are necessary to improve their chances. While these students are the source of some of Pace's most notable successes, they also include many individuals who cannot succeed due to academic weakness and/or financial pressures. As this population continues to grow as a percentage of the total undergraduate population, Pace must insure that it does not neglect its better-prepared students, has reliable indicators of student potential for success, has appropriate academic and financial support available, maintains the integrity of a Pace degree, and controls the total number of students who need special assistance.
>
> In addition, the University faculty members must prepare themselves to deal with the growing diversity of future student populations. Even Pace, which has a history of welcoming and serving diverse populations, will be challenged by the complex identities of future students. This diversity will challenge curricular design, course content, instructional strategies, and communal identity. To address these issues, the university must gain support for a balanced resolution to the quality vs. access tension. (Ewers, 1991, p. 6)

Third, but just as significant, is a faculty perception that to render service is to dig one's professional grave. This perception is a consequence of a paradoxical emphasis by committees on research as a prerequisite for tenure and promotion at Pace, even though the college is historically a teaching institution. From a modern perspective, teaching ranks second to research, while service lags a distant third. This trend is not unique to Pace. A national survey conducted by the Carnegie Foundation for the Advancement of Teaching found that while in 1969, 6% of faculty surveyed indicated that research was required for a tenure award at their institution, in 1989 that figure had leaped to 43%.

From the vantage point of the project director, then, the more immediate question was not "Why partnership?" but rather, "How do we *do* partnership?", given what appeared to be a low-potential proposition all around. Each SSPP program would eventually forge a unique equation that fit its own particular constellation of actors, vectors, and agendas; the Pace program emerged as a gerrymandered, autonomous pocket in which success was possible. Despite wide divergence among models, however, there are common dynamics to school–college partnerships that the author intends to describe. Beyond the context of marginality, four factors are central to the negotiation of any partnership: Stakes, Power, Interest interdependence, and Readiness for trust; the fluctuation of these factors over time provides a framework—the SPIR paradigm—through which to view critical incidents. A case illustrating the dynamic interplay of these factors follows; its lessons are then distilled into a set of recommendations for building partnership.

ANATOMY OF A CONFLICT

The survival of the Pace program was threatened during its second year of operation. Following a pattern of veiled negative signals from the funding agency, the university requested a meeting to clarify the issues. It was divulged that the program suffered from two political flaws that threatened its survival. First, only one school building was being served; second, an insufficient number of African American and Latino youth were being served as a consequence of the school's demographic composition (see the description of School I above). It was made clear to the university that for funding to continue, expansion to a second school with a significant proportion of non-Asian minorities was necessary. Consequently, contact with a nearby alternative high school was facilitated by the School I principal, who was apprised of the necessity of identifying a second site and subsequently supported the goal of program survival through expansion.

School II, for its part, enjoyed a history of collaboration with a large local corporation and a neighboring public community college. Our initial call to arrange a meeting was greeted coolly, and a meeting between the school administration and the Pace program director could only be arranged on the condition that he bring a series of developed, concrete ideas to the meeting, to which the school leaders would react.

Within these parameters, it was my hope that: 1) School II would ultimately agree to a partnership for the following year, within the constraints of SSPP guidelines, funding agency expectations, and resource limits; 2) as a consequence, Pace's SSPP program would meet the political criteria for continuation and survive; and 3) the program at School II would exceed the minimum goal of mere survival, and have a powerful effect on its participants.

Actors

Initial meetings were held between myself and the school principal and assistant principal for administration. Because the Pace psychology department was called into the planning meetings, a psychology faculty member, the school assistant principal for pupil personnel support services, and two highly advanced doctoral students in school psychology were also involved. A second project director from a department of social work at another university became the third party in the conflict that emerged at School II.

Events

At the initial meeting with the School II administration, I described the service plan already in place at School I, noting that program design would of course vary with differences in the characteristic risk profiles of each population. The administrators then provided information about the school's history, mission, and students. The meeting concluded with a bilateral commitment to move forward with a university-sponsored needs assessment and program recommendation, with proposal submission to follow a school-cabinet review of the SSPP plan for School II. The first goal, gaining a second partner school, was thus met.

A service plan was formulated that included, among its other components (e.g., tutoring, mentoring, inservice teacher training) a psychological-services component. During the proposal-design period, a cluster-service model was created to provide student participants with in-school, small-group counseling sessions led by Pace psychologists, and with the principal's approval, this model was proposed to the state. Two Pace psychologists were to be placed into regularly scheduled classes known as "Family Group." Because attendance at Family Group was required, this venue was seen as the vehicle of choice for delivering psychological services.

Ultimately, the third-year continuation proposal to incorporate African American and Latino students from School II into the Pace program resulted in funding of 266% of the previous year's amount. (Some of the increase was attributable to an unexpected, but welcome, legislative increase for SSPP statewide.) Thus, the second goal, that of program survival, was met.

Following the continuation award, Pace attempted to implement the psychological-services component in September, only to discover that Family Group classes had been diverted to social work interns from the other university. The psychologists who had been contracted to deliver services according to the funded SSPP plan were the first to discover the alternative arrangement when the assistant principal attempted to place them into nonclassroom settings (e.g., in the library, guidance office). Their faculty supervisor met with the assistant principal, who finally revealed that School II had received Board of Education funding to place five full-time social work interns into the very classes originally committed to two Pace psychologists.

An attempt to negotiate a collaborative settlement with the other college failed. The Pace team suggested sharing the four Family Group classes in ways that would diminish the student–staff ratios to even more desirable levels, but this suggestion was rebuffed. The social worker took the stand that "we control Family Group," and insisted that the psychologists would need to find an alternative accommodation. An appeal directly to the building principal proved futile as well. While admitting that the commitment of Family Group classes to Pace was made first chronologically, the principal explained that her primary commitment had to be to the grant controlled by her school, noting that five full-time interns provided greater coverage than two part-time doctoral students working 20 and 10 hours per week, respectively.

Pace considered, but never executed, an appeal to the principal's superintendent, as the ill will that such an action might have engendered would have been prohibitive to meaningful partnership. As the Pace dean of education explained, "I will never support forcing school leaders into making unwanted changes in their own buildings." Ultimately, I reluctantly authorized the redesign of the psychological-services component around an intensive individual-counseling model exclusively serving returning long-term absentees, the label for a statistical category of students who have missed 20 consecutive school days. Long-term absentees are temporarily removed from the computation of the school's average daily attendance rate in order to allow the school to continue receiving its per-capita funding allowance.

The new plan called for the returning long-term absentee to enter into a contract with one on-site Pace psychologist. As a condition for readmittance to the school, the student would agree to two initial individual-counseling sessions followed by weekly group sessions. The group, run by both psychologists, would comprise all returning students in this category. Because the membership of groups was capped at 10, new groups would be formed as necessary. As the principal explained, "there is plenty of business here for everybody."

Impact

The third goal—having a powerful effect on students—was most critical from the vantage point of genuineness of intent, and remained unmet. Despite an in-school referral network and office space, the psychological-services component never attained a significant caseload. Few long-term absentee students ever returned to School II. Of the ones who contracted for services, few ever attended their sessions, and most left School II within days of their return. In total, seven students were served on an ongoing basis during the school year, and the group contained only three students at its peak.

The psychologists stoically continued attempting to engage students, in some cases even visiting known student hangouts to find missing clients. The principal continued to deny SSPP access to the Family Group throughout the year, adamant about the position that there was much "business" to be had if only the psychologists would "hustle." Eventually, School II was most meaningfully served by the psychologists' integration into case-management (known as "Talk Kid") meetings. During this period, another problem that the project could address emerged: teacher burnout. A consultation group for teachers was formed and continued through the year's end, and the teachers considered the meetings valuable enough to repeat in subsequent years.

I adopted a conservative resource-allocation approach with School II. Troubled that approximately $15,000 had been spent on an ineffective program component, and concerned that the commitments of school administrators could be abrogated again, we made a program-level decision to allocate resources only to those components that the school could not obtain elsewhere. Consequently, the psychological-services component was discontinued; only tutoring and in-school mentoring services were provided in subsequent years.

ANALYSIS

In this case, the combined efforts and resources of four organizations failed to serve the client population in the richest possible way. Secondary agendas of the state education department, the Pace program, School II, and the second institution of higher education failed to overlap, even at their margins, resulting in an operating space most aptly characterized as a hole. From one perspective, this was a lose-lose outcome for Pace and School II: SSPP was denied an opportunity to realize a primary objective; School II, as a consequence, was denied a broader array of services in subsequent years.

But no organization plays to lose. Nor did these events occur by chance, or through mere bad luck; some incentive for each party's behavior must have existed. Analysis into the way partnerships are structured yields insights into the predictable failures and the successes of school-reform efforts. A useful framework for analysis is the SPIR (Stakes, Power, Interest Interdependence, and Readiness for Trust) paradigm for predicting and explaining the outcome of organizational negotiations. Empirically derived from social psychological research, this model predicts which of five possible outcomes are likeliest in a given negotiation: competition, collaboration, compromise, accommodation, or withdrawal.

Competition denotes an entity's attempt, hostile or otherwise, to gain control of an object, possession, or prize. Wars, lawsuits, and the Olympic Games are all examples of competition. In the case of our program, each of the four parties involved might have engaged in competitive actions.

For example, the state education department could have decided not to refund the Pace SSPP for failing to meet its objectives. Pace University and the second college could have attempted a direct appeal to the principal's superintendent, threatening to immediately withdraw from School II until access to Family Group classes was granted. School II could have rejected all SSPP services and attempted to gain direct access to SSPP funds.

Collaboration refers to a cooperative undertaking between two or more parties, typically involving coordination of actions and sharing of resources to achieve the same or similar goals. It is different from compromise, which results in a fixed pie being divided into more but smaller slices, since collaboration typically increases available resources. In the present case, a true collaborative effort among SSPP, School II, and the second college might have consisted of reprogramming the four family group classes into six smaller units, allowing for closer student–staff interaction.

Compromise denotes a mutually agreeable settlement between opposing interests, based on multilateral concessions in the pursuit of a working relationship. The creation of two family group classes jointly served by both universities would have been a good example of a compromise solution.

Accommodation means capitulation to the demands of another party. Compliance and surrender are two examples of accommodation. The SSPP decision to accept the school's individual-counseling model was an accommodation outcome from the Pace perspective, because not a single family group class was accessed. From the perspective of the second college, compliance with a principal's hypothetical decision to yield all or most of the family group classes to SSPP would have constituted accommodation.

Withdrawal is clearly the least desirable outcome, indicating that one or all of the negotiating parties is simply no longer willing to participate.

A Dynamic Model

Which of the five outcomes is likely to result can be predicted or postdicted by assessing the negotiations along two dimensions: relative assertiveness and quality of relationship. These two dimensions can be thought of as being orthogonal to each other; when two dimensions cross at right angles, four quadrants are created, as illustrated in Figure 1. Through empirical study of negotiation, it has been determined that four of the outcomes defined (competition, collaboration, accommodation, withdrawal) can be represented by these quadrants. The fifth outcome, compromise, overlaps all four. By assessing the relative assertiveness of each party, and the quality of relationship between parties, it is possible

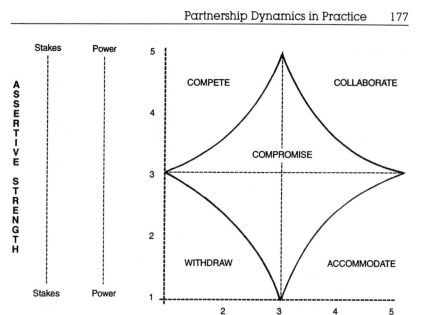

Figure 1. The SPIR dynamic: conflict strategy plotted against strength and quality of relationship.

to anticipate which quadrant a party will fall into, or which outcome will predominate. For example, if a party had high assertive strength and no relationship with an adversary, competitive behavior is likely, with that party adopting a strategy that seeks to maximize its position. If another party has low assertive strength, but an excellent relationship with the adversary, accommodation will be the likely result. Attempts at compromise are always a possibility at any time, because compromise has potential overlap with all the other outcomes.

In this model, assertiveness is assessed by evaluating the **relative power** (P) of the two parties, and the **stake** (S) that each has in the outcome of a given negotiation. Similarly, quality of relationship is assessed by evaluating the degree to which their **interests are interdependent** (I), and their **readiness for trust** (R).

The SPIR model can be used to examine the interactions of the Pace program with the other parties. Although our case involved four players, the focus of this illustration is on explaining the behavioral actions of the Pace program and School II.

Assessing Stakes

While both parties had major stakes in the success of the project, those for the Pace program were higher in the short term. It was unlikely, for instance, that we would have received continuation funding without involvement of the second school. A program such as ours is totally dependent on outside funding, whereas this was not true for the school. Their need was to protect their new dropout prevention grant and demonstrate their ability to get other grants over the longer term.

Intuitively, one might think that the goals of improving attendance and enhancing student performance would be high stakes for School II. Paradoxically, however, if a school starts to do too well in this regard, it can *lose* its special funding. According to this somewhat cynical perspective, it is to the school's advantage to consistently move in a positive direction with respect to attendance rates and academic improvement while managing to always fall just short of the mark, thus guaranteeing another round of funding eligibility and more salary lines for personnel.

Relative Power Assessment

Power can be derived from a number of sources, and the Pace program had only moderate access to any of them during the first year of the partnership. One of these sources is control of rewards and punishments. Pace had discretionary control over the relative distribution of grant resources between School I and School II, and could deny requests for non-grant university resources (e.g., School II's request for meeting space to accommodate non-SSPP business). Another source of power is position in an administrative hierarchy; Pace had none of this type, as the university was not a player on the board of education or in the state funding agency and, worst of all, no prior commitment at the level of school superintendent had been sought. A third source of power derives from moral persuasion. Pace's position was that a signed agreement should be honored, but the other party showed complete indifference to this argument.

School II's position in the first year of the partnership can be conceptualized along the same dimension. School II had no reward power, especially as its ability to provide access to family group classes was severely curtailed when it contracted with the second college. School II had a great deal of punishment power, as it was able to block access to any program service. However, it had no positional power, since it, too, had no particular role in the way the state education department interacted with institutions of higher learning.

Comparing the combined sources of power available to the two parties, it can be deduced that School II had near-absolute power advantage during year one. It is important to note, however, that relationships are dynamic and change over time. During the second year of the relationship between the Pace SSPP and School II, survival issues had been resolved and psychological services withdrawn. This resulted in the relative power of the two parties switching, this time in the favor of the Pace program.

Assessing Interest Interdependence

While the two parties were in dispute as to the best means for delivering SSPP-sponsored psychological services (family group versus individual model), there was agreement that the ultimate goal of the undertaking was to have a beneficial impact on student attendance and achievement. However, we interpreted the school–university partnership as a new path to this end. This in turn created a superordinate goal for Pace of SSPP program survival, whereas for School II there were alternate methods for improving student performance. Thus, from the perspectives of both the Pace program and School II, interest interdependence was only moderate.

Assessing Readiness for Trust

For the SSPP program at Pace University, trust was initially high. We felt that we had addressed initial concerns. A collaborative program-design process had been proposed, and there seemed to be good interpersonal chemistry with the school administrators. We had had no prior history of a partnership with another educational institution ever being abrogated. School II, however, had had the opposite experience. Senior administrators were rather indiscriminate consumers of proposals for educational reform: when SSPP was introduced it was the sixth external "partner" to the school that year. Unbeknownst to us, the school was wary of the relationship, as there had been a past conflict with Pace University over a space-rental agreement. Furthermore, the long-term future and commitment of the Pace program was unpredictable for School II: at the time they contracted with the other college (post-submission of the SSPP proposal, but pre-award), there was no assurance of funding—a factor that further increased the ambiguity of the relationship. Thus, School II's readiness for trust was very low.

IMPLICATIONS[1]

In the formal SPIR model it is possible to assign numerical values to the four dimensions of interest, and thus make specific quantitative predictions regarding the likelihood of competition, collaboration, compro-

---

[1]This section, and the concluding comments, were written by Ian M. Evans.

mise, accommodation, or withdrawal. No such attempt has been made in the above analysis, as the purpose is to illustrate how a dynamic analysis of possible influences could suggest changes that might make a better, truly collaborative outcome more probable.

It is clear, for instance, that although the long-term stakes for all concerned were the improvement of educational opportunities for children at risk, there were more immediate stakes related to funding and survival that created an imbalance. One means of redress is to allow a much larger proportion of the funding to be made directly available to teachers. The SUNY—Binghamton program, for example, began to award "mini grants" directly to teachers who were committed to program goals; this has proved to be a highly successful strategy, as it gives teachers a direct stake. Another important tactic for raising the short-term stake of the school is to make funding contingent upon continued improvement in student achievement, rather than cutting it off when some minimal criterion for progress has been achieved.

It is unlikely that a university-based program will ever command much power in a partnership, other than that derived from the moral force of its goals and intentions. Inevitably, however, the school will always have a considerable amount of punishment power, because teachers can simply refuse to participate and cooperate. Indeed, many do, for a variety of different personal and occasionally professional reasons. Even when programs decide to focus on those individual teachers who are enthusiastic and interested, it is possible for negative teachers who are influential, senior, or closely connected to union politics to sabotage the efforts of teachers who wish to participate. In such circumstances, having a strong alliance with powerful individuals in the district is an enormous advantage. The Binghamton program frequently had to appeal to the district superintendent, Dr. James Lee, who not only was fully supportive of the program but had, in fact, originally contacted the university to initiate it. Dr. Lee was able, through his authority and command of resources, to prevent objections by negative teachers from interfering with program activities: he was able to provide substitute teachers to allow program teachers to attend meetings and inservice training, to negotiate with union representatives, and to reinforce those teachers we knew to be making important changes in educational practices. In addition, of course, programs can elevate the influence of supportive school personnel: a strategy used in the Binghamton program was to organize a group of teacher "ambassadors" who maintained close personal contact with the program and who were asked to represent the program to the school faculty as a whole.

In order to try to make the interests of the school and the university more interdependent, it is critical that there be some agreement on the methods for achieving program goals. This need was illustrated very clearly in the Pace program. Simply because two parties agree on the ultimate objective—prevention of school failure among the pupils at greatest risk—does not mean that there will be agreement on the causes of student failure, and thus on the best solutions to be adopted. As revealed throughout this volume, the overriding principle guiding most of the university programs was that fundamental school reforms are needed to effect meaningful change. SSPP programs that focused primarily on providing schools with extra educational services had less conflictual interactions, since there was agreement on their respective interests. Furthermore, when a program is urging systemic change on the school it is particularly important that those involved not be distracted by less important interests, such as maintaining their funding. Although one can understand why state and other funding sources provide resources for only 1 year (or at best 3 years) at a time, this traditional approach to funding seriously undermines the work of partnerships such as those we describe in this volume.

The erratic nature of funding is also one of the barriers to greater trust among members of partnerships. Schools have all seen university projects come and go, since they are so highly dependent on grant support and the interest of key faculty: as explained in this chapter, universities typically reward faculty research and development activities much more than service, despite their rhetoric to the contrary. SSPP schools were all quite wary of the university programs, having rarely experienced involvement by personnel who were truly dedicated to being there for the long haul. By the time this volume is published, in 1995, many SSPP programs will have been in existence for more than 8 or 9 years, regardless of the stresses and disruptions caused by sporadic funding. Hopefully, such long-term engagement will greatly increase future trust on the part of the schools, which too often in the past have been seen by universities as convenient institutions to provide practicum training or research subjects—or simply as the causes of poor preparation among incoming college students. SSPP program university personnel typically entered school partnerships with trust and optimism and were amazed to find that past abuses resulted in these feelings rarely being reciprocated. It is our recommendation that only through a long-term commitment to maintain partnerships such as these can mutual trust be fully established. New programs will have to realize that true partnerships take time to develop.

CONCLUDING COMMENTS

All of the SSPP programs funded in New York State acknowledged that at one time or another there were conflicts with the schools that needed to be addressed. In fact, at the annual meeting of the project directors, a common theme was just how difficult it was to work constructively with organizations as complex as public school districts. As noted a number of times in this volume, the partnerships formed often represented the first time university personnel had really had direct experience in collaborating with schools in an attempt to resolve a specific issue. Lack of experience, lack of a history of working together, and occasionally simply differences in personal style contributed to the difficulties that arose.

Often, discussions of these problems turned into something very close to "teacher bashing." Difficulties in forming successful partnerships seemed to be attributed to unwillingness on the part of teachers to participate constructively in the process. All projects reported phenomena such as teachers agreeing to attend inservice workshops only if paid to do so, leaving scheduled meetings early, insisting on having oversight committees to review SSPP materials, and attributing student problems to external influences such as family factors or low socioeconomic status. A number of these frustrating experiences have been mentioned throughout this volume. However, it was quickly recognized by all concerned that for program staff to blame teachers was as counterproductive as teachers themselves blaming families. A much deeper understanding of the dynamics of these partnerships was needed.

We all recognized that concepts such as ownership or empowerment were critical, but these conditions could not always be achieved. Sometimes school superintendents had sought participation without letting it be known to their building principals; sometimes principals did the same without informing their faculty. In one case, asking teachers to make decisions about the direction of the project was interpreted as the project staff not knowing what they were doing. We also recognized that the implicit message of the SSPP projects was that the schools needed to change. But rarely was it suggested that the universities might need to change as well. And yet the schools knew perfectly well that the energy and enthusiasm for the various projects was quite dependent upon the continuation of funding: many districts had experienced university-based projects that started with much fanfare, only to end abruptly as grants came to an end or key personnel at the institutions departed. Furthermore, as is made so clear in this chapter, many schools have a variety of resources for responding to the needs of students at risk. Most of the SSPP program personnel were surprised to discover that the schools requesting their services already had in place other state-funded projects for dropout prevention and retention, agreements with mental health agencies (e.g., primary mental health programs), plans such as school and business alliances, volunteer mentoring and tutoring activities, services from county cooperative extensions, and many others. Thus, the problems were often not a lack of specific resources so much as of coordination of services.

For these reasons, the present analysis of a degree of conflict between the SSPP program and the collaborating school is particularly important. By focusing on a formal theory for analyzing such conflicts, it is possible to examine the issues objectively, without identifying villains or attributing the difficulties to the incompetence or intransigence of a particular party. Pace University's SSPP program with School I was known to be highly successful. The principal of School I was a very active player in annual meetings and in presenting the findings and accomplishments of the project. Thus, it is safe to conclude that individual personalities, or lack of sensitivity on the part of Pace SSPP personnel, did not contribute to the problems described here. That is not to say that such factors cannot or do not have an effect; as in any other complex interaction, the individual styles of the various parties affect the chances of success in the relationship. But in the present case, circumstances that are identifiable, that relate to power, trust, interest interdependence, and stakes, can be considered in a simple and practical way. Partnerships, while having many potential advantages, are not entered into without problems and potential conflicts. The experience of the Pace University partnership and the analysis provided should assist other projects to avoid common pitfalls.

10

A Perspective on Students at Risk in the Suburbs

AARON W. GODFREY

After World War II, the suburbs around New York grew dramatically as young couples fled the crowds and problems of the city to raise their children where there was more room, clean air, and patches of green. The dream lasted for a few years, until it became apparent that the suburbs were not impervious to urban problems, many of which migrated with the new arrivals. The schools were not unaffected, especially in working-class districts, where quality education gradually became subordinated to the shrinking tax base as the salaries of residents failed to keep pace with the rate of inflation. Many qualities characteristically associated with urban schools, such as low achievement and social problems, began to also appear in the suburbs, which grew more rapidly in two Long Island counties (Nassau and Suffolk) than in other areas of the state.

Suffolk County is a complex region of great diversity. Outside of New York City, it is the largest county in New York State in both area and population. Since World War II, the population has multiplied fivefold and has changed the rural quality of the region to the extent that Suffolk County is still in search of an identity, especially because there are no urban centers in the county. In the 1990 census, Suffolk County showed a population of 1,322,000, compared with 245,000 residents in 1948. The perception of affluence is misleading, despite the apparent wealth of such areas as the Hamptons and other shore resorts, whose prosperity is seasonal.

The 70 school districts in the county tend to be decentralized, independent, resistant to change, and suspicious of outsiders. In the larger

185

districts that serve predominantly working-class populations, the school boards too often are not prepared to handle the complexities of school financing or educational change, and can be manipulated by school administrators to follow directions without much dissent.

Furthermore, it appears that administrators have not had much impact on the achievements of students, as demonstrated by the decline in reading and math scores on statewide tests. Additionally, the budgets of many of these districts are top-heavy, with highly paid administrators who lack the educational leadership to bring about a reversal of the decline in quality.

The school districts of Suffolk County are enormously diverse in the amounts spent to educate students ($7,500–$18,700 per pupil) and in pupil–teacher ratios, which vary from 9 to 1 to 16 to 1 (New York State Education Department, 1991). The dropout rate is also hard to determine, but official figures vary from 7% to more than 12%. The official figure taken from the annual report of the state education department, which is much greater than the stated dropout rate for Long Island, is at least questionable for some school districts. A low official rate satisfies school boards and district residents that the schools are doing a good job and at the same time helps maintain the level of state aid, which is linked to attendance. Consequently, students who do not officially sign out of school and who might possibly return at some future time are not dropped from the rolls. A more realistic calculation might be made if the number of graduating seniors was compared to the number of those who entered the 9th grade 4 years before. Most schools resist such a study and question its validity because they claim that many students move from the district or transfer to other schools, though the region's population has remained quite stable, actually showing an overall increase. However, it should be noted that of the 70 districts in New York that receive state dropout-prevention funds, 18 are in Suffolk County, which suggests that dropping out of school is a problem that needs serious attention, regardless of how the statistics on which funding is based are calculated.

Over the last 15 years, the University at Stony Brook has had an uneven relationship with the schools in Suffolk County. During the 1976 budget crisis, the university's education department, including the elementary education program, was retrenched, to the dismay of many local school systems. Secondary education preparation and certification remained in the hands of the academic departments and were loosely administered until 1988, when the Center for Excellence and Innovation in Education was established. The center coordinates all teacher preparation and the cooperative efforts between school districts and the university. Prior to the establishment of the Center, contacts with school districts were selective and often random, including programs like Upward

Bound, which some schools perceived as adversarial. The center established a focus for school–university partnerships and has begun to improve relationships so that a great measure of trust has been generated.

In 1987, the first Stay-in-School Partnership was funded at Stony Brook, to be implemented in four school districts that were receiving state funds to reduce the dropout rate. The purpose of this chapter is to provide a case study of a suburban working-class school district and the development of its relationship with the university.

THE STONY BROOK SSPP PROGRAM

A Suburban Community

Brentwood is a large school district (11,500 students), which is largely working class and a primary relocation area for people from New York City. Thirty-nine percent of the students are Latino, sixteen percent are African American, and the balance are white. The Latino population has been growing rapidly, and the character of this population has also changed. Ten years ago, most Latino children in Brentwood came from Puerto Rican families, but because of the volatile political situation in Latin America, there has been an increase in the number of immigrants from the Dominican Republic, Central America, and Colombia, such that Puerto Ricans no longer constitute a Latino majority. Many of the new students are illegal aliens. Some children from Central America have never been to school and need special intensive classes in English and basic skills. Some of the new immigrants live in incredibly crowded conditions—five to six persons in a room—and may share a bathroom and kitchen with four or five other families of the same size in a small development house. Within the district there is a high rate of child abuse, drug use, illiteracy, and poverty. If unusual problems unexpectedly occur, the parents are reluctant to seek help, due to their precarious legal status. The schools consequently have become the only public agency capable of assisting families to resolve chronic problems, even though they are dreadfully understaffed.

Brentwood has a limited tax base, because there is no industry of any significance within the district, resulting in a continuous fiscal crisis. The student–staff ratio of 15–1 is among the highest on Long Island, and the per-pupil expenditure of $7,709 is among the lowest. Forty-four and one-half percent of the students receive free or reduced-rate lunches, which is the fourth highest figure on Long Island.

The Partnership

The Stony Brook Partnership began working in Brentwood at a critical point during which outside funds were drying up and several budget defeats had created particularly austere conditions for the district. Fortunately, the partnership was able to respond flexibly to the changing needs of the district. Early in the partnership it became clear that most chronic learning problems begin earlier than junior high school and that it was necessary to begin intervention at the elementary school level. Since the program was originally funded for junior high and high school students, permission was needed to change focus. The school asked the university for elementary school tutors and social work interns; permission to amend the action plan was readily granted by the funding agency. Subsequently, several interesting and beneficial components were added that have been in successful operation for some years. Social work interns in four of the elementary schools extended services to children and families and began to develop family histories and treatment plans for the participants.

In 1989, when the project began, two interns, both of whom are now licensed social workers, developed a program for those children prenatally exposed to drugs and alcohol who were not functioning at age level, some with fetal alcohol syndrome, and others who had been exposed to crack cocaine. Special classes and techniques were developed to help the children be fully included, with a full commitment from the school to provide resources for the program, despite a desperately tight budget year.

It has become evident that a child born to a mother who uses crack often has physical and emotional disabilities that may never be completely compensated for. Children prenatally exposed to crack are beginning to enter the schools and pose serious problems that the system seems unable to handle. It seems possible, however, that early intervention may help make these children functional by the time they reach elementary school. It is also clear that these programs must begin as early as possible and that the parents must be an integral part of the process, because they too usually need extensive direct services, including attempts at rehabilitation. The social workers identified, and developed family histories of, many of these children. Alternate classroom environments were established, as well as an inventory of needs for children and parents.

The Brentwood schools also asked for help in providing bilingual tutors for newly arrived immigrants. The university was able to provide at least 40 hours of such tutoring per week, and during one year of our program at least 20 such students were included in the high school. All 20 of these students were from the Caribbean or from Central or South America, which tends to support the thesis that immigrant minorities sometimes perform better academically and are more highly motivated than "caste-like" native minorities, groups who are stigmatized because of generations of systematic discrimination and who sometimes appear to repeat cycles of poverty and low self-esteem (Ogbu, 1978).

The school district also asked for help with paraprofessional training, and the university conducted more than a dozen such training sessions, focusing on the needs of students at risk and on how community paraprofessionals can be of practical help in identifying certain kinds of problems, including child abuse. At these sessions, during informal discussion, paraprofessionals were encouraged to continue their education and the university staff made appointments for them with admissions officers. As a consequence, several paraprofessionals graduated from degree-granting programs at local colleges.

Finally, the university sponsored cultural events in Brentwood that enriched the students and community. Two all-day jazz workshops, provided by the organization International Art of Jazz, were attended by nearly all students in the junior and senior high schools. There was also a day-long series of workshops with two authors of books for children and adolescents that was attended by more than 200 elementary and junior high school students. The writers, Pat Cummings and Nicholasa Mohr, who wrote about the Black and Puerto Rican experiences in America, made a deep impression on the students and were a strong and positive motivation for them to remain in school.

EFFECTS OF THE PARTNERSHIP

The university's relationship with the Brentwood schools was positive, mutually beneficial, and like many close relationships, very aggravating (on both sides). It began with mutual need and mutual distrust, but with clear agreement that decisions had to be shared; we also agreed that the tutors and interns were to be screened and to receive orientation by Brentwood personnel before they could start working. The school's overprotective posture initially seemed rhetorical and designed to impress the university, but these perceptions were incorrect. The concern for the young people in the district turned out to be consistent and genuine, unlike other districts, according to reports of colleagues from other areas of Long Island. Although the question of control was always an issue, it was possible to negotiate with Brentwood, because neither party was inflexible. In fact, contact with the Brentwood administration changed the stereotype subscribed to in other districts, in which educational and administrative burnout are considered facts of life. In most Suffolk County districts, superintendents and other senior administrators have tenure of 5 years or less. Many retire at 55, very few beyond 60. The pressures and tensions generated by school boards, parent organizations, and the unions frequently make administration positions untenable. Experienced teachers, too, spurred on by retirement incentives, are leaving schools in unprecedented numbers (Farber, 1991). The SSPP program changed the university, the school, the perception of the university, and the participants, especially those at Stony Brook.

The experience of the university in the schools helped to change attitudes toward both the schools and the way teachers are prepared. In the 4 years of our program, field-based experiences early in the teacher education sequence became an integral part of teacher preparation. Students preparing for teacher certification must now spend time observing classes, as well as tutoring and microteaching in schools, before they can begin their student teaching. They are urged to work in schools that have higher than average concentrations of students at risk. In this the Brentwood schools were especially cooperative, even though the short-term presence of undergraduates could be somewhat disruptive.

It was clear that prospective teachers needed a realistic picture of the schools and better preparation for what they were likely to meet in the classroom (this is discussed in further detail by Allison Alden in Chapter 12 of this volume). Even in the few years of our program, the ambience of many schools changed visibly, even in those considered "good" schools. Scare tactics or "war stories" were entirely out of place, in teacher preparation programs, though it was reported that some professors still liked to tell horror stories about inner-city schools that had become more exaggerated and lurid with the passage of time.

The initial observation of classes is followed by a tutoring assignment, an effective means of easing undergraduates into the rhythm of the school system. Training is necessary, however, before they begin, and anecdotal contact sheets should be completed after tutorial sessions. Although it is a time-consuming task, it is important that the contact sheets be reviewed, and that there be random on-site visits to monitor the tutors. There should also be an adequate reward system. Two viable possibilities are to pay the tutors, or, if credit is to be granted, require the students to attend weekly seminars, write reports, and become conversant with current literature in their content area. Either system ensures quality control by program managers.

It is better when tutors are recruited in their sophomore or early in their junior year, even if they are not in the teacher preparation program. Successful tutors are likely candidates for the teacher preparation program because they have a fairly clear idea of what is involved in teaching, and have probably taken enough courses in a content area to have a solid academic background. The good tutors also help recruit others to keep the tutor/teacher-preparation pipeline active.

Tutors in our program also took creative initiatives with students, orchestrating individual or group visits to the campus, which reduce the awe many first-generation students have of the university (see Chap. 7, this volume). When the younger student "shadows" a university student during a typical day on campus, he or she becomes aware for the first time that college is a possibility, and more fun than hanging out aimlessly in the neighborhood. During our program, several students who never considered college as even a remote possibility entered undergraduate programs.

The tutorial experience also changed the placement of student teachers. Before our program, student teaching was done in districts that were immediately contiguous to the university, fairly standard, overwhelmingly white, and largely middle class. The main challenge in such settings was to break the aggressive apathy that characterized some of the students who had been overindulged by their affluent parents. Our program, however, engendered increased interest in learning how to teach students at risk. In the last 3 years of the partnership, 30 student teachers were placed in schools with critical masses of students at risk of dropping out, including one in a district that had not had a student teacher in more than 10 years.

The curriculum, too, was directly and indirectly changed. In 1988 a new graduate course especially designed for teachers entitled "Teaching the At-Risk Student" was introduced. More than 100 local teachers took the course, which, according to evaluations, changed the way they taught such students. One spinoff from the course was that the material, reworked for the undergraduate level, was integrated into the teacher-preparation program. The course drew on the resources of the university and the community. Individual lectures were given by experts in the field and each class focused on topics such as "child abuse," "the criminal justice system," "special needs of African American and Latino students," and "teaching reading, science, or math to the student placed at risk." This course generated interest in the school districts and the teacher centers, which incorporated components from it into their inservice courses. Presenters of topics in the course were also called on as resources during teacher- or district-conference days.

CONCLUDING COMMENTS

Suburban school personnel now experience many problems that used to be associated with the inner city and are beginning to realize that they must take positive steps to face these problems and to educate those students who might have been overlooked in the past. Some district personnel are unwilling to admit either that there are problems or that they may not be competent to deal with them. They believe that joint programs with outside agencies, including the university, will weaken their control and show their dirty laundry to the general public. However, universities have a tendency to look down on secondary schools and to propose solutions that sound brilliant in theory, but simply do not work in practice because university personnel have not been in the trenches on a regular basis and lack the degree of realism and wisdom that comes with actually having to design workable programs for students with significant social and academic difficulties.

Education can be made more effective through daring and flexible partnerships and coalitions whose members are willing to take risks by deviating from the initial framework of programs. New programs, even if they are conceived with care and precision, often change course over time. The most permanent and positive effects of a program may be those that were never imagined at the time requests for proposals and guidelines were drawn up, and this is why flexible partnerships are so important and can help agencies plan common strategies to address one of the most serious crises affecting the United States today.

11

School-Centered
Teacher Education
School Improvement
Through Staff Development

NORMAN P. SHAPIRO

Most of the state funds for City College's SSPP program were spent on providing supplemental services, including a "Mini-College," a series of enrichment courses offered once a week on our campus (see Chap. 8, this volume). Yet it was our belief that college and university programs had to do more than provide direct services to students, as the benefits of such services would likely be undone when students returned to dysfunctional high schools. While colleges in general, and schools of education in particular, might be able to provide useful services to students at risk (e.g., tutoring, mentoring, social services, and other forms of academic and cultural enrichment) their real work needs to be focused on helping to make schools better.

To the project's credit, SSPP guidelines permitted support not only for direct services for students but also for teacher education and curriculum development. So with funding from SSPP, the Metropolitan Life Foundation, and later the Aaron Diamond Foundation, we were able to undertake a program that sought to improve the high school from which our Mini-College students came. Some of our initial assumptions were that even the most difficult schools could be made better; that teachers and other school staff had to be involved in the improvement process; and that what was needed was a way to combine teacher education and school improvement. Such a synthesis is what is meant by the term *school-centered teacher education.*

THE PROBLEM

In the last two decades, a number of reports have pointed out the major shortcomings of the American education system and have urged that steps be taken to halt the decline in quality. On average, American students do far less well on tests in nearly all academic subject areas than their counterparts in other industrialized nations. The problem is magnified in the inner cities of this country, where much-greater numbers of students fail to complete high school and many more are considered at risk of dropping out. Many educators feel that radical steps must be taken and have called for a fundamental restructuring of schools and a reform of the education system.

Teacher education in America is seen as one of many possible causes for the failure of the public schools. As such, it too is under intense scrutiny and attack. Not only have reports pointed out the inadequacies of institutions that prepare teachers, higher education is faulted for playing only a peripheral role in the movement to improve and restructure schools. University courses for teachers are almost always offered on campus and almost always designed solely by university faculty. As a result, courses are not only physically remote from teachers' classrooms, but psychologically remote from what future teachers come to need in the schools. While ample theory may be provided, too often the opportunity to link theory with practice is not. While simulated problems are often solved, real problems are not. Teacher educators exhibit a concern for training teachers, but little or no concern for the schools into which those teachers are sent. Professors may sometimes talk to teachers about possible solutions to their problems, but seldom do they themselves venture into schools to actually work with teachers to solve them.

The high school that was sending their students at highest risk to our Mini-College—I will call it Uptown High—seemed to be the most likely candidate for our attention. Uptown High is a very large, comprehensive high school located in one of many economically disadvantaged neighborhoods in New York City. The school was cited by New York State as among the most poorly performing in the state based on the number of students who drop out, the average daily attendance, and achievement on state competency tests. Eighty percent of its more than 3,500 students are non–English-speaking immigrants and many are recent arrivals. The school is overcrowded and, as a zoned neighborhood school, it is a school of last resort for students who are not accepted into more choice institutions. While more than 3,000 students attend Uptown High, only about

300 graduate each year. Poor academic skills and low achievement among students on entry as well as on exit complete the picture of this largely dysfunctional high school.

Uptown High runs like most other traditional high schools in this country. The factory model is well entrenched, and students shuffle from one classroom and discipline to another every 40 minutes. The central board of education's initiative to divide the school into houses so as to create smaller, less anonymous, and more caring communities was complied with, like so many other directives from above, in name only. No clear vision or sense of mission existed in the school, and rather than providing support for meaningful teaching and learning, the structure supported little more than a system that simply operated smoothly.

SCHOOL-CENTERED TEACHER EDUCATION: ELEMENTS OF THE NEW MODEL

School-centered teacher education is a way in which schools of education can work to improve and transform schools. We believe that while existing university-based courses often have little impact on schools, school-centered courses can foster school change. The elements of the school-centered model are presented below.

Creating an Advisory Committee

The notion of collaboration was essential to the design of our program. We had no intention of going into a school and unilaterally deciding which courses were needed and which would be offered. Collaboration would be accomplished, in part, through the creation of an advisory committee comprising the principal and other administrators and teachers. The advisory committee would help identify school needs as well as courses that might best address those needs and contribute to school improvement. The committee also served as the focal point for our work at Uptown High, helped advertise the program, and recruited teachers for courses.

Our initial assumption was that teachers and administrators would have a handle on the school's problems and needs and would be able to identify (with our help) the skills, knowledge, and abilities teachers and other staff needed in order to improve the school. This assumption proved to be questionable as the program progressed and we came to more clearly understand how difficult it is for teachers to imagine possibilities other than those that already exist in their schools. From a political perspective, however, our work in the school depended upon the establishment of a truly collaborative and collegial relationship with school personnel, which the advisory committee enabled us to achieve.

Designing New Courses

Rather than offer courses that were part of existing degree programs at the university, we made the commitment to create new courses. These new courses were identified and designed, with titles, descriptions, and content that were mutually agreed upon and suitable for the particular needs of Uptown High. Fortunately, City College's School of Education had a mechanism for easily creating experimental courses without completing the rather formidable task of gaining the approval of various faculty curriculum committees. Experimental courses could be offered, with the approval of the department chair, for 3 years, no questions asked. After that time, a course would have to be "regularized" and the necessary faculty committee approvals obtained. Had such a process not been in place, it would have taken at least a year from the time the school advisory committee planned a course to the time that the course could be offered in the school, a lag that would surely have stifled the program.

It is important to realize that in the early stages of the project we were not attempting to create a new degree program. Instead, we were creating individual courses to solve specific classroom or school problems or to meet specific classroom or school needs. In New York City, as in other school districts throughout the country, teachers receive pay increases for coursework they complete. This coursework does not need to be tied to a particular graduate degree program. While our approach had the advantage of freeing us to design specific courses to meet specific needs as they arose, it had the distinct disadvantage of failing to provide a coherent educational experience for the teacher who decided to take a number of our courses.

Situating the Program at Uptown High

Because courses were open only to staff of Uptown High, and because we felt that it was important to integrate course content with the realities of the school, we decided to offer courses on site at the school, rather than at the university. The convenience of courses offered at Uptown High ensured greater teacher participation. Because all of the teachers taking each course were part of the same school community, they shared common referents and were in a better position to discuss specific strategies to improve their classrooms and the school.

An additional advantage of situating the program at the high school was that college faculty could more easily work with teachers in their classrooms during the school day. Unfortunately, this happened less than we would have wished. Many college faculty were not available during the school day, and our budgets simply did not allow for the additional time.

Offering the courses on site was not the only incentive for teachers to participate; so too was the fact that the program sought the solution to problems teachers might be having in their classrooms and was aimed at trying to find ways of creating a better school. A more-tangible incentive was provided in the form of tuition waivers, thanks to a university provision that permitted grant-supported courses to be offered for free. We believe that tuition-free courses are most appropriate for a program such as this, since, much like inservice programs offered by school districts, the goal of school-centered courses is to improve the school. Another advantage of such courses is that, unlike typical inservice training, which is too often a short-term, hit-or-miss operation, college courses provide the opportunity for more in-depth work over a longer period of time.

Modeling Pedagogy

Our initial approach was rooted in the assumption that the solutions to problems at the high school would be complex and difficult to formulate, that they were not simply "out there," waiting to be transmitted to receptive teachers, but instead, would need to be constructed, to a great extent, by the teachers themselves. We also believed that learning is enhanced when teachers are actively engaged in using knowledge for the purpose of transforming their own classrooms or school. We wanted teachers to engage in inquiry, develop recommendations for change, and actually implement such changes, wherever possible. Having teachers collaborate in the process of identifying needs, developing courses, and making changes in their classrooms and schools has an enormous capacity for empowering teachers and modeling democratic schooling.

Rather than teaching by telling or lecturing, college instructors would utilize small collaborative learning groups that would set their own agendas and ask and answer their own questions. When necessary, instructors and participants would negotiate course content in order to determine the best way of achieving course goals.

School-centered teacher education implies not only that teachers collaborate in the design of courses and that these courses are offered at the school rather than at the university, but also that the goal of such courses is to examine and better understand the problems that a particular school is having and find and implement feasible solutions. University courses often lean more toward reflection than action; we attempted to redress this imbalance through what we call the *product/action approach*. These product and action imperatives were the driving force behind our program. Not only would teachers study the problem and possible solutions, they would implement solutions through the products they created and/ or the actions they took. Through the emphasis on meaningful course outcomes, "praxis," the balance between reflection and action (Freire, 1971), and between theory and practice, is achieved.

THE PROGRAM IN PRACTICE

Entry: Gaining Trust and Acceptance

The first 2 months of our program were spent meeting with our advisory committee and with administrators, sitting in on classes, and informally talking to teachers in the halls, lounges, and cafeteria about their needs and problems. We decided that a more extensive needs analysis was in order and that the process could be furthered by a first course offering entitled "Directions for Uptown High School." This was the only course we offered in the first semester of our program. The Directions course gave teachers an opportunity to critically examine their school and identify some of its most pressing problems. They also read some of the reform literature and developed what we referred to as informed recommendations for school change.

Working with teachers in this course helped us think through the key issues and develop some sense of where we thought the school should be going. Informed by the work teachers did in the course, we developed some 32 separate recommendations for school improvement. These recommendations proved enormously important in helping to guide our thinking about directions for school change. They also set the stage for some of the courses that would follow in later semesters.

Teachers were very positive in their evaluations of the Directions course. The inquiry-based, cooperative learning approach gave them the opportunity to engage in dialogue with their colleagues, something they felt was particularly practical and relevant. One course participant noted, "I don't believe I ever took a course that was really not all lecture." Another said, "The course really came from the class. We chose specific problems and dealt with them. No other course I attended has done this." More important perhaps, was the trust and credibility that we gained as a result of this first course. Teachers felt that their needs would be responded to in ways that were respectful of their knowledge and experience and that the college was in the school in a truly supportive capacity.

The Ongoing Program

Over the next 4 years, the school-centered teacher education program typically sponsored as many as five courses each semester. Courses dealt primarily with efforts to improve teaching and learning in the classroom, or with ways of effecting overall school change. Courses in these areas included:

Alternative Approaches to Teaching and Learning
Improving High School Teaching
Improving Curriculum and Instruction in English
Educational Theory and Practice: Framing a Critical Strategy
Creating a Caring Community at Uptown HS
Alternate Roles for Teachers in a Restructured School
Extending School, Parent, and Community Linkages
School Restructuring
Uptown High School in the 20th Century
Grants Writing for School Development
Models for Restructuring the Secondary School
Conversational Spanish

One major problem with the course offerings was the fact that, with the exception of those offered by the English department, virtually no other courses were devoted to improving curriculum and instruction in a specific academic area. Department supervisors resisted much of what we were trying to do and felt that our approach was far too progressive, and while they did not discourage their teachers' participation in the program, they did not encourage it either.

Program Impact

Determining the effect of school-centered teacher education is a complex task. Even with sufficient resources to conduct extensive evaluation, which we did not possess, accurately measuring the impact of the program would have been difficult. We did collect course ratings and anecdotal data from teachers who took our courses on a routine basis. We also conducted focus-group sessions with teachers who took the greatest number of our courses. Our continuous presence in the school helped to give us some idea of the major changes that came about as a result of our courses.

Attracting Participants   After nine semesters at the high school, it is safe to say that the program was successful in attracting participating staff. Over 4½ years, more than two-thirds of the staff took one or more courses. Many courses had waiting lists. While we limited staff to two courses per term, some teachers managed to complete as many as eight or nine courses all together. Most often, courses were taken by less-senior personnel, who needed the credits for salary increases. While stipends were offered to senior staff who did not need additional credits, the amounts were not large enough to attract more than two or three such teachers per course.

Course Ratings   Evaluation data based on teacher perceptions of the courses were consistently positive. In the first full year, between 80%

and 90% of the participants rated their courses and instructors as "valuable" or "very valuable." In the second and third years (answering a modified questionnaire), between 77% and 92% rated their courses and instructors "above average" or "one of the best." Table 1 presents some of the specific ratings of school-centered courses obtained in the second and third years of our program.

It is interesting to note that while all of the characteristics listed in Table 1 were positively rated by more than three fourths of the respondents, the characteristic consistently rated most positively was "contribution to school development," which is the central goal of most school-centered courses.

Based on our sense of what was going on both in courses and in the school, one of the most important outcomes of this program was that it gave teachers an opportunity to interact with their colleagues in meaningful and important ways, and it also contributed to reducing the isolation teachers often feel in a school the size of Uptown High. Teachers had the opportunity to be learners once again and to feel that they were a part of a community working collaboratively for school improvement. Teachers' comments about the courses seemed to suggest that the program played a role in improving morale, though this effect was never directly measured.

Schoolwide Changes   Specific schoolwide changes were difficult to track. While we asked teachers to note changes in their end-of-term course evaluations, such changes were often instituted long after a course was completed. Some of the changes that had the most significant impact on the school are noted below:

As a result of the school-centered course, a group of teachers felt that it would be important to have a teacher center at the high school. They sought and found resources, space, and financial support for the

Table 1. Ratings of school-centered courses on specific characteristics in the second and third years (N = 300)

	Percentage of teachers who agree or strongly agree	
	1988/1989	1989/1990
My School-Centered Course:		
1. Contributed to school development	88	89
2. Strengthened relations with colleagues	83	88
3. Was based on the needs of teachers	85	82
4. Strengthened relations with students	79	85
5. Helped improve my teaching	84	77
6. Was based on needs of students	77	83

project. They also created a Professional Development Committee that, since its creation, has assumed responsibility for all staff development at the high school.

Teachers who participated in a School Restructuring course designed an alternative mini-school called Varsity House. The house was modeled after two Coalition schools, Central Park East Secondary School and University Heights High School. With City College's commitment to use SSPP funds to help support Varsity House, the school administration agreed to implement it. Varsity House became an alternative program for some 350 students and was intended as a model of a small, caring community of active and collaborative learners (see Chap. 8, this volume).

A school-centered course entitled Extending Parent and Community Linkages helped guide the creation of a number of programs and activities aimed at increasing parent involvement. Partly as a result of this course and of City College's support for closer links with parents, the school assembled the resources to create a Parent Center and developed an evening program for parents and other community members.

In addition to the changes noted above, examples of other, more modest changes at the school included: a hall monitoring plan; the elimination of distracting Walkman radios from the school, which contributed to improved discipline; the establishment of a mentoring program; and a community-service program for a group of students who served at a nearby home for older adults.

Classroom Changes   Changes at the classroom level were also difficult to track; again we had to rely on anecdotal data obtained during the last session of each course. While our hope was that courses would have an impact on the classroom long after they were over, we had no way of measuring such effects. Although we conducted no systematic observation of classrooms, anecdotal reports give an idea of what teachers were saying:

> It drew the students together and also drew me more to them. It made us compassionate toward one another.
> I created a Hispanic Unity Club and the students are enjoying the opportunity to deal with students from different cultures.
> When a teacher understands the problems of students, teaching goes better.
> Students are taking a more active part in the learning process because more of the material is being drawn from their experience.
> I pay more attention to students' needs and feelings than I used to—I even changed the way I teach and organize my class.
> In addition to complying with the curriculum, I have included thought provoking questions which tend to personalize the readings and create relevance. This has improved motivation in the students and in me.

I do not believe that this course will be able to impact the entire school over the short term. But, in time, I believe we will begin to see philosophical changes which will result in the way classes are structured and conducted.

The major change I have noted in my teaching is an increased awareness of the near uselessness of current teaching methods. I have a clearer perception of students needs and have begun to make small adjustments to better meet those needs.

I got insights into how else a curriculum could be designed and how else schools and classes should be run. I am more aware of how useless and futile certain things we teach in school are.

This [change] is difficult to predict, as the Board of Education is somewhat like a five-legged dinosaur with the metabolism of a dead turtle; however, success is occasionally noted, even when not mandated. Perhaps some change may occur on a collegial level and spread like wildfire in the snow to the administrative level, from whence it may even stir the petroglyphs of Court Street.

A thousand points of smiles will be spread throughout the school.

I didn't give a multiple choice final exam. The students had final projects to complete . . . I was amazed by some and disappointed by others. Overall, it was a very meaningful project for both of us.

More people are interested in [doing] something new. That may lead to more small changes, more awareness, more people trying to change what they don't like. The downfall of years of dealing with the "Board of Dead," however, is difficult to overcome.

People are now reflecting on what they do—even if they don't implement the ideas immediately or directly. That reflection is invaluable. Also a community is forming as a result of the City College courses, increasing contact between professionals and the spirit of collaboration among us.

One important dimension of any evaluation of school-centered teacher education is the measure of the ultimate impact courses for teachers have on high school students. While such an analysis was clearly beyond the scope of our resources, those attempting to replicate this program need to think carefully about how such effects might be studied. On the whole, it is probably safe to say that while there are more "points of light" in the school as a result of the program, the high school remains among the most poorly performing in the state.

WHAT WE LEARNED

The Directions course that began our school-centered graduate program was offered in 1986, and we offered our last school-centered course at Uptown High in 1992. The rather long time span gives us a wonderful opportunity to reflect on what we have learned and on how we are applying the knowledge we gained to our current work. Our ideas about the best way to design a school-centered teacher education program continue to evolve as we gain more experience with the model.

Despite teacher enthusiasm for the school-centered courses and the fact that there were a number of changes that were the direct result of the program, bringing change to the school through courses was far more difficult than we had anticipated. Long after our initial Directions course and many subsequent courses, Uptown High School remains one of the most poorly achieving schools in the city. We need to face the fact that the program did not succeed in transforming Uptown High and to try to identify some of the reasons why. While many of the program's strengths are described in the preceding section, an analysis of some of its weaknesses can provide us with some important lessons for our future work.

The Need for a Shared Vision

A major problem with the program at Uptown High was that the school never had a sense of where it wanted to go, let alone of how to get there. In 1994, four principals later, the school had yet to develop a sense of mission or purpose. When the program first started, both university and school faculties had views about some of the specific changes that were needed, but neither had a clear and coherent vision of what the school as a whole could or should look like. Through exposure to the ideas of Theodore Sizer and of the Coalition of Essential Schools, and through the example of two model Coalition schools in New York City (Central Park East Secondary School and University Heights High School), college faculty had developed a much clearer understanding of the kinds of changes that were needed in secondary schools. Yet despite any number of efforts on our part, the leadership of Uptown High School remained unconvinced and unmoved.

School-centered teacher education was initially conceived of as a process, a collaborative way of working with schools. Courses would be negotiated with school staff, in order to best meet school needs. School-centered teacher education was *not* a prescriptive set of courses that represented the particular philosophy of the particular faculty from the university who were coordinating the program. Paradoxically, the more solid our vision of schooling became and the more we pushed courses that would support that vision, the more we felt ourselves in conflict with our own model. We maintain the belief that school-centered teacher education can be a powerful tool in school reform when courses are designed and offered as a means toward this end. For this to happen, however, the school and college must have or must develop a shared vision, a philosophy and a structure that supports this mission. We still think that school-centered courses can help a school arrive at a coherent philosophy and mission and can support schoolwide reform efforts, once the school knows where it wants to go.

The Ephemeral Nature of School Change

All change is, perhaps, ephemeral. Hampel (1986), who has studied high schools since 1940, argues that few American institutions have managed to retain their routines as tenaciously as the secondary school. He also notes that the regimentation in high schools is too deeply rooted to give way and pointed out that progressive reform never dislodges traditional schooling. Many of the changes that were brought about by school-centered courses at Uptown High have been undone. The Parent Center was dissolved, not long after it was created, because of a change in school leadership, the press for space, and the fact that while the space for the Center was committed, no one thought through the programs that would be needed to sustain the Center. Varsity House, our alternative mini-school, no longer exists. After City College left the school, the school culture attacked the very elements that distinguished the house from the rest of the school. First, family group classes, intended to make the house more responsive to student problems and needs and to strengthen house cohesiveness, were dismantled. Then the notion that the house should have its own teachers was abandoned, returning it to the old factory model. Finally, a new principal simply did away with it. The Teacher Center, while still in existence as of 1994, also suffered from repeated attempts to cut back the school's contribution to the Center or diminish the importance of its work. Many of the other changes were equally ephemeral and as easily done away with.

Lasting change requires that the college and high school share a vision of their ultimate goal and work collaboratively to bring that vision about. School-centered teacher education cannot be just another program in the school, one of the many programs that the principal can boast about to colleagues. It must be at the very top of the school's agenda. We thought that it was possible to work at Uptown High without that level of commitment; in fact, we could not.

Supporting Course-Based Changes

Our school-centered courses often resulted in specific recommendations for changes, yet there was no adequate mechanism for bringing teachers' ideas to the school for implementation. We were encouraging teachers to utilize more active approaches in their classrooms and to experiment with cooperative learning, special projects, and inquiry-based instruction. Yet even these approaches were often blocked by supervisors who had their own, time-honored approaches to teaching. The fact that their approaches were not working seemed to be of minimal concern. Attempts at wholesale change in curriculum and/or teaching could and often did run up against the intransigence of the department chair. The work teachers do in school-centered courses needs to be supported and teachers have to feel that changes encouraged by a course will be supported by their superiors.

Designing a Comprehensive Program

While we pinned our hopes on changes arising from individual courses, the typical course, offered over a single semester, was often too short to accomplish all that we were expecting. It was perhaps too much to expect teachers to identify needed changes, examine existing literature, make informed recommendations, and implement changes, all in the same semester. Two possible solutions to this problem are: 1) holding courses over a longer period of time than a single semester, and 2) viewing teachers, and not courses, as the agents of change. While change might not arise from a single course, it might come from a single teacher who has taken a comprehensive set of courses over a sustained period of time.

The journey that we took over 8 years deeply affected our ideas about the process of school change and about the way school-centered teacher education can play a role in that process. While we still believe that school-centered teacher education can have an enormous impact on schools, that impact may depend on how the process is implemented. If its strengths can be maximized and its weaknesses minimized or avoided, it has the potential to help in improving and restructuring schools.

POSTSCRIPT: A NEW LOOK FOR
SCHOOL-CENTERED TEACHER EDUCATION

After a 3-year hiatus, a grant from the Danforth Foundation in 1992 provided us with the opportunity to redesign our school-centered teacher education program. While we think that individual school-centered courses that are designed to achieve specific and limited objectives and that have the strong support of the school in which they are offered can be successful, we decided to move in a different direction. We designed a new, school-centered master's degree program in School and Classroom Design and as of this writing are in the process of having the program approved by the university.

Working with an advisory committee, we spent a year developing the courses of the new graduate program and began to pilot test the program at a Manhattan middle school. We chose this particular school because although it appeared to be dysfunctional in many respects, its principal, who had been there for 16 years, expressed an interest in learning about school reform and school change. She indicated a willingness to participate in the process and a commitment to make it the central activity of the school for the next 2½ years. As of 1994, the principal had not disappointed us; she had attended all of the graduate courses offered, encouraged teachers and administrators to participate, and expected schoolwide changes to result from each course.

Half of the courses in the new graduate program deal primarily with classroom redesign and half deal with school redesign. Those that deal primarily with classroom redesign are:

Fostering Inquiry in the Classroom
Alternative Strategies for Teaching and Learning
Alternative Assessment
Curriculum Development for the Middle School I
Curriculum Development for the Middle School II

The courses that deal primarily with school redesign include:

Schools as Caring Communities
Strengthening Linkages Between School, Parents, and Community
Democratic Classrooms and School Governance
School-Based Research
School and Classroom Design

We worked with the principal and the school leadership to write a school development plan, and each of the graduate courses was created to provide direct support for that plan. While we expect specific changes to result from individual courses, the cohort of teachers who participate in the entire program will be well trained in school and classroom design in general. They will become the core group in the school supporting the reform process and will work to move the rest of the school along.

CONCLUDING COMMENTS

We agree with the report of the Holmes Group, who argue that "American students' performance will not improve much if the quality of teaching is not much improved. And teaching will not improve much without dramatic improvements in teacher education" (p. 3). Schools of education need to do more than pay lip service to the crisis in urban education. They must become more actively and directly involved in trying to make schools better. The only way for schools of education to start turning out better teachers is by becoming actively involved in trying to solve some of the most pressing problems that teachers face. We think that school-centered teacher education provides that opportunity, and that it can be as significant to the schools it serves as it is to the colleges from which it originates.

12

Preparing Teachers for Student Diversity
Educational Course Curriculum

ALLISON F. ALDEN

T he following comments represent the perspectives that often lead to a stalemate between educators at universities and those in public schools:

> The kind of relationship we have with the local university is generally one-sided; they use us to provide sites for pre-service teacher training and to conduct research that they never end up sharing with us.

> Schools don't appreciate the resources that are available to them here at the University. They ask us to speak at Superintendent's days and other one-shot workshops, but seem uninterested in long-term collaboration that could lead to meaningful change.

Through SSPP funding, the New York State Department of Education sought to expand the limited roles described above. The main goal in establishing strong relationships between schools and universities was the development of true partnerships. These alliances used the knowledge and skills of people in both constituencies in a team format to address the problem of school dropout (Driscoll & Nagel, 1992; Stowitschek & Smith, 1990; Williams, Gold, & Russell, 1993). Strong partnerships have served to improve the quality of programs offered in both local school districts and universities. Making use of university expertise, schools have critically reflected on current practices and made informed decisions about

---

The author would like to give special thanks to Karen Bromley, Ph.D., Professor of Education, Binghamton University, who helped design and teach the course described in this chapter. Her guidance and support are greatly appreciated.

change. Guided by feedback from practicing teachers, teacher-preparation programs have begun to close the reality gap between the content of university courses and the practices necessary to meet challenges in the classroom.

THE GENERAL MODEL

SSPP funding was provided in the Fall of 1986 to create the Binghamton School Partnership Project (BSPP), a joint effort by professionals in the fields of education and psychology at Binghamton University and the Binghamton City School District. The underlying premise of the project was that school failure and dropout are symptoms of complex educational problems that begin during the first years of school. BSPP focused on establishing active partnerships between teachers and parents of children in pre-kindergarten through 2nd grade who were having difficulty in school (Chapter 2 of this volume includes a full description of the BSPP partnership model). By fostering a home–school partnership early in a student's career, we hoped to reduce academic and behavior problems, improve attendance and involvement, and encourage overall positive attitudes about learning and education in general. In addition to the strategies suggested to parents by "School Partners" who made visits to students' homes, the design of the program and implementation process targeted school-based changes in structures, policies, and instructional practices.

While the home-visitation component of the model was well received by both teachers and parents, we discovered that establishing alliances with teachers and suggesting school-based intervention strategies were more difficult. A significant number of teachers reacted to our ideas with varying degrees of resistance and defensiveness. Some appeared embarrassed when they admitted that they had little knowledge about, and great difficulty understanding, the complex emotional challenges that many of their students face.

However, during the first 2 years of BSPP, we began to notice that similar questions came from a number of teachers in different buildings, and it became obvious that they were interested in investigating some issues in greater depth. These teachers were struggling to gather information, understand issues, and solve very complex problems independently. We decided that it would be beneficial to bring interested teachers together to discuss these topics in detail.

Since many of the teachers did not have a thorough understanding of the issues involved in the concept of being "at risk" and a workshop seemed insufficient to address so important and complex a topic, we felt that a course format was most appropriate. So we developed "Issues in Meeting the Needs of Students Placed At Risk," a 2-credit graduate education course focusing on the concerns and questions that teachers had raised. To provide an extra incentive, we supported teachers from participating Binghamton schools with a full-tuition scholarship. It was decided that the course would be further enriched by including a variety of perspectives, so enrollment was opened to other teachers and teachers-in-training.

Like Binghamton, nine other universities supporting SSPP programs developed graduate education courses to assist preservice and inservice teachers in learning about student diversity and the education of students placed at risk (Alden & Bromley, 1991). These courses were created to provide a knowledge base from which could be explored the phenomenon of students who are placed at risk for school failure, and later school dropout, as well as the educational practices, policies, and services that might best address the needs of the growing numbers of these students.

Clearly, there is a need to better understand the complexities involved in the phenomena of student diversity and at risk status so that parents, teachers, and administrators can more effectively provide educational environments and opportunities for students to succeed in learning. One strategy suggested by the American Association of Colleges for Teacher Education is to better prepare teachers to assess the strengths and weaknesses of individual learners (1992). Often, the limited backgrounds and inappropriate training of teachers result in feelings of inadequacy and frustration when they attempt to provide for the needs of students from diverse backgrounds. In particular, many educators lack the knowledge base from which understanding and effective curricular and instructional practices can grow.

Research conducted by Rieck (1992) confirms that although "recent and necessary attention is being paid to the 'at-risk' student, more than two thirds of our institutions are graduating teachers with less than complete preparation in this area" (p. 18). The creation of new university courses is one way to deliver this knowledge and foster attitudinal changes that can lead to success in school for a wide range of students and enhance the probability of their eventual graduation. Many university faculty members teaching existing courses do not incorporate issues of diversity as they pertain to students who are not succeeding in school, but do focus on multiculturalism. New and revised courses are required to meet teachers' needs, as well as to heighten the awareness of university faculty of the critical nature of the new composition of school populations. The 10 graduate education courses developed and offered through SSPP programs achieve these goals.

This chapter presents an overview of, and insights from, the course "Issues in Meeting the Needs of Students Placed at Risk," developed and taught at Binghamton University in conjunction with BSPP. Included in the discussion are the common topics and guidelines found in this and the other nine SSPP courses.

GUIDELINES FOR PLANNING

The guidelines below were followed while developing and teaching "Issues in Meeting the Needs of Students Placed at Risk."

Meeting Teachers' Needs

The course was developed to help meet the current and anticipated needs of teachers. Input was sought from local teachers, parents, administrators, and other educators about what they believed were the greatest problems concerning the education of students experiencing failure. Their suggestions helped identify relevant topics to include in the course and increased the likelihood that the course content met their needs. Not only did this allow participants to direct the course in a more meaningful way, it also encouraged the development of a cooperative relationship between the university and the local educational community as they followed a more focused problem-solving approach.

A Systemic Approach

In the course, we avoided suggesting that educators merely "help" certain students by inundating them with remediation and other support services, as this focuses on the deficits of students at risk and ignores the societal problems of disadvantage and unequal access to resources that are the ultimate causes of many student difficulties. Often, these larger societal problems result in a lack of knowledge, skills, and perceived aptitude on the student's and family's part, and these factors alone are addressed (the deficit model), while the district and the schools it comprises continue to operate in a way that perpetuates social injustice.

While services may be necessary to assist students who are at an academic disadvantage, equal attention should be given to responsibilities at both the building and district levels. We encouraged teachers and personnel at the educational institutions in which they worked to look into ways they could become more involved with and supportive of the communities and families they served, demonstrating increased understanding and flexibility. If, for example, it is felt that parents of students at risk tend not to participate in school, and if this is a real concern, rather than simply an excuse to give up on those students, the district can have a significant impact on the situation. District policies regarding open-house programs, parent visitations, and parent–teacher conferences, as well as parent involvement in educational decisions, can be examined to see if improvements can be made by increasing access and content in order to interest under-represented parents.

One guidance counselor enrolled in our course seemed to consistently defend practices and policies that she recognized and admitted were not effective. She reasoned that there were no real opportunities for change, so she and her colleagues were forced to operate within a system designed for failure. Only after a lengthy discussion of the district-wide change process, New York State's New Compact for Learning, and the NYS Department of Education's encouragement of district requests for educational waivers would she acknowledge that perhaps *real* change was a possibility in her district. Although she seemed anxious to share this with her colleagues, the prospect of eliminating their reasons for inaction seemed to cause some trepidation. While teachers can do much within their own classrooms to address the needs of a varied student body, in order to fully enable teachers, district priorities should reflect and support these needs as well.

Avoiding Labels

Teachers and school personnel were encouraged to avoid identifying individual students as being "at risk." Although an understanding of the factors that contribute to at-risk status is vital in any discussion of the topic, it seems imperative that students not be seen in that context alone, but rather as whole people who react to their environments. An identification process that focuses on the negative adaptive behaviors (skipping classes, drug use, aggressiveness, etc.) that students have developed in response to the challenges they face tends to blame the victim for his or her circumstances, while failing to recognize the more significant underlying problems that have led to and further compound the current situation. An elementary principal taking our course stated that although she was already acutely aware of the issues surrounding at-risk status, because of class discussions she examined the way she disciplined students sent to her office for disruptive behaviors. She realized that she was mentally grouping students with similar behaviors and carefully assigning equal punishments, rather than attempting to understand children as individuals and addressing their needs on a more personal level.

The class participants concluded that educators would be more effective if they understood that many negative student behaviors that cause them great concern are not inherent character flaws, but rather expressions of unfulfilled inner needs. When reflecting on strategies to use with students they were having difficulty reaching, teachers considered possible causes for the unacceptable behaviors. They then developed approaches aimed at their immediate cessation, but that would not further compound the suspected causes. They recognized that their ultimate goal was to help the students develop self-regulation skills, and so were thoughtful in their selection of short-term strategies.

If *all* students are fairly evaluated to identify their strengths as well as their weaknesses in a nonjudgmental way, it becomes easier to implement positive reinforcing strategies. The more realistic appraisal also helps children to feel accepted as worthwhile members of the class.

Local Factors

Local case studies were examined to provide immediate relevance. Regardless of which communities course participants come from, there are examples of children who are experiencing difficulties in school due to a number of severe, complex factors in their lives. Statistics and other supporting evidence were provided to substantiate the degree to which the success of local schools was being challenged by these factors. We also included several case studies of actual children and the details of their lives (anonymously, of course). Class members discussed these cases, in addition to some of their own, and talked about improvements that could be made at the classroom, building, and district levels. This process enabled teachers to comprehend the relevance of the issues and to practice reflecting on and developing strategies to address student needs. The issue papers that were required focused on the environments in which the teachers worked, their views, and how they could encourage change— making the entire topic more relevant.

One new teacher in the course verbalized her doubts that her small, white community included any students experiencing disadvantage. She was quickly informed by other class members that her community was well known for its rural poverty. She then seemed to gain new interest in the topic and began making attempts to get to know the children in her classroom better.

Diversity

The positive nature of diversity was emphasized in the course. A major goal was to help educators understand that societal and classroom diversity is a strength, rather than a problem. As Vivian Paley concludes in *White Teacher* (1979), "Homogeneity is fine in a bottle of milk, but in the classroom it diminishes the curiosity that ignites discovery" (p. 56). First, we attempted to help teachers develop a knowledge base and understanding of the varied backgrounds from which students come and how these differences can strengthen curricula, teaching, and learning. Second, we worked to help participants overcome any personal discomfort they felt about their lack of knowledge and understanding by discussing personal feelings often and in a comfortable, nonjudgmental environment. Often, teachers who were ill at ease with students from varied backgrounds perceived "different" as meaning "deviant," with an overwhelmingly negative connotation that prevented them from accepting children so described. A short emotional writing and read-aloud, followed by a discussion of the feelings and insights they evoked, was quite valuable in this regard (Ballard, no date). The mix of practicing teachers and teachers-in-training significantly added to the diversity within the class and often enriched the course discussions, demonstrating for teachers the unique contributions and perspectives of each participant.

Personal Engagement

Teachers were encouraged to engage personally with content. Selected readings, such as *White Teacher* (Paley, 1979), encouraged the taking of a different perspective and continual re-evaluation of classroom practices (see Alden & Bromley, 1991, for a bibliography of useful readings). Teachers engaged in discussions with each other regarding personal reactions and interpretations of readings and course content. Other methods, such as role playing, demonstrations, and simulations, were used to provide a number of opportunities for teachers to interact on a personal level. When confronted with the realities that many of these children face on a daily basis, some teachers were shocked, even horrified, but the insensitivity barrier was broken down as a result, and many teachers demonstrated greater empathy for children. A 17-year veteran teacher participating in our course showed little interest in class discussions until the topic of poverty surfaced. She then stated how surprised she was at the number of children from their schools who were described as having very difficult lives. She began to reassess her conclusions about her own class and decided that she had become numb to the pain of her students over the years. Before the course ended, she was actively making voluntary home visits to work with parents on providing positive educational supports at home.

In addition to leaving with tangible ideas for classroom methodology that supports learning, teachers acquired a better understanding of the importance of the affective environments they create. Discussions, simulations, and role playing demonstrated that teachers' knowledge and attitudes regarding students at risk had actually evolved on both the personal and intellectual levels—that personal biases, discriminatory beliefs, and invalid assumptions had been challenged.

Benefits for All Students

The course reinforced the concept that *all* students benefit from effective teaching. Another important goal of the course was to help educators acknowledge that fine educational practices for students at risk are, in fact, fine educational practices for *all* students. While many high-performing students succeed even with poor teaching, the achievement of students at risk will particularly suffer under those circumstances; in other words, at-risk learners reap the greatest benefits from overall good teaching. This concept entails a number of principles:

Educating *all* students effectively means employing a variety of instructional methods and taking all learning styles into consideration.

It implies using a discipline strategy that does not concentrate on punishments and humiliation, but uses a number of positive approaches to encourage the development of student self-regulation.

It involves providing all students with the support they need to succeed, even if levels of assistance appear unequal on the surface. (Medical interventions, by way of analogy, are not the same for everyone; only people who have severe heart problems have expensive open-heart surgery.)

It means relating to children as people with feelings by breaking down the insensitivity barrier.

It means refusing to ignore the sad realities in the lives of many children and their families by addressing relevant topics in class (child abuse, pregnancy, drug abuse, alcoholism, violence, etc.)—not simply preaching "shoulds" and "don'ts," but helping students to share how these things affect people, and in particular themselves.

It involves moving away from conformity-based practices and designing classrooms that encourage individual student growth.

It means accepting that teachers play a tremendously vital role in the lives of *all* students.

Field Experience

Many of the class participants were teaching while taking the course, so they could observe students, plan instruction, engage in guided practice, and discuss these experiences with colleagues in the course. For those who were not teaching in a classroom themselves, these discussions about classroom experiences and student reactions further enriched the course content.

COMMON COURSE TOPICS

Although there are countless meaningful topics that could be covered in a course about students at risk, the following themes seemed most significant and provided a basis for knowledgeable discussions. Undoubtedly, the course is further enriched as additional subjects are included, providing that depth is not sacrificed for breadth. Generally, the topics focused on the educational issues related to student diversity and students placed at risk.

Definitions of *At Risk*

Since almost everyone has a different definition of *at risk*, it was helpful to hear the meanings presented by course participants. Some teachers referred to the profile of "typical" students who are statistically most likely to drop out of high school. Others focused on those they knew who were already having difficulty functioning in school according to established standards. Several mentioned environmental factors that tend to put students at a disadvantage in school. All agreed that there are a number of areas in which students exhibit wide diversity that may partially account for the frustration and difficulty teachers have in meeting their needs: family structure, health, psychological status, race, economic situation, ethnicity, sexual orientation, physical characteristics, language, religion, learning style, and ability.

Two topics seemed to be of particular interest to teachers: 1) poverty and its impact on education and family life, and 2) the emotional turmoil students experience due to divorce in the family; death; victimization through emotional, sexual, or physical abuse; and depression.

Although it was difficult, we found it extremely useful to discuss the complex definitions of the term *at risk* and the factors that can result in a student's being labeled as such.

Classroom Strategies to Improve Instructional Effectiveness

Our general conclusion was that most methods that benefit students at risk also improve the performance of others in the school. Although remediation in reading, writing, and mathematics was commonly mentioned, few felt that these were effective enough to reduce the necessity of overall classroom instructional change.

Approaches to Engaging the Support of the Family

Most teachers realized that one key to working more effectively with students is to increase parents' involvement in the education of their children. Parents can act as true partners to help children succeed in and come to value education. There are many successful models for increasing parental knowledge and participation. Teachers seemed to be unaware of the benefits of utilizing local community resources and programs to increase parental involvement. They also seemed unaware that there is often great community interest in providing support for schools, parents, and children. Fortunately, community partnerships targeting home factors that affect student performance in school are becoming much more common across the country.

Exemplary Programs

It was very helpful to identify programs that had experienced successes in addressing the needs of students at risk, as this provided educators with some specific and tangible examples of the types of innovations that have been found to be effective. Teachers were cautioned, however, against adopting a program wholesale, or with only minor modifications, without considering the specific characteristics of their schools.

Current Research

Teachers were given a number of articles summarizing recent educational research on students experiencing difficulties in school. These different, and at times conflicting, perspectives stimulated thought-provoking discussions. It soon became obvious that this is a complex problem that does not have clear or concise solutions. This topic was useful in helping teachers to understand and discuss the importance of possible implications for future educational policies and practices.

Classroom Environments that Foster Learning

Although not specifically identified as separate topics, some concepts and ideas were infused throughout the course, such as: 1) student self-concept, 2) student motivation, 3) creation of a comfortable social and physical environment conducive to learning, 4) the necessity of positive school experiences in generating student success, 5) curriculum revisions and textbook selection to create a more realistic and unbiased reflection of society, and 6) the need for greater awareness and acceptance of diversity/multiculturalism. A number of more theoretical and philosophical topics were also presented to provide a thorough understanding of some of the larger issues: 1) evaluating educational program effectiveness, 2) the historical/theoretical perspectives on societal factors leading to disadvantage, 3) systemic change to influence the environmental factors that lead to school dropout, and 4) teacher empowerment and responsibility. The overall orientation of these topics was one of enabling the teacher to accommodate the learner.

COURSE EVALUATION

Each semester for the 3 years that this course was taught, it was always full, with a substantial waiting list. Inevitably, at its conclusion each semester, the majority of teachers remarked on their evaluations that the course should be expanded, offered more often, and made mandatory for graduating teachers. Teachers regularly commented that this course enabled them to apply many guiding principles and theories to the situations they actually dealt with in their classrooms, something that they had experienced little success with in the past. In fact, a number of teachers recommended that more time be spent on strategies and less on issues, even though this course was initially designed primarily to focus on issues.

The feedback collected from teachers reinforces my belief that there is a substantial need for *several* courses in teacher preparation programs addressing the topic of diversity, as it is such a broad topic. Although we were not able to accomplish this through BSPP, it became apparent that several courses, each with a different focus, should be offered—for example, an issues or theories class and an educational methods class. This enables teachers to understand the theoretical complexities of the topic, as well as gain insights into practical methods for immediate implementation. In developing a curriculum course on diversity, however, it is advisable to avoid the temptation to recommend a separate curriculum for students at risk if that means segregation, diluted course content, or lowered expectations.

Another common comment made by teachers on their course evaluations was that they were more committed than ever to confronting the problems they faced, while still recognizing the magnitude of the challenge. As one class participant explained:

> Each Wednesday, I was excited to come to class, yet I dreaded it!! The professional discussion was incredible and helpful. But the frustration level was horrible. I left class each night wondering why more people are not concerned (or don't voice their concerns) with our society's educational system. And I felt lost and very small and incapable of making a difference. Don't worry, though, I will *not give up or lose my idealistic views*!

Judging by the feedback received through evaluations, courses that better equip teachers for the realities of today's schools are greatly needed.

CONCLUDING COMMENTS

The issues relating to the education of students placed at risk are extremely complex. For many, it is much easier to label children and blame their difficulties on them or their families than to identify and address the actual *causes* of problems. This "blame the victim" mentality usually results in ineffective, short-term efforts to alleviate symptoms. Thus, many educators choose to apply pre-packaged educational programs that have been promoted as a cure-all for kids at risk, while paying little attention to the underlying risk factors that permeate some children's lives in both their home and school environments. Although educators have had a difficult time appreciating the nature of this most complex societal phenomenon, the development of effective intervention strategies begins with understanding.

Classroom teachers cannot be expected to overcome these tremendous obstacles on their own. Establishing a positive, supportive relationship with a student who is struggling is a good start, but by no means will this address societal problems that perpetuate and compound the problem. Those making budgetary decisions, voting on educational policies, and preparing educators and administrators for service need to re-evaluate their priorities concerning this issue. Only then will the necessary attention and financial support be focused on the development of effective solutions.

Districts have a responsibility to support the creation of flexible, responsive environments that best meet the needs of their students. With the commitment of school districts behind them, teachers are in a better position to face problems and overcome the extreme frustration that they may feel when struggling with these issues on their own.

There are many reasons for attempting to improve the school experience for youngsters. Some argue that it is good for America, since we will need these children in the work force in the near future; others say that if students drop out, they become a financial and social burden on society. But the most important reason is that everyone deserves a positive, rewarding experience at school; that we are obligated to promote a happy, fulfilling life for *all* children, including those with seemingly limited prospects or overwhelmingly difficult living circumstances.

There is a commonly held illusion about American education, attributed to Horace Mann, which holds that education in the United States serves as "the great equalizer." Some continue to believe this despite the fact that children are obviously sorted, channeled, tracked, promoted, and failed in ways that strongly correlate with socioeconomic levels. Schorr (1988) contends that

> The "golden age" in American education, with schools as the great leveler, may well have been a myth, compounded with successes heralded by history and ignoring failures lost in history. In fact, then as now, most pupils found it difficult to surmount class barriers, and schools tended more to reinforce social inequality than to facilitate escape from it. (p. 217)

According to Schorr (1988), we have the knowledge and capabilities to help children avoid "rotten outcomes" in their lives. As a society, we need to demonstrate our concern for the youth in this country by re-evaluating educational practices and policies, by implementing programs that have proven successful, and by validating and supporting those teachers who currently use effective practices.

Universities can take a leadership role in this effort by providing the kind of training and support required to address these issues. Offering quality graduate courses with an emphasis on diversity, as described in this chapter, to prospective teachers and future administrators is an excellent way to positively influence the futures of children placed at risk. Thanks to SSPP funding, universities and schools have demonstrated that, working together as partners, we can meet these great challenges with innovative and effective solutions.

What might the fictitious educator with whose comments I began this chapter say *after* working in a partnership with the university to address educational concerns? Probably something like this:

> Now that we are working together, I can see just how complicated these problems really are! But with different perspectives and support, I believe we may actually be able to deal with them. These people have access to information and resources that we would not otherwise have. Also, I am continually amazed at how much we have in common. I feel that we are a solid team and have hopes for expanding our partnership in the future!

Epilogue

Learning Together
Practical Lessons from School–University Partnerships

IAN M. EVANS,
NORMAN SHAPIRO,
MARVIN COHEN,
AND TERRY CICCHELLI

There is no simple prescription for the enhancement and restructuring of the educational system in a highly pluralistic society like our United States. We do not expect that you will have acquired a precise, practical set of guidelines for educational change after having read these chapters. Though we did roll up our sleeves to actually *do* something, we cannot pretend that we have absolute answers to the complex question of how best to help students stay in, and succeed in, school. But one of the clearest lessons from these chapters is that wisdom arises from action, or perhaps more accurately, from interaction— from the actual working partnerships between universities and schools.

It should be remembered that our original mandate from the state was relatively specific. Activities were simply decreed, as though solutions were already known and understood. Often, the proposed range of activities that the programs were to comprise was based on faddish notions that were some administrator's idea of what was needed: you must have mentoring, or tutoring, or summer programs. University faculty, for obvious reasons, are more used to relying on a set of abstract principles for generating recommendations. These conceptual foundations helped to shape projects in important ways, many of which are described in this volume. It is our belief that if you wish to emulate our efforts, what you need most is the partnership itself—the commitment to do something together according to a shared vision or plan. We hope that we have provided enough detail on conceptualizations, concerns, and feelings that you the reader can develop a model for your own multi-unit collaborative team.

It took the various SSPP programs some time to recognize that the influence arose from the partnership itself, and not from the specific activities. To be really successful, a program needs to focus on certain outcomes and goals but leave the precise means of achieving them open and ambiguous enough that a range of creative solutions can be developed. In SSPP, this was not achieved without some conflict. For instance, the state agency administering the program was very interested in documenting "success" according to the outcomes for specific numbers of students. Personnel in many of the programs, however, began to realize the critical importance of a plethora of systemic changes and resisted the rather constant pressure to provide direct services to individuals. Eventually, the state education department started to understand this need as well, and SSPP projects that were being criticized for not concentrating on individual students began to be recognized for the broader restructuring impact that they were having.

It is people who actually make changes, but a positive atmosphere is also essential. An illustration of this phenomenon came very early in SSPP, at the annual meeting of the programs. These meetings were originally suggested in the SUNY–Binghamton proposal, which had requested funds to host such an event that then became a regular feature of SSPP. At the meetings, the element that was found to be least useful was when the different programs carried out show-and-tell presentations, simply describing what they were doing and boasting about their successes. The really important discussions concerned issues—the conceptual themes discussed in this volume.

The role of the agency staff turned out to be critical to the process of interchange, collaboration, and sharing of ideas and insights. The state education department had assigned a number of employees to serve as SSPP liaison staff, acting as project officers, making site visits, helping with problems, and generally administering the funds according to legislative mandates. These individuals had personal qualities that made interactions with them positive and encouraging, and all SSPP personnel will remember with affection the laughter, enthusiasm, and energy that characterized our group meetings. But more importantly, these administrators were able to allow control to remain in the hands of the project personnel themselves, resisting the temptation to micromanage programs instead of trusting participants to do the job. Thus, an ostensibly unitary program became much more like a group of thinkers pursuing issues that were important, spending money as wisely as we could, and trying to focus on the task of serving schools, students, and communities, rather than serving as bureaucratic extensions of the state agency. It is an accepted fact that effective programs need to comply with mandates and guidelines, but they must also have the freedom to follow new ideas, so that they may grow and change and respond to new needs.

JUDGING EFFECTIVENESS

We all accept that the bottom line in judging the effectiveness of any of the programs described in this volume must be the hard data on the numbers of students who would have otherwise dropped out, but instead remained in successful educational programs. Thinking about the futures of these young people and the difference that adequate schooling makes reveals the tremendous responsibility that our program had. Although the administrative agency attempted valiantly to maintain records of the students served and their educational outcomes, the reality is that we need more solid data on the results of our efforts. These projects were not designed as formal research studies, and only a very limited part of the budget was earmarked for the task of evaluation.

Many of the authors of this volume have been genuinely honest in their chapters about the limitations and difficulties of their projects. Obviously, none of the programs were failures. Many of the students who participated in SSPP liked the programs and appeared to benefit from them in ways not always measurable. There is no question that our efforts saved some students: students who have since completed high school and gone on to postsecondary education, who were completely turned around as a result of our work. Individual successes with such students justify the time, effort, and resources spent on SSPP. From the outset, we all shared a sense of optimism and enthusiasm about our ability to succeed with those students at greatest risk. We soon learned that the work would be more difficult, and the problem far more resistant to simple solutions than we initially thought. And yet there *were* many changes, and these must be recognized.

Many of the partnerships described continue to the time of this writing (though not necessarily at the same schools), despite the end of the original source of funding. This is a remarkable outcome, and some would see it as an example of seed monies successfully yielding long-term growth. And yet it should be noted that the termination of this funding was incredibly short-sighted. As repeatedly demonstrated in the foregoing chapters, the only way we can really accomplish our goals is by entering into serious, long-term partnerships with schools, particularly the schools that need our support the most, and this requires the kind of supportive funding originally represented by the Stay-in-School initiative. With only a very small outlay of state funds, a very vibrant and expanding product emerged that depended on these funds, and yet was able to bring together many elements that did not: esprit de corps among the professionals and educators who participated in the projects, changes in university faculty competencies and sensitivities, and contributions from program alumni and other community sources are but a few examples. When one considers the start-up costs of these projects, the anxiety of the staff and students over uncertain funding from year to year, and finally the cost of dismantling highly trained teams of professionals who were really bridging the gap between public schools and postsecondary education in ways that many policy makers are continuously calling for, it seems especially regrettable that funding should have been withdrawn.

CHANGING PERCEPTIONS IN THE UNIVERSITY

A recurring theme in this volume has been the issue of the limitations of direct services, particularly those provided by universities. For many of us, the frustration of trying successive interventions with little effect led us to reexamine our original assumptions. For example, the assumption that a college student serving as a tutor or mentor will help improve students' attendance, achievement, and ultimately their likelihood of graduation from school seems, in retrospect, somewhat naive. While it is clearly possible for a tutor or mentor to have a significant influence on individual students, more often than not this does not occur. Similarly, while it is possible for a campus enrichment program to inspire a particular student, it will typically not be successful with all students.

The programs we provided were sometimes not powerful enough relative to the needs of our students and the problems that they faced. The good work a tutor can do may help for a while, but it won't solve every problem. And the effects of our various interventions can so easily be undone by very powerful forces—those forces responsible for having put students at risk in the first place. When students leave their tutors or on-campus enrichment programs, they return to schools, families, and communities that do not always serve them well. Schools can be very effective "collectors of programs"; buildings that may still be failing children can produce a long list of impressive-sounding procedures that are part of the school and serve certain groups of children, but do not necessarily contribute to making the school as a whole a better place for children. As we came to understand these facts, we began to work in very different ways.

Universities seem ill-equipped to be the providers of direct services, and as the years went by we shifted our focus to teachers, schools, and families. We began to look for more systemic solutions. Teacher retraining, curriculum development, and school redesign grew critically important as more of the project personnel became convinced that the solution required intervention on a broader scale. However, having to initially provide direct services did have a very salutary effect on most of us. We learned firsthand what students "at risk" were really like and how difficult it was to serve them. We learned how rewarding, and at the same time how frustrating, the task can be. By our willingness to serve some of the students most at risk and by sharing the schools' struggle to educate these young people, we strengthened our credibility with the education system. As a result, real and lasting partnerships were formed.

The partnership experience was both invigorating and humbling. It provided college and university personnel with an unusual window into the operation of schools. We feel that we have benefitted enormously from seeing the problems firsthand. Understanding the students, truly knowing the kids who are the focus of concern, inspired a new sense of confidence among university faculty and graduate students and a renewed realization that much can be accomplished by motivated, committed individuals.

LEARNING ABOUT SCHOOLS

The chapters in this volume do not pull any punches concerning experiences with schools and the frustrations caused by the partnerships. Should one really expect anything different? But there is an equally clear message from our contributors that the public schools are richly endowed with many excellent and caring people who are ready to work hard and to learn. The universities are in an ideal position to provide opportunities for professional development among such teachers. But university faculty often had to discover how to approach teachers as colleagues and equals, and both groups had to be interested in learning and willing to change based on the needs of children. We had to learn to adapt to the needs and circumstances of the individual school sites—without compromising what we understand to be beneficial to children. The university became the source of new information for what has traditionally been a closed public education system; only the teachers themselves could determine the best ways to use this information.

All this while, the universities learned about what works best in urban and rural schools. We learned much about the structural obstacles to reform. We discovered that there is a great deal of instability in school administration, that it takes time to do such a large job, and that there are various myths in education that stand in the way of action. Systemic school reform does not require a single specific program or charismatic leader. Instead, it requires a constellation of programs that affect all levels of the schooling process and include teachers, parents, administrators, and school boards. All must be involved, and all must be committed to participating in the improvement of children's school experiences, to re-thinking and redefining what school is for the student. The process of teachers learning together can then become the model for the way the students interact with one another.

The challenge for university personnel remains to discover how best to collaborate with schools without assuming that we have all the an-swers, or giving the impression that we do. As we have explained, we do not, in fact, have all the answers. If we did, it would be nothing short of immoral for us to fail to go in and fix the schools—and even university faculty are not ready to assume *that* responsibility. We must, therefore, learn to collaborate in a way that allows school personnel to draw on the information available in the universities and then create their own solu-tions to their problems. Then, perhaps, we at the universities will be smart enough and humble enough to invent and refine theories that are easily translated into practice. We will all learn, and the children will be the biggest winners.

CLOSING THOUGHTS

We will not attempt to list a final set of recommendations. Rather, in clos-ing, we will pose certain questions into which SSPP provided some insights.

How should schools and universities collaborate to make school a better place for children? The first step is to acknowledge that the purpose of school is to provide an environment in which all children can learn. In order for this to occur, schools will probably also have to be places where adults—the professional and nonprofessional staff—are treated respect-fully and given the opportunity to learn and grow. It is only through this process that expectations can be modeled that will affect behavior in the classroom.

Schools will therefore have to provide opportunities for other mem-bers of the educational community, including university personnel, to interact with the staff. This will require changes in programming and shared discussion about what role each can play. Though the initial bur-den will appear to fall on the school as the "host," there will also be sig-nificant changes necessary among the university faculty. Timetables, def-inition of student teaching assignments, delineation of valid coursework, and faculty schedules will all need to be revised. Both groups will have to redefine their beliefs about what is possible, and both will have to develop new shared meanings for words and work that have long been defined by each in their own context and that they have often used to criticize the other.

What does the successful school look like? What do students and teachers do in the successful school? How do families served by such a school interact with the educational community and each other? What do they learn, and how? Once these questions have been answered, the new issue becomes: is the process for reaching this goal the same for every school, or are successful schools defined by the communities they serve, each of which has its own agenda?

How do we encourage ongoing professional growth for all those involved in the education of children? It seems important for children to be exposed to a model of "life-long learning," and we educators can set such an example. For too long, schools have operated as closed information systems, without the benefit of new knowledge available in universities and other schools. For schools to serve students as they should, there needs to be manageable access to this information, so that the professionals in the school can frame new programs that achieve the community's goals, whatever these may be. So too, universities must have knowledge of the experiences of experts in the educational system, so that we can prepare the next generation of teachers for the realities of schools, such that graduates will not have to sacrifice their idealism when they enter their invariably grueling first few years as teachers.

Perhaps the solution to the problems facing the public schools does not lie within the schools, nor with the universities, but rather, with the interaction of the two in a collegial way. This was the lesson we began to learn through SSPP.

References

Ainscow, M. (Ed.). (1991). *Effective schools for all*. London: David Fulton Publishers.

Alden, A.F., & Bromley, K. (1991). *Preparing teachers for student diversity: Graduate program curricula* (Technical Report #13). Binghamton, NY: Binghamton School Partnership Project.

Alden, A.F., Brown, B., & Chanecka, M. (1988). *Linking home and school to prevent dropout: An introduction to a home-visitor program in the early elementary grades* (Technical Report #3). Binghamton, NY: Binghamton School Partnership Project.

American Association of Colleges for Teacher Education. (1992). *The national education goals: The AACTE member response*. Washington, DC: AACTE Publications.

Armstrong, D.G., Henson, K.T., & Savage, T. (1993). *Education: An introduction* (4th ed.). New York: Macmillan.

Ashton, P.T., & Webb, R.B. (1986). *Making a difference: Teachers' sense of efficacy and student achievement*. New York: Longman.

Baecher, R.E., & Cicchelli, T. (1992, April). *One option for school restructuring: A school–university partnership*. Paper presented at the annual meeting of the American Educational Research Association, San Francisco.

Baldwin, B.A. (1990). Educating parents. *USAir magazine, 12*(9), 24–33.

Ballard, E.S. (no date). *Three letters from Teddy*. Unpublished story.

Beaudry, J., & Sanders, W. (1990, February). *Results of a program for "at-risk" high school students: The first year*. Paper presented at the annual meeting of the Eastern Educational Research Association, Clearwater, FL.

Beaudry, J., & Sanders, W. (1991, February). *Evaluation of Project LEARN*. Paper presented at the annual meeting of the Association of Teacher Educators, Washington, DC.

Berman, S. (1990). The Real Ropes course: The development of social consciousness. *ESR Journal: Educating for Social Responsibility, 1*, 1–18.

Berrueta-Clement, J., Schweinhart, L., Barnett, W., Epstein, A., & Weikart, D. (1984). *Changed lives: The effects of the Perry Preschool Program on youth through the age of 19*. Ypsilanti, MI: High/Scope Education Research Foundation.

Biber, B. (1973). *What is Bank Street?* (Convocation speech). Bank Street College, New York.

Biklen, D. (Producer). (1988). *Regular lives* [Video]. Washington, DC: State of the Art.

Blechman, E.A., Kotanchik, N.L., & Taylor, C.J. (1981). Families and school together: Early behavioral intervention with high risk children. *Behavior Therapy*, 12, 308–319.

Bossert, S.T. (1988). Cooperative activities in the classroom. In E.Z. Rothkopf (Ed.), *Review of Research in Education*, 15, 225–250.

Brantlinger, E. (1991). Social class distinctions in adolescents: Reports of problems and punishment in school. *Behavioral Disorders*, 17, 36–46.

Brookover, W.B., Brody, N.V., & Warfield, M. (1981). *Educational policies and equitable education: A report of studies of two desegregated school systems*. East Lansing: Center for Urban Affairs, Michigan State University.

Burkett, C. (1982). Effects of frequency of home-visits on achievement of preschool standards in a home-based early childhood education program. *Journal of Educational Research*, 76, 41–44.

Carnegie Council on Adolescent Development. (1989). *Turning points: Preparing American youth for the 21st century: The report of the task force on education of young adolescents*. New York: Carnegie Corporation of New York.

Casavant, P.J. (1987). *A study of school dropouts in the Syracuse City Schools: Summary results*. Syracuse, NY: Syracuse City School District.

Center for Educational Development. (1986, March). *A call to action: A report from the Center for Educational Development and the Urban League community task force on education*. Rochester, NY: Author.

Clark, D., & Astuto, T. (1988). Paradoxical choice options in organizations. In D. Griffiths, R. Stout, & P. Forsyth (Eds.), *Leaders for America's schools: The reports and papers of the National Commission on Excellence in Educational Administration* (pp. 112–130). Berkeley, CA: McCutchan Publishing.

Coalition of Essential Schools. (1988). Prospectus, RI: Education Department, Brown University.

Cochran, M. (1987). The parental empowerment process: Building on family strengths. *Equity and Choice*, 3, 9–23.

Cohen, B., & Lukinsky, J. (1985). Religious institutions as educators. In M. Fantini & R. Sinclair (Eds.), *Education in school and nonschool settings* (pp. 140–158). Chicago, IL: University of Chicago Press.

Cohen, M. (1993, May). Changing schools from within. *Journal of School Leadership*, 3, 269–287.

Cohen, M., Gaines, L., & Monroe, L. (1989). *The Center Minority Achievement: An early adolescent program*. New York: Bank Street College of Education.

Coleman, J., Campbell, E., Hobson, C., McPartland, J., Mood, A., Weinfeld, F., & York, R. (1966). *Equality of educational opportunity*. Washington, DC: U.S. Government Printing Office.

Coleman, J.S., & Hoffer, T. (1987). *Public and private high schools*. New York: Basic Books.

Colligan, L. (1987). *Scholastic's A+ junior guide to studying*. New York: Scholastic, Inc.

Comer, J.P. (1984). Home–school relationships as they affect the academic success of children. *Education and Urban Society*, 16, 323–337.

Comer, J.P., (1986). Parent participation in the schools. *Phi Delta Kappan*, 67, 442–446.

Cooper, M. (1988). Whose culture is it anyway? In A. Lieberman (Ed.), *Building a professional culture in schools* (pp. 102–132). New York: Teachers College Press.

Coopersmith, S. (1986). *Self-esteem inventories*. Palo Alto, CA: Consulting Psychologists Press.

Counts, G. (1969). *Dare the schools build a new social order?* New York: Arno Press.

Cremin, L. (1980). *American education: The national experience—1783–1876.* New York: Harper & Row.

Crichlow, W. (1988, April). *Dropout prevention in an urban district: Integrating policy, practice, and research.* Paper presented at the annual meeting of the American Educational Research Association, New Orleans.

Dalton, T.H. (1988). *The challenge of curriculum innovation: Ideology and practice.* New York: Falmer Press.

Darling, R.B. (1983). Parent—professional interaction: The roots of misunderstanding. In M. Seligman (Ed.), *The family with a handicapped child* (pp. 95–121). New York: Grune & Stratton.

Deal, T., & Nutt, S. (1983). Planned change in rural school districts. In A. Baldridge & T. Deal (Eds.), *The dynamics of organizational change in education.* Berkeley, CA: McCutchan Publishing.

DeFranco, T.C. (1987. *Metacognition and mathematical problem solving.* New York: St. John's University Press.

Deutsch, M. (1973). *The resolution of conflict: Constructive and destructive processes.* New Haven, CT: Yale University Press.

Dewey, B.E., & Gardner, D.C. (1983). Do you really want to teach? Fifteen job search rules. *College Student Journal, 17,* 80–82.

Dillon, J.L. (1982). Problem finding and solving. *Journal of Creative Behavior, 11*(2), 38–42.

Driscoll, A., & Nagel, N. (1992, April). *University/school district reflection in teacher education: A collaborative inquiry approach.* Paper presented at the annual meeting of the American Educational Research Association, San Francisco.

Dryfoos, J.G. (1991). *Adolescents at risk: Prevalence and prevention.* New York: Oxford University Press.

Dunst, C.J., & Trivette, C.M. (1987). Enabling and empowering families: Conceptual and intervention issues. *School Psychology Review, 16,* 443–456.

Dylan, J.L. (1982). Problem finding and solving. *The Journal of Creative Behavior, 11*(2), 38–42.

Eccles, J.S., & Midgley, C. (1990). Stage/environment fit: Developmentally appropriate classrooms for early adolescents. In R.E. Ames & C. Ames (Eds.), *Research on motivation in education, (Vol. 3).* New York: Academic Press.

Education for All Handicapped Children Act of 1975, PL 94-142. (August 23, 1977). Title 20, U.S.C. 1401 et seq: *U.S. Statutes at Large, 89,* 773–796.

Ekstrom, R.B., Goertz, M.E., Pollack, J.M., & Rock, D.A. (1987). Who drops out of high school and why? Findings from a national study. In G. Natriello (Ed.), *School dropouts: Patterns and policies* (pp. 52–69). New York: Teachers College Press.

Epstein, J.L. (1986). Parents' reactions to teacher practices of parent involvement. *The Elementary School Journal, 86,* 277–294.

Epstein, J.L. (1987). Parent involvement: What research says to administrators. *Education and Urban Society, 19,* 119–136.

Evans, I.M. (1985). Building systems models as a strategy for target behavior selection in clinical assessment. *Behavioral Assessment, 7,* 21–32.

Evans, I.M. (1989). A multi-dimensional model for conceptualizing the design of child behavior therapy. *Behavioural Psychotherapy, 17,* 237–251.

Evans, I.M., & DiBenedetto, A. (1990). Pathways to school dropout: A conceptual model for early prevention. *Special Services in the Schools, 6,* 63–80.

Evans, I.M., & Matthews, A.K. (1992). A behavioral approach to the prevention of school dropout: Conceptual and empirical strategies for children and youth. In M. Hersen, R.M. Eisler, & P.M. Miller (Eds.), *Progress in behavior modification* (Vol. 28, pp. 219–249). Sycamore, IL: Sycamore Press.

Evans, I.M., & Meyer, L.H. (1985). *An educative approach to behavior problems. A practical decision model for interventions with severely handicapped learners.* Baltimore: Paul H. Brookes Publishing Co.

Evans, I.M., & Okifuji, A. (1992). Home–school partnerships: A behavioural-community approach to childhood behaviour disorders. *New Zealand Journal of Psychology, 21,* 14–24.

Evans, I.M., Okifuju, A., Engler, L., Bromley, K., & Tishelman, A. (1993). Home–school communication in the treatment of childhood behavior problems. *Child & Family Behavior Therapy, 15,* 37–60.

Ewers, P.O. (1991). *A vision for the future of Pace University: A discussion paper.* Unpublished manuscript, Office of the President, Pace University, NY.

Fantini, M. (1985). Stages of linking school and nonschool environment. In M. Fantini & R. Sinclair (Eds.), *Education in school and nonschool settings* (pp. 46–63). Chicago: University of Chicago Press.

Fantini, M., & Sinclair, R. (Eds.). (1985). *Education in school and nonschool settings.* Chicago: University of Chicago Press.

Farber, B.A. (1991). *Crisis in education: Stress and burnout in the American teacher.* San Francisco: Jossey-Bass.

Feltz, D., Landers, D., & Becker, B. (1988). A revised meta-analysis of the mental practice literature on motor skill learning. In *Enhancing human performance: Issues, theories, and technologies.* Background papers. Washington, DC: National Academy Press.

Fine, M. (1991). *Framing dropouts.* Albany: SUNY Press.

Fine, M.J. (1984). Parent involvement. In J.E. Ysseldyke (Ed.), *School psychology: The state of the art* (pp. 195–224). Minneapolis: National School Psychology Inservice Training Network.

Firestone, W., & Wilson, B. (1985). Using bureaucratic and cultural linkages to improve instruction. *Education Administration Quarterly, 21*(2), 23–29.

Freire, P. (1971). *Pedagogy of the oppressed.* New York: Herder and Herder.

Friesen, J.W., & Wieler, E.E. (1988). New robes for an old order: Multicultural education, peace education, cooperative learning and progressive education. *The Journal of Educational Thought, 22,* 46–56.

Fullan, M. (1991). *The meaning of educational change.* Elmsford, NY: Principals' Exchange, Lower Hudson Principal's Center.

George, P.S. (1983). *The Theory Z School: Beyond effectiveness.* Columbus, OH: National Middle School Association.

George, P.S., & Oldaker, L.L. (1985, December–1986, January). A national survey of middle school effectiveness. *Educational Leadership, 14,* 1–8.

Goodlad, J.I. (1984). *A place called school.* New York: McGraw-Hill.

Goodlad, J.L., & Anderson, T. (1987). *The nongraded elementary school.* New York: Teachers College Press.

Goodson, B.D., & Hess, R.D. (1975). *Parents as teachers of young children: An evaluative review of some contemporary concepts and programs.* Washington, DC: U.S. Department of Health, Education, and Welfare.

Grannis, J. (1991). Dropout prevention in New York City: A second chance. *Phi Delta Kappan, 77,* 143–149.

Grannis, J., & Torres-Guzman, M. (1990). Hispanic students in the New York City Dropout Prevention Program. In J. Grannis & C. Riehl (Eds.), *Evaluation of the*

New York City dropout prevention initiative 1986 through 1988: Final longitudinal report (pp. 45–67). New York: Institute for Urban and Minority Education, Teachers College, Columbia University.

Grant, C.A., & Secada, W.G. (1990). Preparing teachers for diversity. In W.R. Houston (Eds.), *Handbook of research on teacher education* (pp. 403–422). New York: Macmillan.

Greene, M. (1978). *Landscapes of learning.* New York: Teachers College Press.

Hall, G.S. (1904). *Adolescence in psychology, and its relations to physiology, anthropology, sociology, sex, crime, religion, and education: Vols. I and II.* New York: Appleton.

Hammack, F. (1986). Large school systems dropout reports: An analysis of definitions, procedures, and findings. *Teachers College Record, 87,* 324–341.

Hampel, R.L. (1986). *The last little citadel: American high schools since 1940.* Boston: Houghton Mifflin.

Henderson, A.T. (1986). *The evidence continues to grow: Parent involvement improves student achievement.* Columbia, MD: National Committee for Citizens in Education.

Henderson, A.T., Marburger, C.L., & Ooms, T. (1986). *Beyond the bake sale: An educator's guide to working with parents.* Columbia, MD: National Center for Citizens in Education.

Henning-Stout, M., & Goode, L.A. (1986). Parent involvement in a low-income neighborhood primary school: A program illustration. *Special Services in the Schools, 2,* 63–76.

Henson, K.T. (1986, April). Middle schools: Paradoxes and promises. *The Clearing House, 59,* 345–347.

Henson, K.T. (1993). *Methods and strategies for teaching in secondary and middle schools* (2nd ed.). New York: Longman.

Hersh, R.J. (1982). What makes schools, teachers more effective. *Catalyst for Change, 12*(1), 4–8.

High school: Sometimes 7 years to diploma. (1990, June 22). *New York Times,* p. B1.

Hirsch, B.J., & Dubois, D.L. (1989). The school–nonschool ecology of early adolescent friendships. In D. Belle (Ed.), *Children's social networks and social supports* (pp. 260–274). New York: John Wiley & Sons.

Houston, R.L., & Joseph, S. (1993). *Parent involvement.* Resource document. Philadelphia: Research for Better Schools.

Individuals with Disabilities Education Act of 1990 (IDEA), PL 101-476. (October 30, 1990). Title 20, U.S.C. 1400 et seq: *U.S. Statutes at Large, 104,* 1103–1151.

Jenkins, J.R., Jewell, M., Leicester, N., Jenkins, L., & Troutner, N. (1990, April). *Development of a school building model for educating handicapped and at risk students in general education classrooms.* Paper presented at the annual meeting of the American Educational Research Association, Boston.

Johnson, D.W., & Johnson, R. (1982). *Learning together.* Englewood Cliffs, NJ: Prentice Hall.

Johnson, D.W., & Johnson, R.T. (1989). *Cooperation and competition: Theory and research.* Edina, MN: Interaction Book.

Johnson, R.T., & Johnson, D.W. (1985). Student–student interaction: Ignored but powerful. *Journal of Teacher Education, 36,* 22–26.

Kaufman, A.S., & Kaufman, N.L. (1985). *Kaufman Test of Educational Achievement: Brief form manual.* Circle Pines, MN: American Guidance Service.

Klepper, W.M. (1987). The role of institutional research in retention. *New Directions for Higher Education, 15,* 27–37.

Levin, H. (1986). Educational reform for disadvantaged students: An emergency crisis. *NEA Search.* West Haven, CT: National Education Association.

Levin, H. (1989). Financing the education of at-risk students. *Educational Evaluation and Policy Analysis, 11,* 47–60.

Levy, J.E., & Copple, C. (1989). *Joining forces: A report from the first year.* Alexandria, VA: National Association of State Boards of Education.

Lew, M., Mesch, D., Johnson, D.W., & Johnson, R. (1986). Components of cooperative learning: Effects of collaborative skills and academic group contingencies on achievement and mainstreaming. *Contemporary Educational Psychology, 11,* 229–239.

Lightfoot, S. (1978). *Worlds apart: Relationships between families and schools.* New York: Basic Books.

Linney, J.A., & Vernberg, E. (1983). Changing patterns of parental employment and the family-school relationship. In C.D. Hayes & S. Kamerman (Eds.), *Children of working parents: Experiences and outcomes* (pp. 73–99). Washington, DC: National Academy Press.

Lipsitz, J. (1984). *Successful schools for young adolescents.* New Brunswick, NJ: Transaction Books.

Loucks, S., & Crandall, D. (1982). *The practice profile: An all-purpose tool for program implementation, staff development, and evaluation and improvement.* Andover, MA: The Network.

Maccoby, E., & Martin, J. (1983). Socialization in the context of the family: Parent–child interaction. In E.M. Hetherington (Ed.), *Handbook of child psychology: Vol. 4. Socialization, personality, and social development* (pp. 1–101). New York: John Wiley & Sons.

MacIver, D.J., & Epstein, J.L. (1991). Responsive practices in the middle grades: Teacher teams, advisory groups, remedial instruction, and school transition programs. *American Journal of Education, 99,* 587–622.

Marlowe, J., & Sartor, T. (1983). Before retooling your curriculum, determine what your kids must do. *American School Board Journal, 170,* 45–49.

Mcloughlin, C.S. (1987). *Parent–teacher conferencing.* Springfield, IL: Charles C Thomas.

McMaster, E. (1982). *McMaster Family Assessment Device.* Providence, RI: Brown University, Butler Hospital Research Program.

Meier, D. (1987). Success in East Harlem. *American Educator,* Fall, p. 34ff.

Melnick, C. (1988). *A search for teachers' knowledge of the out-of-school curriculum of students' lives.* Chicago: University of Illinois Press.

Meyer, L.H., & Biklen, D. (1993). Preparing teachers for inclusive schooling: The Syracuse University Inclusive Elementary and Special Education teacher preparation program. In the fifth annual *University Leadership Institute Proceedings,* New York State Office for Special Education Services, Albany.

Meyer, L.H., Harootunian, B., & Williams, D. (1991, April). *Identifying at-risk status and preventing school dropout.* Paper presented at the Annual Meeting of the American Educational Research Association, Chicago.

Meyer, L.H., & Henry L. (1993). Cooperative classroom management: Student needs and fairness in the regular classroom. In J.W. Putnam (Ed.), *Cooperative learning and strategies for inclusion: Celebrating diversity in the classroom* (pp. 93–121). Baltimore: Paul H. Brookes Publishing Co.

Meyer, L.H., Mager, G.M., & Sarno, M. (1994). *Inclusive Elementary and Special Education Teacher Preparation Program.* Syracuse, NY: Syracuse University School of Education.

Meyer, L.H., & Putnam, J.W. (1988). Social integration. In V.B. Van Hasselt, P.S. Strain, & M. Hersen (Eds.), *Handbook of developmental and physical disabilities* (pp. 107–133). New York: Pergamon Press.

Meyerhoff, M.K., & White, B.L. (1986, November). New parents as teachers. *Educational Leadership*, 42–46.

Meyers, J., & Rowan, B. (1983). The structure of educational organizations. In J.V. Baldridge & T. Deal (Eds.), *The dynamics of organizational change in education* (pp. 60–87). Berkeley, CA: McCutchan Publishing.

Moles, O.C. (1987). Who wants parent involvement? Interest, skills and opportunities among parents and educators. *Parents and Urban Society, 19*(2), 137–145.

Monroe, L. (1985). *Principalships in the metropolitan centers.* Unpublished doctoral dissertation, Teachers College, New York.

Muncey, D.E., & McQuillan, P.J. (1991). *Preliminary findings from the field: Results from a five-year study of the Coalition of Essential Schools.* (Unpublished Study): Providence, RI: The School of Ethnography Project, Brown University.

National Assessment of Educational Progress. (1985). *The reading report card, progress toward excellence in our schools, trends in reading over four national assessments, 1991–1984.* Princeton, NJ: Educational Testing Service.

National Association of State Boards of Education. (1993a). *The American tapestry: Educating a nation. A guide to infusing multiculturalism into American education.* Alexandria, VA: Author.

National Association of State Boards of Education. (1993b). *Winners all.* Alexandria, VA: Author.

National Center on Effective Secondary Schools. (no date). *Wisconsin youth survey.* Madison: School of Education, University of Wisconsin.

Natriello, G. (1987). Introduction. In G. Natriello (Ed.), *School dropouts: Patterns and policies* (pp. 1–19). New York: Teachers College Press.

New York State Board of Regents. (1987). *Increasing completion rates: A framework for state and local action.*

New York State Education Department. (1987a). *More effective schools through parent involvement.* Albany: Author.

New York State Education Department. (1987b). *Increasing high school completion rates: A framework for state and local action.* Albany: Author.

New York State Education Department. (1991). *The state of learning: A report on the educational status of the state's schools.* Albany: Author.

New York State Education Department. (1992). *Proceedings of the 5th University Leadership Institute: A state conference.* Albany: Author.

Noddings, N. (1992). *The challenge to care in schools: An alternative approach to education.* New York: Teachers College Press.

Odynak, E. (1985). *Review of cooperative learning research and methods.* A discussion paper prepared for the Ad-Hoc Committee of Multiculturalism and Education, Secretary of State, Edmonton, Canada.

Ogbu, J. (1978). *Minority education and caste: The American system in cross-cultural perspective.* New York: Academic Press.

Okun, B.F. (1984). Family therapy and the schools. In J.C. Hansed & B.F. Okun (Eds.), *Family therapy with school related problems.* Rockville, MD: Aspen Publishers, Inc.

Oxley, D. (1994). Organizing schools into small units: Alternatives to homogeneous grouping. *Phi Delta Kappan, 7,* 521–526.

Paley, V. (1979). *White teacher.* Cambridge, MA: Harvard University Press.

Pitman, A., & Romberg, T. (1985). *The urban mathematics collaborative projects.* (Annual report to the Ford Foundation.) Madison: The Wisconsin Center for Education Research.

Polansky, N., Chalmers, M., Buttenwieser, E., & Williams, D. (1978). Assessing adequacy of child caring: An urban scale. *Child Welfare, LVII*(7), 439–449.

Popkewitz, T.S. (1983). The sociological basis for individual differences: The relation of solitude to the crowd. In J. Goodlad & G. Fenstermacher (Eds.), *Individual differences and the common curriculum. Eighty-second yearbook of the National Society for the Study of Education [Part I].* Chicago: University of Chicago Press.

Rich, D. (1985). *The forgotten factor in school success: The family—A policymaker's guide.* Washington, DC: The Home and School Institute.

Rieck, W.A. (1992, April). *A study of current practice on the pre-service preparation of secondary school teachers.* Lafayette: Department of Curriculum and Instruction, University of Southwestern Louisiana.

Rist, R. (1970). Student social class and teacher expectations: The self-fulfilling prophecy in ghetto education. *Harvard Educational Review, 40,* 411–451.

Romberg, T.A. (1986). *Mathematics for compensatory school programs.* Paper presented at conference on "Effects of alternate designs in compensatory education," Washington, DC.

Roos, P. (1979). Parents of mentally retarded children: Misunderstood and mistreated. In A.P. Turnbull & H.R. Turnbull (Eds.), *Parents speak out: Growing with a handicapped child* (pp. 12–27). Columbus, OH: Charles E. Merrill.

Rumberger, R.W., Ghatak, R., Poulos, G., Dornbusch, S.M., & Ritter, P.L. (1988, April). *Family influences on dropout behavior: An exploratory study of a single high school.* Paper presented at the annual meeting of the American Educational Research Association, New Orleans.

Rutter, M., Maughon, B., Mortimer, P., Ouston, J., & Smith, A. (1979). *Fifteen thousand hours: Secondary schools and their effects on children.* Cambridge, MA: Harvard University Press.

Salisbury, C. (1987). *Parental perceptions of home and school relationships.* Technical report #1, Binghamton School Partnership Project, SUNY–Binghamton, NY.

Salisbury, C., & Evans, I.M. (1988). Comparison of parental involvement in regular and special education. *Journal of The Association for Persons with Severe Handicaps, 13,* 268–272.

Sattes, B.D. (1985). *Parent involvement: A review of the literature* (Occasional paper #021). Charleston, WV: Appalachia Educational Laboratory.

Schnorr, R., Ford, A., Davern, L., Park-Lee, S., & Meyer, L. (1989). *The Syracuse curriculum revision manual: A group process for developing a community-referenced curriculum guide.* Baltimore: Paul H. Brookes Publishing Co.

Schorr, L. (1988). *Within our reach: Breaking the cycle of disadvantage.* New York: Doubleday.

Schubert, J.G., & Steel, L. (1983). *The effectiveness of upward bound in preparing disadvantaged youth for postsecondary education.* Palo Alto, CA: American Institute for Research in the Behavioral Sciences.

Seeley, D. (1984). Educational partnership and the dilemmas of school reform. *Phi Delta Kappan, 65,* 383–393.

Simmons, R.G., & Blyth, D.A. (1987). *Moving into adolescence: The impact of pubertal change and school context.* Hawthorne, NY: Aldine.

Siobhan, N., & Ramos, C.L. (1990). *Together is better: Building strong relationships between schools and Hispanic parents.* Washington, DC: Hispanic Policy Development Project.

Sirotnik, K., & Goodlad, J. (Eds.). (1988). *School–university partnerships in action.* New York: Teachers College Press.

Sizer, T. (1985). *Horace's compromise*. Boston: Houghton Mifflin.

Sizer, T. (1992). *Horace's school*. Boston: Houghton Mifflin.

Smey-Richman, B. (1991). *School climate and restructuring for low-achieving students*. Philadelphia, PA: Research for Better Schools.

Steiner, L. (1987). Field trips provide learning experience for students, staff. *Journalism Educator, 42,* 39–41.

Stinnet, T.M., & Henson, K.T. (1982). *America's public schools in transition: Future trends and issues*. New York: Teachers College Press.

Stowitschek, J.J., & Smith, A.J. (1990). *Implementing the C-STARS interprofessional case management model for at-risk children* (Contract #OEG-S201B81048). Washington, DC: U.S. Department of Education.

Swap, S.M. (1990). Comparing three philosophies of home–school collaboration. *Equity and Choice, 6*(3), 9–19.

Turnbull, A., & Leonard, J. (1981). Parent involvement in special education: Emerging advocacy roles. *School Psychology Review, 10,* 37–44.

Tyack, D.B. (1974). *The one best system*. Cambridge, MA: Harvard University Press.

Wahler, R.G. (1980). The insular mother: Her problems in parent–child treatment. *Journal of Applied Behavior Analysis, 13,* 207–219.

Walberg, H.J. (1984). Improving the productivity of America's schools. *Educational Leadership, 41*(8), 19–27.

Walker, B. (1989). Strategies for improving parent–professional cooperation. In G.H.S. Singer & L.K. Irvin (Eds.), *Support for caregiving families: Enabling positive adaptation to disability* (pp. 103–119). Baltimore: Paul H. Brookes Publishing Co.

Wehlage, G.G., & Rutter, R.A. (1987). Dropping out: How much do schools contribute to the problem? In G. Natriello (Ed.), *School dropouts: Patterns and policies* (pp. 70–88). New York: Teachers College Press.

Wehlage, G.G., Rutter, R.A., Smith, G.A., Lesko, N., & Fernandez, R.R. (1989). *Reducing the risk: Schools as communities of support*. London: Falmer Press.

Weiss, H. (1989). Family support and education in early childhood programs. In S.L. Kagan, D. Powell, B. Weissbourd, & E. Zigler (Eds.), *Family support programs: State of the art*. New Haven, CT: Yale University Press.

Wentzel, K.R. (1991). Social competence at school: Relation between social responsibility and academic achievement. *Review of Educational Research, 61,* 1–24.

Whittaker, J.K., Kinney, J., Tracy, E.M., & Booth, C. (Eds.). (1990). *Reaching high-risk families: Intensive family preservation in human services*. New York: Aldine de Gruyter.

Williams, D.R. (1993). Cooperative learning and cultural diversity: Building caring communities in the cooperative classroom. In J.W. Putnam (Ed.), *Cooperative learning and strategies for inclusion: Celebrating diversity in the classroom* (pp. 145–162). Baltimore: Paul H. Brookes Publishing Co.

Williams, D.R., Meyer, L.H., & Harootunian, B. (1992). Introduction and implementation of cooperative learning in the heterogeneous classroom: Middle school teachers' perspectives. *Research in Middle Level Education, 16,* 115–130.

Williams, E.U., Gold, V., & Russell, S.C. (1993, February). *Collaboration: A potential solution in teacher education for addressng at-risk and special education students in today's schools*. Paper presented at the annual meeting of the American Association of Colleges for Teacher Education, San Diego.

Winn, D.D., Regan, P., & Gibson, S. (1991, March–April). Teaching the middle years learner. *The Clearing House, 64,* 265–267.

Index

YORK COLLEGE OF PENNSYLVANIA 17403

0 2003 0083690 1

LB2331.53 .S73 1995

Staying in school :
partnerships for
c1995

LIBRARY

GAYLORD FG